CAMBRIDGE SO

WORSHIP AND CONFLICT UNDER COLONIAL RULE

A SOUTH INDIAN CASE

CAMBRIDGE SOUTH ASIAN STUDIES

These monographs are published by the Syndics of Cambridge University Press in association with the Cambridge University Centre for South Asian Studies. The following books have been published in this series:

1 S. Gopal: *British Policy in India, 1858–1905*
2 J. A. B. Palmer: *The Mutiny Outbreak at Meerut in 1857*
3 A. Das Gupta: *Malabar in Asian Trade, 1740–1800*
4 G. Obeyesekere: *Land Tenure in Village Ceylon*
5 H. L. Erdman: *The Swatantra Party and Indian Conservatism*
6 S. N. Mukherjee: *Sir William Jones: A Study in Eighteenth-Century British Attitudes to India*
7 Abdul Majed Khan: *The Transition in Bengal, 1756–1775: A Study of Saiyid Muhammad Reza Khan*
8 Radhe Shyam Rungta: *The Rise of Business Corporations in India, 1851–1900*
9 Pamela Nightingale: *Trade and Empire in Western India, 1784–1806*
10 Amiya Kumar Bagchi: *Private Investment in India, 1900–1939*
11 Judith M. Brown: *Gandhi's Rise to Power: Indian Politics, 1915–1922*
12 Mary C. Carras: *The Dynamics of Indian Political Factions*
13 P. Hardy: *The Muslims of British India*
14 Gordon Johnson: *Provincial Politics and Indian Nationalism*
15 Marguerite S. Robinson: *Political Structure in a Changing Sinhalese Village*
16 Francis Robinson: *Separation among Indian Muslims: The Politics of the United Provinces' Muslims, 1860–1923*
17 Christopher John Baker: *The Politics of South India, 1920–1936*
18 David Washbrook: *The Emergence of Provincial Politics: The Madras Presidency, 1870–1920*
19 Deepak Nayyar: *India's Exports and Export Policies in the 1960s*
20 Mark Holmström: *South Indian Factory Workers: Their Life and Their World*
21 S. Ambirajan: *Classical Political Economy and British Policy in India*
22 M. M. Islam: *Bengal Agriculture 1920–1946: A Quantitative Study*
23 Eric Stokes: *The Peasant and the Raj: Studies in Agrarian Society and Peasant Rebellion in Colonial India*
24 Michael Roberts: *Caste Conflict and Elite Formation: The Rise of a Karāva Elite in Sri Lanka 1500–1931*
25 J. F. J. Toye: *Public Expenditure and Indian Development Policy 1960–70*
26 Rashid Amjad: *Private Industrial Development in Pakistan 1960–70*

WORSHIP AND CONFLICT UNDER COLONIAL RULE

A SOUTH INDIAN CASE

ARJUN APPADURAI

Department of Anthropology
University of Pennsylvania

CAMBRIDGE UNIVERSITY PRESS

Cambridge
London New York New Rochelle
Melbourne Sydney

CAMBRIDGE UNIVERSITY PRESS
Cambridge, New York, Melbourne, Madrid, Cape Town, Singapore, São Paulo

Cambridge University Press
The Edinburgh Building, Cambridge CB2 8RU, UK

Published in the United States of America by Cambridge University Press, New York

www.cambridge.org
Information on this title: www.cambridge.org/9780521231220

First published 1981
This digitally printed version 2008

A catalogue record for this publication is available from the British Library

Library of Congress Cataloguing in Publication data

Appadurai, Arjun, 1949–
Worship and conflict under colonial rule.
(Cambridge South Asian studies; 27)
Bibliography: p.
1. India – Religion – Case studies. 2. Religion and
state – India – Case studies. 3. India – Politics and
government – 1765–1947 – Case studies. I. Title.
II. Series.
BL2003.A66 294.5′09548 80–24508

ISBN 978-0-521-23122-0 hardback
ISBN 978-0-521-05358-7 paperback

CONTENTS

PREFACE

This study is part of a larger ongoing effort to develop methods and models for the study of colonialism from a cultural point of view. As such, it draws upon the materials and techniques of social history but shares the methods and comparative concerns of anthropology. It follows, also, that the findings of this case study are relevant to the intrinsically cross-cultural problem of colonialism.

These larger aims, however, do not occupy the bulk of the pages that follow. Their content is culturally and historically specific and consists of an ethnohistorical analysis of conflict in a single South Indian temple over a two-hundred-year period. The arguments of the substantive chapters bear directly on the institutional formation of a set of South Asian ideas concerning power, ritual, and authority, especially in the colonial context. These arguments result from deliberately juxtaposing ethnographic fieldwork and archival research.

The results of this enterprise bear the marks, both for better and for worse, of a serious effort to achieve two goals, for which there are few clear precedents in the scholarship on South Asia: first, to provide a sustained analysis at the micro level of the cultural processes of an institution over a substantial period of time; second, to conduct an "archeology" of the ethnographic present, which entails a particular type of historical journey.

In the course of researching and writing this study I have incurred many debts to both individuals and institutions. At various stages I received financial support from: the Danforth Foundation, St. Louis, Missouri; the Committee on South Asian Studies of the University of Chicago; the Center for the Study of World Religions at Harvard University; and the American Institute for Indian Studies.

During my fieldwork, which was conducted in 1973–4, I was privileged to be affiliated with the Institute for Social and Economic Change in Bangalore and was permitted scholarly access to the Śrī Pārtasārati Svāmi Temple by the Hindu Religious and Charitable Endowments (Administration) Department of the State of Tamiḻnāṭu. Officials at the India Office Library in London, the Tamiḻnāṭu

Archives in Madras city, and the High Court of Judicature at Madras were also good enough to give me access to their archival holdings.

Of the many individuals who helped me with my research in Madras, I can name only a few: Mr. M. Rajah, who was then second assistant registrar of the High Court of Judicature at Madras; Shri M. G. Anantha Bhattachariar, head priest of Cinnai Murai Miras at the temple; Mr. Arumugam, then superintendent of the temple, and Mr. and Mrs. T. K. Ramanujadoss of Triplicane.

My natal family in Bombay and many relatives in Madras were throughout a source of encouragement. My father, the late Mr. S. A. Ayer, and my mother, Mrs. Alamelu Ayer, continued to believe in me even when my scholarly pursuits seemed esoteric and aimless. My late paternal uncle, Lieutenant Colonel Annaswami, and his family in Madras, were throughout a home away from home. My late brother, Vatsal, was a model of scholarship and humility to me all his life, and it is to his memory that this book is dedicated. Vatsal and his wife, Tusi, helped me through difficult times in Madras.

In the shaping of my thought and the crafting of this book, I have benefited from the advice, encouragement, and criticism of many academic colleagues: Victor Turner, A. K. Ramanujan, Bernard S. Cohn, Ronald Inden, Nur Yalman, S. J. Tambiah, K. K. A. Venkatachari, and John Carman. I owe a special debt to Burton Stein, who, by his own scholarly example, patient criticism, and steady encouragement, has helped make this study much stronger than it would otherwise have been. Professor M. N. Srinivas, who supervised my original fieldwork, has been generous in his support and impressive by his example throughout. My colleagues in the Departments of Anthropology and South Asia Regional Studies at the University of Pennsylvania have helped me refine my thought in more ways than they are likely to suspect. I would also like to acknowledge the patient assistance of Peter Just, without whom I would not have been able to prepare the Index, and the South Asia Regional Studies Department at the University of Pennsylvania for financial aid toward the preparation of the Index.

My greatest intellectual and personal debt, however, is to my wife and colleague, Carol A. Breckenridge. Because she has been engaged in her own study of a South Indian temple, our own collaboration has been a very special one. Many of the ideas contained in this study are equally hers. Her generosity and self-sacrifice, in a period of frequent professional and personal strain, have made this study possible.

NOTE ON TRANSLITERATION

Technical words

In general, this study follows the system of transliteration of the *Madras University Tamil Lexicon*.[1] However, in two kinds of case the system followed here departs from the *Lexicon*.

In the case of words whose usage has become standardized in English, and particularly in South Indian English usage, the strict *Lexicon* form has been abandoned and the more conventional usage adopted; namely, *pūjā, bhakti, varna, Brahmin, Sūdra, Āgama, Vēda, dubāshi, mirās, dharmakarta, mahout, Prabandam.*

For words in Sanskritized Tamil whose *Lexicon* transliteration would render them virtually unrecognizable, this study follows the system appropriate to modern *maṇipravāḷam,* that is, the normal Tamil script with the five most common Grantha additions: *j, s, ṣ, h,* and *kṣ*. In this style, Sanskritic consonant clusters and the contrasts indicated by the foregoing Grantha additions (but not voicing and aspiration) are represented. Sanskritists should note that the words, although recognizable, are *not* Sanskrit and therefore do not follow *its* normal transliteration. The following is a sample of words transliterated according to this system, accompanied by their equivalents in the official *Lexicon* system.

Maṇipravāḷam system	*Lexicon system*
arccakaṉ	aruccakaṉ
brahmōtsavam	piramōṟcavam
jīyar	cīyar
karpakkriham	karuppakkirukam
nakṣattiram	naṭcattiram
prāṇa pratiṣṭai	pirāṇa-p-piratiṣṭai
prasātam	piracātam
samskāram	camakkāram
utsavam	uṟcavam

[1] *Madras University Tamil Lexicon*, 8 vols. (Madras, 1925–63). I am grateful to Professor David McAlpin, University of Pennsylvania, for his help in formalizing my system of transliteration. The inconsistencies that remain are my responsibility.

Names

In transliterating the names of persons, castes, and places, the principle followed in this study is based on the *context,* both the context provided by the source on which the relevant portion of the text is based (namely, Vijayanagara inscriptions, British revenue records, and Anglo-Indian legal records) and the context of the usage of the period in question. Thus, the word for a given personal name or caste name might appear in different portions of the study variously, as *mutaliyār, moodeliar,* or *mudaliar.* In the case of place names, compromises have been arrived at to balance strict *Lexicon* transliteration and common scholarly usage, namely, Śrīrangam instead of Śrīraṅkam.

INTRODUCTION

Anthropological theory and ethnohistory

Making the "implicit" meanings in other cultures explicit is a dialectical task in which the anthropologist potentially exposes his or her own principles to sociological scrutiny.[1] Because the body of this study is concerned with describing some "implicit" aspects of South Indian society, it is only fair that some of the analyst's own methodological assumptions be made explicit at the outset. These assumptions have influenced my choice of subject (a single South Indian temple), my methodological approach, which is ethnohistorical, and my findings.

The theoretical context for the procedures and arguments of this study is provided by a set of interlocking ideas generated by social and cultural anthropologists in the last two decades. The common element in these ideas is the aspiration to transcend some of the characteristic limitations of functionalism, especially as it was exemplified by Malinowski and Radcliffe-Brown. Theoreticians who are otherwise distinct, such as C. Geertz, C. Levi-Strauss, V. Turner, and E. Leach, share this aspiration. It is to various aspects of their thought that I owe my own premises.

Following Clifford Geertz, I take culture to be "an ordered system of meanings and symbols, in terms of which social interaction takes place."[2] The social system, according to Geertz, is the pattern of social interaction itself. But Geertz rightly recognizes that such a distinction, although heuristically important, is only a reification:

> On the one level there is the framework of beliefs, expressive symbols, and values in terms of which individuals define their world, express their feelings, and make their judgements; on the other level there is the ongoing process of interactive behaviour, whose persistent form we call social structure. Culture is the fabric of meaning in terms of which human beings interpret their experience and guide their action; social structure is the form that action takes, the actually existing network of social relations. Culture

[1] Mary Douglas, *Implicit Meanings: Essays in Anthropology* (London and Boston, 1975), Preface and Introduction.

[2] Clifford Geertz, *The Interpretation of Cultures* (New York, 1973), p. 144.

and social structure are then but different abstractions from the same phenomena.[3]

But Geertz takes this distinction further when he argues that culture and social structure have characteristically different modes of integration. Following Sorokin, he argues that what holds culture together is "logico-meaningful integration," that is, "a unity of style, of logical implication, of meaning and value."[4] Social structure, on the other hand, is characterized by "causal-functional integration," the kind of integration "one finds in an organism, where all parts are united in a single causal web."[5]

To make such a distinction, in Geertz's view, is not simply to avoid the functionalist tendency to make one of these terms a "mirror image" of the other, a dependent and unoriginal variable. It also opens up the possibility of dealing with change in ways that functionalists have not done. For, because culture and social structure are characterized by different modes of integration, "because the particular form one of them takes does not directly influence the form the other will take, there is an inherent incongruity and tension between the two, and between both of them and a third element, the pattern of motivational integration within the individual which we usually call personality structure."[6] Geertz argues that this disharmonic view of the relationship between culture and social structure is more accurate than the functionalist one, "and the functional analysis of religion can therefore be widened to deal more adequately with processes of change."[7] In his own analysis of the breakdown of a funeral ritual in Java, Geertz provides a striking example of this possibility when he demonstrates that the disruption of a particular Javanese funeral was rooted in a single source, "an incongruity between the cultural framework of meaning and the patterning of social interaction."[8]

The idea that moments of disruption and, in general, occasions of conflict provide lenses into the key principles of the social and cultural order and focuses for the study of change is a major methodological principle of the dramatistic, symbolic, and processual analysis of Victor Turner. In his seminal essay, "Social Dramas and Ritual Metaphors,"[9] Turner provides an extended methodological

[3] Ibid., pp. 144–5.
[4] Ibid., p. 145.
[5] Ibid.
[6] Ibid.
[7] Ibid., p. 146.
[8] Ibid., p. 169.
[9] Victor Turner, *Dramas, Fields and Metaphors: Symbolic Action in Human Society* (Ithaca and London, 1974).

discussion of the relationship between conflict, structure, and process, which has considerably influenced the arguments of this study. Conflict, according to Turner, "seems to bring fundamental aspects of society, normally overlaid by the customs and habits of daily intercourse, into frightening prominence."[10] Accordingly, "disturbances of the normal and regular often give us greater insight into the normal than does direct study."[11] The pivots for Turner of a genuinely processual analysis are what he calls "social dramas," which are "units of aharmonic or disharmonic process, arising in conflict situations."[12] The analysis of such dramas, for Turner, reveals "temporal structures," that is, structures that are organized "primarily through relations in time rather than in space."[13] In his own analyses of such social dramas, Turner is interested in testing a particular sequence of phases in given social dramas for its cross-cultural regularity.

But the methodological implications of this approach are more fundamental. He suggests that "religious and legal institutions, among others, only cease to be bundles of dead or cold rules when they are seen as phases in social processes, as dynamic patterns right from the start."[14] It is this larger implication of the dramatistic approach that is reflected in this study, for it suggests the link between occasions of conflict and those dynamic principles of "temporal structure" that they reveal in condensed form. Although my own, largely archival, data do not permit the detailed processual analysis of social dramas that Turner has conducted, I share his concern for "temporal structure" and agree with his recommendation that more extended case studies are required before such "temporal structures" can be cross-culturally compared. His argument, in this regard, provides the major justification for the detailed historical aspects of this study:

> An extended case-history is the history of a single group or community over a considerable length of time, collected as a sequence of processual units of different types . . . This is more than plain historiography, for it involves the utilization of whatever conceptual tools social anthropology and cultural anthropology have bequeathed to us. "Processualism" is a term that includes "dramatistic analysis." Processual analysis assumes cultural analysis, just as it assumes structural-functional analysis, including more static comparative morphological analysis. It negates none of these, but puts dynamics first.[15]

[10] Ibid., p. 35.
[11] Ibid., p. 34.
[12] Ibid., p. 37.
[13] Ibid., p. 35.
[14] Ibid., p. 37.
[15] Ibid., pp. 43–4.

It is in the above sense, following Turner, that this is a case study, for its primary object is to put dynamics first, to explore the dynamic links between the regularities of social structure and the dramatistic moments of conflict. This processual orientation converges methodologically with Geertz's suggestion that the locus of change might lie in those areas of tension where culture and social structure do not fit each other coherently.

Extended case studies have always been the hallmark of ethnography. In his recent essay "Thick Description: Towards an Interpretive Theory of Culture,"[16] Geertz has placed this distinctive feature of ethnography in a broader theoretical context. His central insight concerning ethnography is that it ought to constitute "thick description" (a phrase he borrows from Gilbert Ryle), by which he means descriptions generated in narrow spatial confines of aspects of social life (seen as discourse) whose strength is their specificity, their circumstantiality, their density, and their particularity. But Geertz's encouragement of such "thick description" has a tacit synchronic bias with textual and cognitive metaphors underlying it:

> Doing ethnography is like trying to read (in the sense of "construct a reading of") a manuscript – foreign, faded, full of elipses, incoherencies, suspicious emendations, and tendentious commentaries, but written not in conventionalized graphs of sound but in transient examples of shaped behaviour.[17]

This book is an ethnohistory,[18] rather than an ethnography, for it seeks to apply the idea of "thick description" across major units of historical time. Thus it departs somewhat from the inclusive cognitive approach of Geertz, according to whom one of the many compacted conceptual structures in a given instant or action ("winks upon winks upon winks") may involve a reference to the past. "Thick description," in the ethnohistorical sense in which it is used here, entails the analysis of all the traces, structural or cultural, that the institution under study has left on the past. But the collection of such traces, however minute and detailed, would not constitute "ethnohistory," but rather history, pure and simple. What makes it ethnohistory is its link to the present, to the cognitive and structural

[16] Geertz, *Interpretation of Cultures*, pp. 3–30.

[17] Ibid., p. 10. This bias, of course, has not prevented Geertz from making extremely important diachronic studies in Indonesia and Morocco.

[18] I have presumed to define "ethnohistory" for my purposes partly because of the diverse traditions that currently place themselves under this rubric: see Bernard S. Cohn, "Ethnohistory," *International Encyclopaedia of the Social Sciences* (New York, 1968), 6:440–6.

ways in which these traces have become compacted in the meaning systems of actors in the present.

Ethnohistory, in this sense of "thick description" across time, presents one route through which to avoid the twin illusions of synchronic functionalism that Levi-Strauss has so eloquently warned against:

> When, in addition, one completely limits study to the present period in the life of a society, one becomes first of all the victim of an illusion. For everything is history: What was said yesterday is history, what was said a minute ago is history. But above all, one is led to misjudge the present, because only the study of historical development permits the weighing and evaluation of the interrelationships among the components of the present-day society. And a little history – since such, unfortunately, is the lot of the anthropologist – is better than no history at all. How shall we correctly estimate the role, so surprising to foreigners, of the *aperitif* in French social life if we are ignorant of the traditional prestige value ascribed to cooked and spiced wines ever since the Middle Ages? How shall we analyse modern dress without recognizing in it vestiges of previous customs and tastes? To reason otherwise would make it impossible to establish what is an essential distinction between primary function, which corresponds to a present need of the social body, and secondary function, which survives only because the group resists giving up a habit. For to say that a society functions is a truism; but to say that everything in a society functions is an absurdity.[19]

This critique of crude functionalism by Levi-Strauss offers an interesting perspective from which to consider a somewhat different critique from an anthropologist working far more directly within the functionalist tradition. In *Political Systems of Highland Burma*, Edmund Leach proffered a number of interrelated criticisms of his own British structural-functionalist heritage, of which one is of central importance, namely, the question of "how different structures can be represented by the same set of cultural symbols."[20] Although my own understanding of the key terms in this question is somewhat different from Leach's, I do share his view that a "one-to-one" model of the relationship between culture and social structure might, in many contexts, prove to be a dangerous fiction. Leach's position, in this regard, is consistent with both the Levi-Straussian critique of functionalism and Geertz's idea of the disharmonic fit between culture and structure. Given Leach's own synchronic-functionalist tendencies, however, his notion of different social structures sharing a

[19] C. Levi-Strauss, "History and Anthropology," in *Structural Anthropology* (New York, 1967), pp. 12–13.

[20] E. R. Leach, *Political Systems of Highland Burma: A Study of Kachin Social Structure* (Boston, 1965), p. 17.

common culture remains static, although his study of the Kachin is filled with historical information. My own concern, given the ethnohistorical premise of this study, is slightly different. I hope to show how alterations in social structure, *over time*, interact dialectically with a fundamentally unaltered cultural system.

Briefly, this book is an ethnohistorical study of a single South Indian temple, over a period of two centuries, whose primary data are provided by occasions of conflict and whose purpose is to evaluate the present state of the temple in light of its particular past. But to understand this particular choice of subject, it is necessary to make a detour into the current state of South Asian, as well as South Indian, ethnography.

South Asian ethnography: the problematic in context

Since the early 1950s, published ethnographic works on South Asia have appeared in immense quantity, and it is both irrelevant and impossible to review that literature here. One aspect of this body of ethnography, however, is of great importance: its virtual concentration on the institutional and ideological complex known as caste. The history of this interest, starting from the major sociological synthesis of Max Weber[21] and including the recent ethnological synthesis of Louis Dumont,[22] conceals a shared and tacit premise, namely, that the sociological understanding of South Asian religion can largely be achieved by concentrating on the ideas and practices associated with caste as a sociological and cultural entity. Instead of reviewing this immense literature, I shall simply describe the following three issues, which a century of heated debate on caste has not been able to resolve.

1. What is the relationship between the economic and political domains of South Asian society and South Asian ideas concerning such things as salvation, pollution, ritual, and worship? With one important recent exception,[23] sociologists and anthropologists working on South Asia have approached this issue in terms of (culturally inappropriate) dualistic categories: secular versus sacred, interactional theories of rank versus attributional theories of rank, ritual status versus secular status, status versus power, and so on. These shared

[21] Max Weber, *The Religion of India* (Glencoe, Ill., 1958).

[22] Louis Dumont, *Homo Hierarchicus: The Caste System and Its Implications* (Chicago, 1970).

[23] M. Marriott and R. Inden, "Caste Systems," *Encyclopaedia Brittanica* (1974), 3:892–91.

and interconnected dualisms have resulted in an isomorphic division within the scholarly community itself, which has retarded the resolution of the question.

2. What is the authoritative basis of ritual, economic, and social arrangements in South Asia? Much is known about power and dominance as an *aspect* of the caste system, and much is also known, from a textual and prescriptive point of view, about Hindu notions of power (in the sense of both royal *kṣatra* and divine *śakti*, for example). But little is understood about authority, that is, the way in which shared cultural understandings order relationships of obedience between men and preempt or resolve conflict of a disruptive sort.[24] This is largely due to the fact that castes, denuded today of their traditional context of king and state, appear to have a political life of their own, whether this be reflected in the "substantialization" of castes as Dumont analyzes it,[25] the seemingly modern feature of conflict between castes that concerns Srinivas and Leach,[26] or the pan-regional political organization of castes which were previously highly segmented on a territorial basis. Whichever of these developments one considers, what is less than clear is the authoritative basis, in cultural terms, of the caste system. Such attempts as have been made to link the present authoritative basis of the caste system to the textual wisdom of the Hindu tradition, on varna, on the political order, and on the role of the king, often reflect the present strained relationship between Indology and ethnology, "text" and "context."

3. How is change in the caste system to be defined and measured, and how can analysts actually test models of change? This problem has generated almost as many positions as there are theorists and the phantom scheme of "modernity and tradition," though in disrepute, continues to haunt and obfuscate scholarly discussion of change in the caste system. This is partly because, from a strictly ethnographic point of view, Indian villages (which provide the context for most caste studies) often resist historical analysis. Because there is inadequate documentation, historical information on particular systems of caste (local or regional) is partial, scattered, and cryptic. This encourages a reification of the "traditional" system, based on a synthesis of textual information, odd bits of pre-British records, and scattered

[24] An important exception is the work of Bernard S. Cohn, for example, "Anthropological Notes on Disputes and Law in India," *American Anthropologist* 67, No. 6 (December 1965): 105, Pt. 2.

[25] Dumont, *Homo Hierarchicus*, pp. 227–8.

[26] Ibid., pp. 225–7.

information from the early British records.[27] Thus, the attempt to genuinely assess the impact of colonial rule on caste is repeatedly confounded by the lack of adequate information on caste as a functioning institution immediately before and during British rule.[28] This encourages arbitrary definitions of the "traditional" system and, therefore, of the nature of contemporary change.

In fact, the three problems in caste studies identified above are related. The absence of a coherent notion of the authoritative basis of the caste system both supports and is encouraged by the dualist notions that dominate most analyses of the relationship between the economic/political domain and the religious/cultural domain. Both these problems are, in turn, exacerbated by the difficulty of conducting intensive *diachronic* studies of caste in particular regional contexts. And finally, the inadequate understanding of caste, as a historical phenomenon, supports the theoretical confusions in the literature about the relationship of authority, economics, and ritual as various components of caste society.

In South India, at any rate, the Hindu temple presents an alternative locus[29] from which to consider these larger issues that plague and intrigue students of caste. In many ways the Hindu temple is the quintessentially South Indian institution. The extensive construction of temples in South India goes back to at least the Pallava period (circa A.D. 700). The vast number of temples in South India is indicated by a recent census report which, "reckoning only the important and well-known temples in Tamil Nadu," identified 10,542 temples in the fourteen districts of the state. Temples come in every

[27] Needless to say, there are important exceptions to this state of affairs: B. S. Cohn's numerous articles on the Benares region at the beginning of British rule; Tom Kessinger, *Vilyatpur, 1848–1968: Social and Economic Change in a North Indian Village* (Berkeley, 1973), is a pathbreaking attempt to discuss various aspects of a single village over a century, although its substantive concerns are somewhat different from those of this study; Ronald B. Inden, *Marriage and Rank in Bengali Culture: A History of Caste and Clan in Middle-Period Bengal* (Berkeley, 1976), is an outstanding ethnohistorical analysis of a single regional system in pre-British India.

[28] Two recent historical studies of caste in the modern world are exceptions to this statement: Karen Leonard, *Social History of an Indian Caste* (Berkeley, 1978), and Frank Conlon, *A Caste in a Changing World* (Berkeley, 1977). Although matters of ritual play an especially important role in Conlon's study, neither Conlon nor Leonard is principally concerned, from a theoretical point of view, with the relationship between authority, ritual, and economy. Nevertheless, these studies, especially Conlon's view of the Saraswat Brahmins, do suggest that the theoretical argument of the present study may be applicable in useful ways to the study of caste.

[29] Geertz has recently argued that "the locus of study is not the object of study" (*Interpretation of Cultures*, p. 22). In Geertz's spirit, I believe that the grand South Asian issues are the same, whether one starts with caste, temple, or any other institution.

size and scale, from small family shrines to village temples, to lineage temples, to regional temples, to great pan-regional pilgrimage centers.

The importance of temples in South Indian history has been the subject of numerous references in the historical literature. In South Indian ethnography, the economic, social, political, and cultural importance of temples has been frequently noted, though rarely analyzed.[30] Temple architecture, temple economics, and temple ritual have been the subject of many learned monographs. Information on medieval temples in South India, in the form of published stone inscriptions, constitutes a vast, though relatively untapped, scholarly resource. Given their number, cultural importance, and economic status, temples had to be dealt with by British administrators and judges, thus often generating a rich and continuous body of information concerning many temples from the beginnings of British rule.

This wealth of information about South Indian temples is, however, matched by its frustratingly disaggregated quality. Among historians, the standard view of temples has been a "loose-leaf" model, with observations on temple management, temple ritual, temple economics, and temple iconography simply juxtaposed but not synthesized.[31] More specialized studies suffer from the opposite drawback, namely, an excessive emphasis on one or another aspect of the temple, without any analysis of the temple as an institutional whole. In South Indian ethnography, the temple generally appears as a subordinate and marginal arena in which ritual and status issues, primarily enacted in the context of caste, lineage, and village, are seen to have a secondary manifestation. In part, it could be argued that it is precisely the methodological insulation of historians and anthropologists from each other, in respect to the study of temples, that has resulted in the present state of affairs, wherein much is known about various aspects of temples but no coherent analysis exists of the temple *as such*, as a total functioning institution viewed from the "inside."[32]

[30] Notable ethnographic reports and analyses of various aspects of temples in contemporary South India can be found in L. Dumont, *Une sous-caste de l'Inde du Soud: organisation sociale et religion des Pramalai Kallar* (Paris, 1957); B. E. F. Beck, *Peasant Society in Konku: A Study of Right and Left Subcastes in South India* (Vancouver, 1972); S. A. Barnett, "The Process of Withdrawal in a South Indian Caste," in M. Singer, ed., *Entrepreneurship and the Modernization of Occupations in South Asia* (Durham, N.C., 1974), pp. 179–204; A. Beteille, "Social Organization of Temples in a Tanjore Village," *History of Religions* 5, No. 1 (1965): 74–92.

[31] Some important exceptions to this characterization are cited in Chapter 2.

[32] An important exception to this methodological rift is the work of Carol A.

This analysis is, in part, an effort to remedy this situation by tracing a single temple over an extended period of time, linking the historical past with the ethnographic present. The following section presents a general, factual picture of the cultural ecology of the Śrī Pārtasārati Svāmi Temple, the case on which this work is based.

The Śrī Pārtasārati Svāmi Temple

The Śrī Pārtasārati Svāmi Temple is located in the neighborhood of Triplicane in Madras city, which is the capital of the state of Tamiḻnāṭu in India. The state of Tamiḻnāṭu, which came into existence in 1956 (previously Madras State), is situated at the southeastern extremity of the Indian peninsula and Tamil is its dominant language (Figure 1). Bounded on the north by the states of Mysore (now known as Karnātaka) and Andhra Pradesh, on the east by the Bay of Bengal, and on the south by the Indian Ocean, and on the west by Kerala State, it has a coastline of 620 miles and a land boundary of 750 miles. It lies between 8°5′ south latitude and 13°35′ north latitude, and 76°15′ west longitude and 80°20′ east longitude. It covers an area of approximately 50,000 square miles, making it the eleventh largest state in the Indian Union. As reported in the 1961 census, its population was 33,686,953.

The city of Madras, which is an administrative district in itself, was founded by the British in 1639 and is now a major industrial, commercial, political, and religious center.[33] The city occupies an area of 48.9 square miles and is situated on the coast, at the virtual northeastern extremity of the state of Tamiḻnāṭu (Figure 1). According to the 1961 census, Madras had a population of 1,729,141; it is divided into numerous zones and subdivided into divisions (Figure 2), of which Triplicane is one. Some impression of the sacred geography of Madras city can be gained from Figure 3, although it covers only a small number of the 296 important temples reported to exist in Madras city by the 1961 census.

Breckenridge, "The Śrī Mīnākṣi Sundarēsvarar Temple: A Study of Worship and Endowments in South India, 1800–1925" (Ph.D. diss., University of Wisconsin, 1976). Some of our joint conclusions concerning the cultural system of the South Indian temple in a schematic form have appeared in Arjun Appadurai and Carol A. Breckenridge, "The South Indian Temple: Authority, Honor and Redistribution," *Contributions to Indian Sociology*, N.S., 10, No. 2 (Delhi, 1976):187–211.

[33] Susan Lewandowski, "Urban Growth and Municipal Development in the Colonial City of Madras, 1860–1900," *Journal of Asian Studies* 34, No. 2 (February 1975): 341–60; also see Lewandowski, "Changing Form and Function in the Ceremonial and the Colonial Port City in India: An Historical Analysis of Madurai and Madras," *Modern Asian Studies* 2, No. 2 (1977): 183–212.

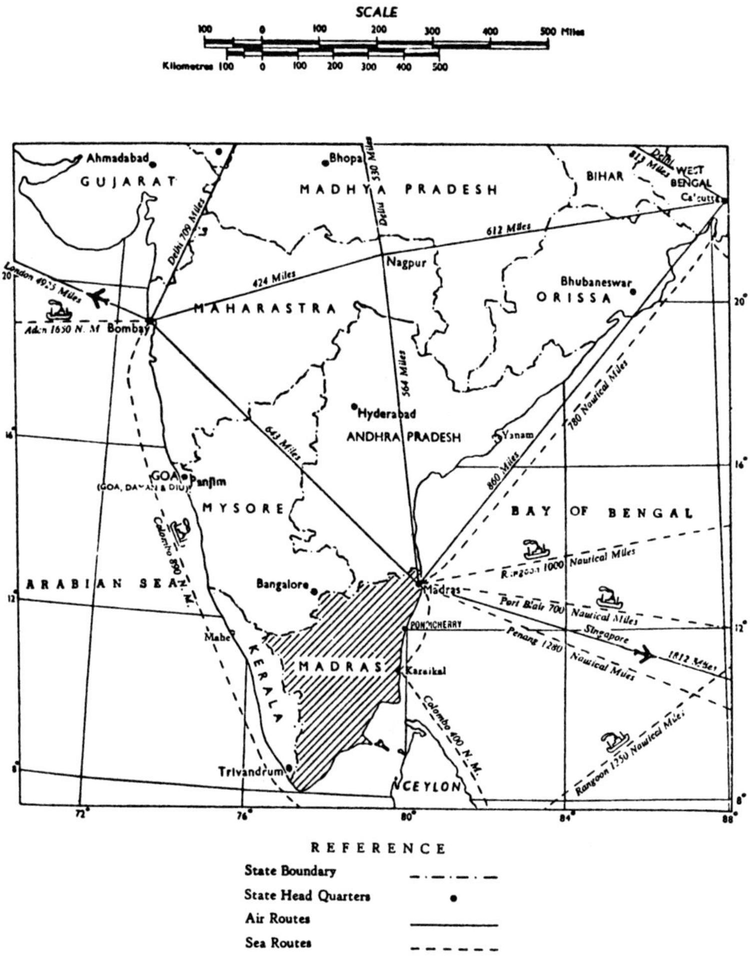

Figure 1. Position of Madras State (*Census of India 1961,* Vol. 9, Pt. 9)

Triplicane, which is division No. 75 of Madras city in Figures 2 and 3, is today a crowded and immensely active urban neighborhood. Covering an area of only .16 square miles, it has a population of approximately 20,000 persons. The Śrī Pārtasārati Svāmi Temple, whose inscriptional history goes back to the eighth century A.D.,[34] is one of the most ancient temples in the city and certainly

[34] V. R. Chetty, *History of Triplicane and the Temple of Sri Parthasarathi Swamy* (Triplicane, 1948), p. 87.

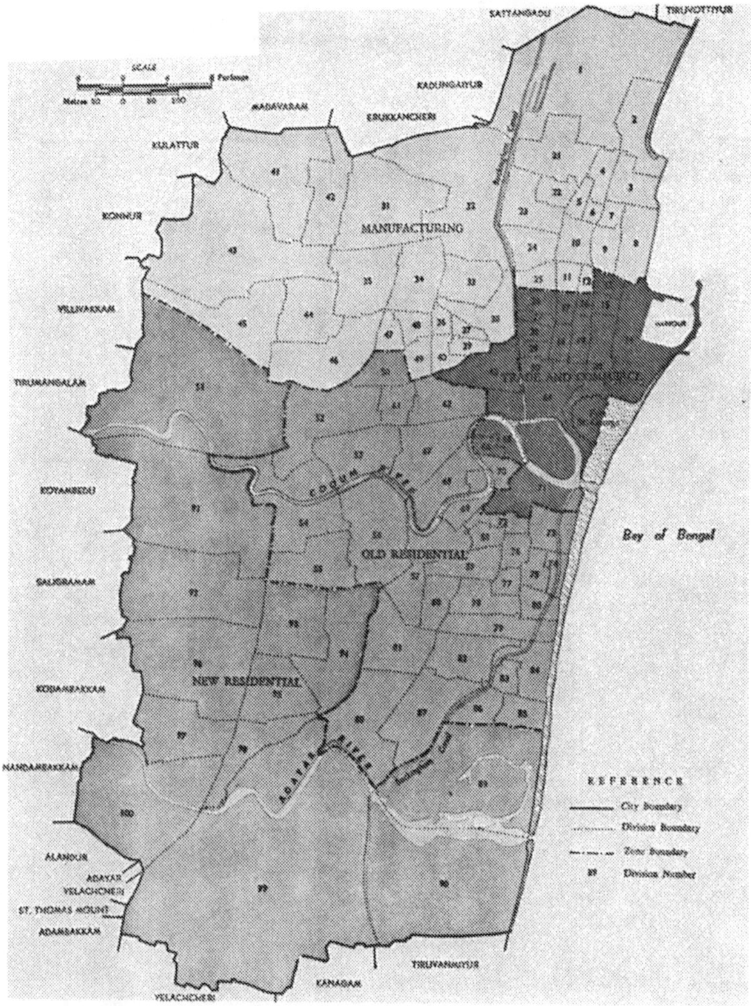

Figure 2. Map of Madras city (*Census of India 1961*, Vol. 9, Pt. 10, iii)

the most important shrine of the local adherents of the Śrī Vaisnava tradition. The temple occupies an area of 1.4 acres and is enclosed by four Triplicane streets. Figure 4 is a replication (not to scale) of the ground plan of the temple, which displays the location of the sanctum (*karpakkriham*), the various shrines (*caṉṉiti*) of the chief deity, Śrī Pārtasārati Svāmi, and the various subordinate deities, sev-

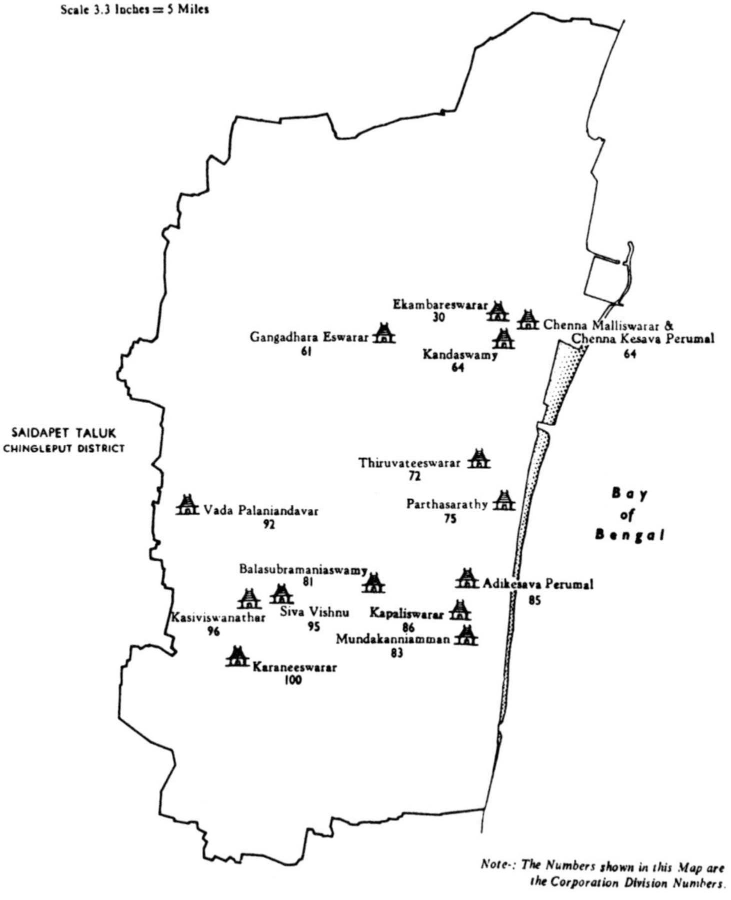

Figure 3. Map of location of important temples in Madras city (*Census of India 1961*, Vol. 9, Pt. 7-B)

eral pillared halls, which have grown around these shrines, and the two temple flagstaffs.

Any visual description of the sacred geography of the temple, however, is too static to be accurate. A more genuine picture of the sacred ecology of the temple can be obtained by noting the processional routes of the various deities of the temple during various calendrical festivals.[35] Most processional routes only traverse the

[35] Processional festivals are discussed in detail in Chapter 1; see also, Chetty, *History of Triplicane*, pp. 34–43, for a description of various processional routes and halting places of the various deities during calendrical festivals.

INDEX TO NUMBERS

1 Glass Room
2 Sri Narasimhaswami Kalyana Mandapam
3 Sri Varadarajaswami Sannithi
4 Sri Andal Sannithi
5 Sri Vedavalli Thayar Sannithi
6 Sri Narasimhaswami Sannithi
7 Sri Parthasarathiswami Sannithi
8 Garbagraham
9 Hanumar Sannithi
10 Ranganathar Sannithi
11 Ramar Sannithi
12 Maha Mandapam
13 Madapalli
14 Dwaja Sthambam
15 Balipeedam
16 Dwaja Sthambam
17 Balipeedam
18 Glass Room
19 Kalyana Mandapam
20 Neerali Mandapam
21 Hanumar Temple
22 Swarga Vasal

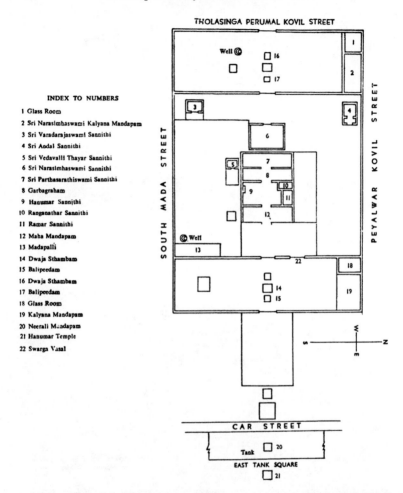

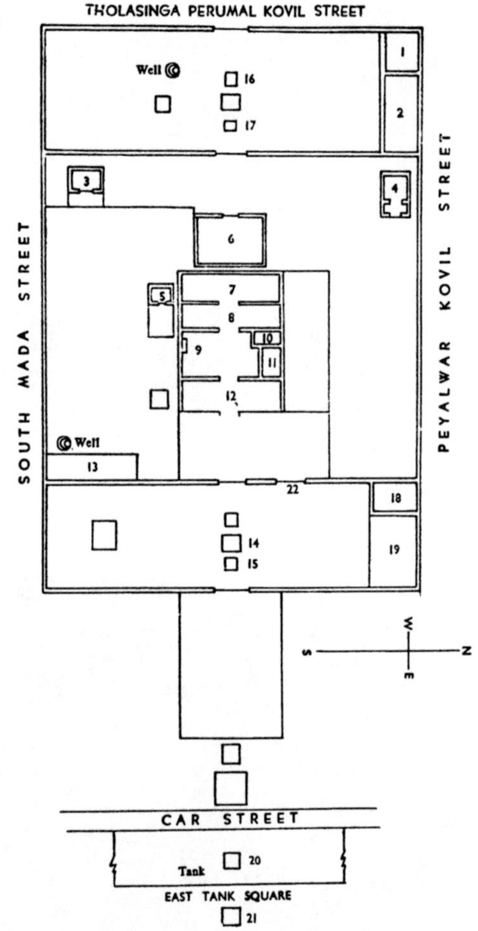

Figure 4. Śrī Pārtasārati Svāmi Temple, not to scale (*Census of India 1961*, Vol. 9, Pt. 11-D)

four streets that form a direct square enclosure for the temple. A few follow a route that also circumambulates the temple tank in addition to the temple walls. And during certain special calendrical festivals, the chief deity and various subordinate deities go even farther out into the heart of the commercial and residential areas of Triplicane.[36]

In the streets immediately bordering and adjoining the temple, the atmosphere is evocative of what the environs of the temple must have been like in the past. Many residents of the houses immediately

[36] Chetty, *History of Triplicane*, pp. 34–43.

surrounding the temple have intimate connections with the temple, as priests, donors, or other temple servants. Many of the neighboring houses, in fact, support endowments in the temple through their rents. The portals of many of the houses are decorated with woodcarvings of the feet of Lord Viṣṇu, which are the iconic model for the forehead mark (*nāmam*) worn by devout South Indian Śrī Vaisnavas today. The general ambience of the temple and its environs is intensely Vaisnavite and, on closer examination, Vaisnavite in the spirit of the Teṉkalai subtradition of South Indian Śrī Vaisnavism, a category that is discussed throughout the study.

The rhythms of activity in and around the temple are complex. They vary, by the hour of the day, the day of the week, the week of the month, and the month of the year.[37] During the year that I spent in Madras, I tried to adjust my own activities to these rhythms. When the temple was at its liveliest, in the mornings and evenings, and especially during processionals, I tried to observe as much as I could and asked my various informants to interpret as much as they could. I spent some of the dormant parts of the ritual day in the temple office, looking at temple records of various kinds and talking to various people in and around the temple. But I also spent a good part of these dormant periods, in both a daily and a calendrical sense, with "texts" of various sorts: books on temple ritual and monographs on other temples which I found in various libraries around Madras city; British administrative records at the Tamiḻnāṭu Archives; and legal documents pertaining to the temple at the High Court of Madras.

Thus, my own daily peregrinations were, albeit erratically, attempts to link "text" and "context," documented past and ethnographic present. For the first half of my year in Madras this was an immensely frustrating dialectic. My informants seemed to me difficult, even obtuse: their language (although I spoke Tamil with them) seemed private and arbitrary, their concerns either petty or pedantic. The texts and records I encountered seemed equally perverse, equally dominated by the seemingly arbitrary concerns of scholars of South Indian religion, British bureaucrats, and Anglo-Indian judges. The fit was far from neat. But I persisted, persuaded by the stubbornness of my informants and the force of the ritual and political dramas I witnessed, in trying to make sense of the "present," the living concerns and categories that I saw around me.

After many months I gradually began to appreciate that the texts and the archival records were not, after all, so distant from what I

[37] For a description of the ritual calendar, see Chapter 1.

saw and heard in the temple. Some common themes began to emerge, themes that linked the past and the present and, more important, themes that revealed the connection between the seemingly confused domains of authority, ritual, and redistribution in the temple. This discovery of diachronic continuity (in spite of significant change) and structural coherence within the various meanings and functions of the temple is what I have sought to describe and develop. It underlies the organizational logic of the book as well as the nature and rhetorical form that its arguments have taken.

Method and organization

The overall organization of the study reflects the complexities of doing an ethnohistory in the sense that I have defined the term. I have deliberately sought to preserve, in the sequence of chapters, the ambiguous and dialectical way in which the past and the present appeared to me to interact in this particular temple.

The first section of Chapter 1 presents a highly schematized description, rooted in the ethnographic present, of the "cultural system" of the temple, the core meanings, beliefs, and rules for action. These govern particular aspects of the life of the institution, and their interrelationship provides a kind of grammar through which we can understand the endless real combinations of ritual, authority, and resource management in the active life of the temple. The central idea here is the sovereignty of the deity and its ethnosociological consequences for behavior. The second section of this chapter, seemingly abruptly introduced, is a detailed report of a recent series of conflicts between the Teṉkalai subsect at Triplicane and the government of Madras over control of the Śrī Pārtasārati Svāmi Temple.

These two perspectives on the "present" have been juxtaposed in order to suggest that the universe of beliefs that makes sense of the temple, although coherent, is also problematic. But the real purpose of this juxtaposition is to show that the link between the *shared* beliefs that unite the temple community and the *divergent* beliefs that create conflict between two important sets of participants in the temple can only be sought in the "past." Nor is it adequate to extract the pictures of the "past" provided by the participants themselves, for these portraits of the past (like the "foreign manuscripts" of Geertz) themselves require interpretation. Such interpretation of the various "pasts" constructed by participants today requires contexts, and informants rarely can provide such contexts: Only the historical sources, with their own hermeneutical problems, can do so. The problematic present, therefore, compels us to make an excursion into the past. The results of that excursion are presented in Chapters 2, 3, 4, and 5.

In Chapter 2 a general argument is developed concerning the dynamic social and cultural context within which temples thrived in pre-British South India. The concentration on Vaisnavite institutions and on sectarian developments within South Indian Śrī Vaisnavism is meant to serve two purposes: to suggest, first, that the cultural understandings underlying the temple in pre-British South India were themselves part of a dynamic and evolving sociohistorical context, and, second, to develop a sort of historical lexicon for a series of key terms, rules, and beliefs that took shape in this period but which are important and alive in the Śrī Pārtasārati Svāmi Temple today. Of these, the term *Teṉkalai*, and the sectarian affiliation it indicates, is only one, though the dominant one. The brief analysis of some late Vijayanagara inscriptions pertaining to the Śrī Pārtasārati Svāmi Temple is meant simply to indicate that this larger universe of relations did encompass this particular temple as well. Thus, the function of this detailed pre-British chapter is not to fulfill one's chronological compulsiveness but rather to provide an overall idea of the *actual* context in pre-British South India, which provides the source for many key meanings and issues today. Also, it represents the broad cultural universe to which the British, from the early eighteenth century, had to address themselves as the new rulers of South India.

Chapter 3 uses largely British administrative data in order to assess the ways in which the British came to deal with the Śrī Pārtasārati Svāmi Temple. Its argument is that British efforts to "manage" conflict in the temple had the twin effects of forcing the British to act in accordance with the structural and cultural needs of the temple community and of providing natives with a fresh set of categories within which to frame their interests in the redistributive process of the temple.

Chapter 4 uses British administrative as well as legal records to analyze the ambivalent response of British administrators to their role as "protectors" of the Hindu temple, their relinquishment of this role, and the "natural" shift of the temple to the judiciary for the resolution of conflict. The category *Teṉkalai* emerges as the bureaucratic charter for temple control but in a way that is discontinuous with its meaning in the pre-British period.

Chapter 5 discusses the interaction between the temple and the Anglo-Indian courts in Madras on the basis of data generated in a series of "legal dramas" involving the temple during this period. The argument of this chapter is that the product of interaction between Anglo-Indian judges, working with English legal categories, and native litigants, expressing their rather different concerns in this new language, was paradoxical. On the one hand, the term *Teṉkalai* acquired a coherent and comprehensive interpretation as an authoritative source for defining the nature of temple control; but at the same time, this interaction between temple and court encouraged the legal reification of the diverse rights of various groups in the temple in such a way as to seriously fragment the distribution of authority in the temple.

In Chapter 6 these empirical arguments are brought together in order to formulate a general argument about continuity and change in the temple as a social and cultural system and in order to evaluate, in retrospect, the theoretical and methodological premises with which this Introduction was begun.

The argument

The overall argument, in its most elementary form, has two parts, the first having to do with continuity in the cultural system of the temple and the second having to do with the question of change.

1. What is the South Indian temple? By way of a highly condensed definition, I would argue that to merit being called a temple an institution must fulfill three requirements: (a) as a place, or a *sacred space*, the temple is an architectural entity that provides a royal abode for the deity enshrined in it, who is conceived as a paradigmatic sovereign; (b) as a *process*, the temple has a redistributive role, which in this cultural context consists of a continuous flow of transactions between worshippers and deity, in which resources and services are given *to* the deity and are returned *by* the deity to the worshippers in the form of "shares," demarcated by certain kinds of honors; (c) as a *symbol* or, more accurately, as a system of symbols, the temple has a "metasocial," or reflexive, quality. It serves to dramatize and define certain key South Indian ideas concerning authority, exchange, and worship at the same time that it provides an arena in which social relations in the broader societal context can be tested, contested, and refined. These three elementary features of the South Indian temple, whereby it is a special sort of royal abode, a

specific sort of redistributive process, and a powerfully reflexive symbolic system, provide the basic cultural elements of continuity in the temple from the pre-British period to the present.

2. How has the temple changed? Because this study argues that no essential cultural change has occurred in the temple, it follows that we must look elsewhere for indices of change. Put baldly, what has changed is not the temple as a cultural entity but the principles that determine how to control or manage the temple. Thus, it might be said that the social system of the temple (defined particularly in terms of the authoritative codes that determine the day-to-day regularities in the functioning of the institution) has undergone some important changes. The primary consequence of British rule, and its post-independence successor, has been to radically complicate the idea of temple control and, specifically, to fragment key authoritative relations in the temple. In the case of the Śrī Pārtasārati Svāmi Temple, the specific category whose history best captures the changes in the principles of temple control is denoted by the word *Teṉkalai*: What this word denoted in the pre-British period and has gradually come to denote since then, in relation to the control and management of this temple, is a condensed guide to the larger contextual changes. The term *Teṉkalai*, therefore, plays an important role throughout this study.

At the heart of my ethnohistorical argument, therefore, lies an irony: What has survived in the temple is a certain idea of the deity as an authoritative figure; what has changed, however, are precisely the rules and actions that determine how to manage and control the processes presided over by this authoritative figure. Authority, in an important cultural sense, is the locus of continuity. But authority, in an equally important social-structural sense, has become fragmented. This book is concerned largely with the documentation and explication of this irony.

1

THE SOUTH INDIAN TEMPLE: CULTURAL MODEL AND HISTORICAL PROBLEM

The Śrī Pārtasārati Svāmi Temple is only one of thousands of temples in the state of Tamiḻnāṭu in South India. These temples vary organizationally, ritually, doctrinally, and iconographically. But all these temples, whether large or small, wealthy or poor, share a common cultural and institutional model, although they might reflect it only partially and in more or less truncated forms. This model, composed of a series of beliefs and rules for action, is analyzed in this chapter and contextualized in ethnographic data from the Śrī Pārtasārati Svāmi Temple.[1]

At the moral and iconographic center of the South Indian temple is the deity. This deity, however, is not a mere image. It is conceived to be, in several thoroughly concrete senses, a person. The problem of how a stone figure can be a person has engaged legal and philosophical scholars for almost the last ten centuries and has been a particular subject of contention since the advent of British legal systems in South India.[2] But regardless of the philosophical and legal biases of those concerned with this question, what is clear is that they were faced with a post-Vedic cultural situation in which the worship of deities that were concretely treated as persons had become popular. Both high-level philosophical treatments and popular behavior provide evidence that the deity is considered fully corporeal, sentient and intelligent.[3] The ceremony of vivifying the idol (*prāṇa pratiṣṭai*) in Puranic and Agamic texts having to do with temples does not seem to imply allegory or metaphor. The daily

[1] All the basic ideas presented in this chapter pertaining to the underlying principles of the South Indian temple are equally shared by my colleague and wife, Carol A. Breckenridge, in "The Śrī Mīnākṣi Sundarēsvarar Temple: A Study of Worship and Endowments in South India, 1800–1925" (Ph.D. diss., University of Wisconsin, 1976). These shared ideas have been generated over six years of continuous interaction and collaboration, and it is, therefore, impossible to draw clear boundaries or to make specific acknowledgments. I remain, however, particularly grateful to her for giving me the benefit of her careful research into the concept of *pūjā* and her theoretical insight into the role of donors and the structure of temple endowments.

[2] Gunter-Dietz Sontheimer, "Religious Endowments in India: The Juristic Personality of Hindu Deities," *Zeitschrift fur Vergleichende Rechtswissenschaft* 67 (1964): 45–100, Pt. 1.

[3] Ibid., pp. 44–59.

cycle of worship in temples, involving waking up the deity, dressing and periodically feeding it, and putting it to sleep at night,[4] implies the literal personality of the deity.

Gifts are made and property is dedicated to deities, who are invariably mentioned by name and in the dative case.[5] The gifts to deities (*tēvatāṉam*) are given for the personal benefit of the deity, and the donor , in return, *expects* a reward. Such evidence that the deity in a South Indian temple is not a mere idol (*pratimā*) can be multiplied. The Vedic notion of giving gifts to Brahmins must have been threatened by this idea of a personal relationship between worshipper and deity, with only a subordinate role for the priesthood. Accordingly, certain Brahmin legal scholars attempted to render this whole model into an allegorical variant of the Vedic sacrifice.[6] This allegorical view of the personality of the deity is still alive in certain judicial circles,[7] but, on the whole, legal and scholarly opinion is fundamentally in accord with the popular notion that the deity in a South Indian temple is a "juridical" person, although these legal categorizations often generate other difficulties for Indian judges.[8]

The extensive legal and scholarly literature on the subject of the personality of Hindu deities, however, has not paid particular attention to another enduring feature of the popular conception of deities in South India, namely, that these deities are understood not to be merely persons, but very special persons. In fact, all South Indian ethnographic evidence, particularly linguistic signs, suggests that the deity is conceived to be the paradigmatic sovereign. The Tamil word *kōyil* means both temple and royal palace. Temple servants are referred to as *paricaṉaṉkaḷ* (courtiers, servants of the king). Much of the paraphernalia attached to temple deities, especially when they are taken out in processions, is indistinguishable from the paraphernalia of human kings: conches, palanquins, umbrellas, elephants, fly whisks, and so on.[9] The language of service to the deity is the idiom of bonded servitude (*aṭimai*), and the deity is referred to explicitly in terms that indicate universal lordship and sovereignty (*iṟaivaṉ*, *svāmi*, *perumāḷ*). This family of terms, which strongly suggests that

[4] This ritual process is more fully analyzed later in this chapter.
[5] Sontheimer, "Religious Endowments in India," pp. 70–1.
[6] Ibid., pp. 60–1.
[7] Ibid., pp. 45–6.
[8] Ibid., pp. 78–97.
[9] For evidence that this set of objects is strongly associated with kingship in South India, see T. V. Mahalingam, *South Indian Polity* (Madras, 1967), pp. 87–92.

the deity is a sovereign person, is fully sustained by the attitude of worshippers in temples, which is not merely one of piety and veneration but one of awe, fear, and enthusiastic subordination. If the deity is a sovereign, then one might ask what this sovereign exercises rule over.

At one normative level the domain of this sovereign ruler is the temple. In the symbolism of temple architecture, the various parts of the temple are considered to be parts of the body, not simply the human body but the divine body as well. This physiological analogy, given the biophysical theories of Hinduism, is simultaneously a cosmological analogy, so that the temple is a cosmic body, that is, the universe conceived as a body. However, in Indian texts there are numerous versions of this basic paradigm (temple : body : cosmos), which emphasize different physiological and cosmological traditions within this shared framework.[10] But this imagery answers explicitly the question of where the deity resides, rather than the question of what the deity rules. The deity is a sovereign ruler, not so much of a *domain* as of a *process*, a redistributive process. In what does this process consist?

The core of temple ritual is described by the term *pūjā* (Tamil, *pūcai*: worship, adoration). *Pūjā* consists of sixteen rites of adoration (*upacāram*) directed to the deity. Although some sources vary the number by disaggregating or synthesizing some of these rites, the standard number is sixteen: (1) *āvākaṉam* (invocation); (2) *stāpaṉam* (fixing); (3) *pāttiyam* (water for the washing of the feet); (4) *ācamanam* (water for sipping); (5) *arkkiyam* (water for hand-washing); (6) *apiṣēkam* (bathing of the idol); (7) *vastiram kaṇṭam cātuttal* (dressing and perfuming); (8) *puṣpancātuttal* (offering of flowers); (9) *tūpatīpam camarpittal* (offering of incense and light); (10) *naivēttiyam* (offering of food); (11) *pali* (sacrifice); (12) *hōmam* (oblation through fire); (13) *nityōtsavam* (daily festival); (14) *vāttiyam* (music); (15) *narttaṉam* (dancing); (16) *utvācanam* (send-off).[11]

This core set of adoration ceremonies together comprise *pūjā*.[12] But to understand temple ritual fully, it is necessary to appreciate the subdivisions of *pūjā* into (1) *nittiyam* (daily); (2) *naimittikam* (on

[10] S. Viraswami Pathar, *Temple and Its Significance* (Tiruchi, India, 1974), pp. 155–61; also see the Introduction to *Speaking of Siva*, trans. and Introduction by A. K. Ramanujan (Baltimore, 1973), for an extremely interesting analysis of the temple:body analogy in the radical devotional poetry of the Vīrasaiva movement in medieval Kannada country.

[11] C. G. Diehl, *Instrument and Purpose* (Lund, Sweden, 1956), p. 90, fn. 1.

[12] For an elaborate description of *pūjā* in Vaisnava temples, see K. Rangachari, *The Sri Vaishnava Brahmins* (Madras, 1931), pp. 141–9.

special occasions, such as consecrations, *pratiṣṭai*, and festivals, *utsavam*); and (3) *kāmiyam* (for expiation in times of evil influences).[13] Most temples have between three and six daily *pūjās*. All ritual in South Indian temples, whether daily, occasional, or calendrical, reflects this basic model of *pūjā* offered to a sovereign deity,[14] although ritual variations are determined by the specific Agamic code that governs a particular temple,[15] as well as other local factors.

The ritual cycle at the Śrī Pārtasārati Svāmi Temple

Although the daily cycle of worship at this temple is focused on its chief deity, the full complexity of worship can best be appreciated by considering the annual cycle of festivals at the temple.[16] In addition to the main shrine for the chief deity of this temple, Śrī Pārtasārati Svāmi, named after the incarnation of Krishna who was Arjuna's charioteer in the *Mahabharata*, there are six subshrines. They are for the four other incarnations of Viṣṇu, Rāma, Narasimha, Gajēntira-Varatan, and Ranganātha; for the goddess-consort of Ranganātha, Vētavaḷḷi Tāyār; and for Āṇṭāḷ, the sole female member of the twelve poet-saints of medieval Vaisnavism, the *āḻvārs*.[17] Deified also are the other eleven *āḻvārs*[18] and nine *ācāriyas*, the great sectarian leaders of the *Teṉkalai* tradition of South Indian Vaisnavism.[19] The festival cycle is oriented to these twenty-eight deified figures, among whom the chief deity, Śrī Pārtasārati Svāmi, has the sovereign and preponderant role.

Dates are set for festivals in two ways:[20] The first is by reference to one of the fourteen days in the bright or dark half of the moon in a given month; the second is by reference to *nakṣattirams* (star days or lunar asterisms), the twenty-seven named positions through which the moon moves during a month, with a twenty-eighth if needed to

[13] Diehl, *Instrument and Purpose*, pp. 49–54.

[14] Jan Gonda, *Visnuism and Sivaism: A Comparison* (London, 1970), pp. 76–7.

[15] For a brief review of the corpus of Agamic texts, both Saivite and Vaisnavite, see Diehl, *Instrument and Purpose*, pp. 43–6. This corpus is yet to be exhaustively catalogued, edited, and analyzed.

[16] For a careful account of this annual cycle, see James L. Martin, "The Cycle of Festivals at Pārthasārathi Swāmi Temple," in Bardwell L. Smith, ed., *Journal of the American Academy of Religion: Asian Religions* (1971), pp. 223–40.

[17] Ibid., p. 224; for a brief account of the iconography and architecture of these shrines, as well as the endowments that support them, see V. Chetty, *History of Triplicane and the Temple of Sri Parthasarathi Swamy* (Madras, 1948), pp. 10–34.

[18] For a brief account of the twelve *Āḻvārs*, see K. C. Varadachari, *Āḻvārs of South India* (Bombay, 1966), passim.

[19] See Chapter 2.

[20] Martin, "Cycle of Festivals," pp. 224–5.

fill out the month. Tamil months begin on the fourteenth to the eighteenth day of months in the Gregorian calendar, which are:

Cittirai (April–May)	Aippaci (October–November)
Vaikāci (May–June)	Kārttikai (November–December)
Āṉi (June–July)	Mārkaḻi (December–January)
Āvaṇi (August–September)	Māci (February–March)
Puraṭṭāci (September–October)	Paṅkuṇi (March–April)

The monthly cycle of festivals consists of the new moon, the full moon, the two *ēkātaci* days (eleventh day after the new and full moons), and the first day of the Tamil month (*mācappiravēcam*), all presided over by the chief deity, Śrī Pārtasārati Svāmi. There are also monthly festivals for all the five main deities, the incarnations of Viṣṇu, on their own star days (*tirunakṣattiram*) and in the case of Śrī Pārtasārati Svāmi, monthly festivals on both the star day of tiruvōṇam, common to all forms of Viṣṇu, and rōhiṇi, for Kriṣṇā.[21] Finally, there are brief monthly festivals on the star days of the deified *āḻvār*s and *ācāriya*s.

In addition to these monthly festivals, there are forty-two annual festivals, which taken together occupy 218 days of the year: sixteen 10-day festivals, twenty-one 1-day festivals, and five festivals of between 1 and 10 days.[22] The basic and most elaborate paradigm for all these festivals is the great festival (*brahmōtsavam*) for the sovereign deity of the temple, Śrī Pārtasārati Svāmi, which occupies ten days in the month of Cittirai (April–May). It is worth describing this festival in some detail, so as to get some of the flavor of all the other festivals.[23]

The elementary units of the great 10-day festival are two processions (morning and evening) on each of the first nine days of the festival and one evening procession on the tenth day. The central feature of each of these processions is the *utsavar*, the processional form of the deity, which is considerably smaller and hence more portable than the main deity in the sanctum, known as the *mūlavar* (the first One). This processional form of the deity is carried on an elaborate vehicle (*vākanam*) or palanquin (*pallakku*) in a clockwise direction around the four streets (known as *māṭā*, or "car," streets) that immediately border the temple. These vehicles are borne on the shoulders of a set of non-Brahmin temple servants, *śrīpātam-*

[21] Ibid., p. 224.
[22] Ibid., p. 225.
[23] The following description combines Martin's descriptions (ibid., pp. 226–8) with my own observations of the festival celebrated in April 1974.

tāṅkīs (literally, bearers of the feet of the Lord), who have the special right to perform this service.

Each such procession is led by the temple elephant, which bears a Teṉkalai sectarian mark.[24] The elephant is ridden by a mahout, who is also a temple servant, and is followed by a bull bearing drums that are beaten by a walking attendant. A horse, ridden by another temple servant and also bearing drums, comes next. It is followed by the various sets of temple musicians, who walk backwards while playing their instruments in order to face the deity. Finally, there is the vehicle bearing the processional form of the deity, on which the *arccakaṉ*s (temple priests) themselves are standing.

The mass of devotees follows behind this royal entourage as it proceeds slowly through the four sanctified streets around the temple. This whole processional nexus pauses at various points, so that residents and worshippers along the route can make offerings to the deity. Sometimes worshippers construct *pantal*s (temporary thatch-roofed structures) under which the deity rests. The most elaborate of these halts is at stone structures called *maṇṭapam*s, erected by individuals generally representing various collectivities, who have established the right to worship the deity and to make offerings to it during these processions. Worship thus offered to the deity during a procession is referred to by the term *maṇṭakappaṭi* (or *maṇṭapappaṭi*).[25]

In each of these processions that make up the total festival the deity travels on a different vehicle, which denotes its link to a particular aspect of the mythology of Viṣṇu.[26] Also, throughout the festival, elaborate rituals, both of a Vedic sacrificial kind and those involving more elaborate versions of the daily *pūjā* model, are directed to the chief deity. These stationary, inner-temple ritual performances during the great festival follow closely the prescriptions of the ritual texts known as the Vaikānasa Āgamas.[27]

The Vaikānasa Āgamas are the ritual texts of the Vaikānasa priesthood, a Vedic school of the Taittiriya branch of the Black Yajur Vēda, and were probably codified some time after the fourth

[24] See Chapter 2, where the evolution of this subsectarian formation within South Indian Śrī Vaisnavism is discussed.

[25] The cultural form, as well as the historical role of the *maṇṭakappaṭi* in the attempts of mobile groups to "enter" South Indian temples, is analyzed by Breckenridge, "Śrī Mīnāksi Sundarēśvarar Temple," in relation to group formation and maintenance and in relation to the segmented organization of authority in the temple.

[26] Martin, "Cycle of Festivals," pp. 226–8.

[27] See Jan Gonda, *Aspects of Early Visnuism* (Utrecht, 1954), pp. 244–55, for an elaborate paraphrase of the relevant portions of these texts.

century of this era.[28] Gonda notes that the main objects of these agrarian festivities were "appeasement of evil, rain, health, opulence, prosperity, fertility, increase of the power of the king – who is not only the protector of his peaceable subjects, but also the mediator in their interest, in stimulating the powers of fertility."[29] In these ancient texts, the two goals of this ritual process, which are mentioned frequently in the texts, are those of *śānti* (destruction of evil influences) and *puṣṭi* (a well-nourished condition).[30]

In the *brahmōtsavam* celebrated today in the Śrī Pārtasārati Svāmi Temple, this basic and ancient cultural model of the great festival in honor of Viṣṇu is followed very closely. But some special and elaborate features of the present-day festival deserve emphasis, because they represent elaborations or innovations upon the textual prescriptions of the old Vaikānasa texts. The first of these is the role given to the recitation of the Prabandam corpus of devotional poetry composed by the poet-saints of the medieval period, the *āḻvārs*, in these processions.[31] The group of Teṉkalai Śrī Vaisnava males who share the privilege of reciting these sacred poems precede the deity in the procession, whereas those who recite the Vēdas follow the deity, indicating the tremendous contemporary significance of this poetic corpus for practical Śrī Vaisnavism in South India.

The second feature, noted already, which is more an elaboration than an innovation, involves the vehicles on which the deity is transported on any given occasion: Their variety and complexity reflect a process of mythological elaboration and ritual pomp that clearly postdates the relative austerity of the early Vaikānasa texts. Third, of all the adorations (*upacāram*) offered to the deity in the course of those festivals, a preponderant importance attaches to *naivēttiyam* (offerings of cooked food), which is done on a massive scale. Again, this elaboration of the simplicity of the original Vaikānasa texts probably occurred at the great temple at Tirupati in the period after the twelfth century A.D.[32] Finally, great importance attaches to the redistribution (*viṉiyōkam*) of the offerings made to the deity by the donor, a feature that is discussed later.

All the festivals at the Śrī Pārtasārati Svāmi Temple, whether they are focused on the main deity, one of the subordinate deities, or

[28] Ibid., pp. 234–5.
[29] Ibid., p. 242.
[30] Ibid., p. 255.
[31] For the entry of this specifically sectarian element into temple ritual, see Chapter 2.
[32] See Chapter 2.

one of the deified *āḻvārs* or *ācāriyas*, and regardless of their length and grandeur, reflect more or less elaborate versions of the above model of the *brahmōtsavam*, with special attention on the given day to certain elaborate inner-temple rituals, extra-temple processions on the royal model, and major food offerings by various donors. The specific dramatic and ritual variations in these festivals are determined by the varied mythologies and hagiographies that have developed around these various deified figures.[33]

In addition to *pūjā*, the elementary daily form of worship, and the processional/festival extension of *pūjā* in calendrical festivals, there is a third form of worship, *arccaṉai*, which is for the benefit of the worshipper (*ātmārttam*) rather than for the benefit of the cosmos (*parārttam*), as in the case of *pūjā* or *utsavam*.[34] *Arccaṉai* involves the offering of selected items such as flowers, fruits, incense, and saffron to the deity, via the priest, while the deity's several names and titles are recited by the priest, generally after the regular daily *pūjā* has been completed. *Arccanai* worship is more or less elaborate and expensive, depending on the number of names recited, a fact that is subject to customary prescription. The offering of *arccanai* may be occasioned by a crisis (illness, court case, sterility, poverty), a change in status (marriage, parenthood, studenthood), or gratitude for a wish fulfilled. *Arccaṉai* offerings are the form of worship that is most widespread and popular among the numerous and less affluent worshippers at South Indian temples who cannot afford the more expensive subsidy of a daily *pūjā* or a part of a calendrical festival.

The temple publishes an annual calendar of its ritual cycle, which excludes the daily *pūjā*.[35] The sample of its contents (Table 1), translated from the original Tamil, for the month of Cittirai (April–May) 1974 illustrates both its density as well as the diverse collection of disparate donors who make possible the actualization of this ritual process.

In addition to displaying the sheer density of the ritual process at this temple, this one-month sample from the ritual calendar also places considerable emphasis on the great diversity of the donors who subsidize the various elements of this ongoing ritual process. What accounts for the interest of these individuals and corporate

[33] Martin, "Cycle of Festivals," pp. 226–35; also, Chetty, *History of Triplicane*, passim.

[34] Diehl, *Instrument and Purpose*, p. 56.

[35] *Pirammātica Varucattiya Utsava Vivaram 1973–1974* (Triplicane, 1973).

Table 1. *Ritual calendar for the month of Cittirai (April-May)*

Tamil date	English date	Day	Lunar phase	Lunar asterism	Festival details/donors
Cittirai	April				
1	13	Fri.	Ēkātaci	Makam	Tirumaḻicai Āḻvār; procession of Śrī Pārtasārati Svāmi for the new year
2	14	Sat.	Tvātaci	Pūram	Śrī Āṇṭāl
3	15	Sun.		Uttiram	Monthly festival of Vētavaḷḷi Tāyār (donor: Śri Attanki Svāmi)
4	16	Mon.		Astam	Great Festival (Prahmōtsavam) of Śrī Pārtasārati Svāmi: The Lord's Festival (donor: Messrs. Ramachandra & Co.) Kūrattāḻvān
5	17	Tues.	Paurṇami	Cittirai	Aṅkurārppaṇam (Ceremony of Sprouting); Annual Festival of Maturakavi Āḻvār (donor: ex-trustee T. A. Varadachariar); Bath for main deity (donor: Mr. P. Krishnamachariar)
6	18	Wed.		Cuvāti	1st day of Great Festival: morning flag hoisting (donor: Mr. T. S. Chinnaswami Chettiyar); arch vehicle (donors: ex-trustees Mr. T. V. Tiruvenkatachariar and Mr. E. Bhoopathy Naidu); evening: tree vehicle (The Ātivalam Brothers Club)
7	19	Thur.	Vicākam		2nd day of Great Festival: morning snake vehicle (donor: Mr. T. P. Raju Pillay Trust); evening: lion vehicle (donor: Mrs. T. K. Kannamal Trust). Dēsayis (a Naidu subsect)
8	20	Fri.		Aṉuṣam	3rd day of Great Festival: vehicle of *karuṭāi* (sacred bird of Viṣṇu) (donor: Mr. T. Shanmugham Estate; *maṇṭakappaṭi* (subritual) in Gangaikoṇṭān pillared hall (donor:

Table 1 (*cont.*)

Tamil date	English date	Day	Lunar phase	Lunar asterism	Festival details/donors
					Mr. Narayanaswami Pillay); evening: swan vehicle (donor: Mr. R. M. Muttukumarappa Rettiyar)
9	21	Sat.		Kēṭṭai	4th day of Great Festival: morning: sun vehicle; evening: moon vehicle (donor: Mr. C. Ramanujam Pillay Trust)
10	22	Sun.			5th day of Great Festival; morning: adornment of the deity in the female form, Mōhini (donors: Mavalur Srimati Etukuri Ammal and Mr. A. R. Rao); evening: vehicle in the form of Hanumān, the monkey god (donors: P. Srinivasa Ayyangar Trust and Mr. K. Krishnamachariar & Bros.); *maṇṭakappati* (subritual) in Hanumān subshrine (donor: Mr. Subramanya Achari)
11	23	Mon.		Mūlam	6th day of Great Festival: vehicle in the form of the superstructure of the temple (*vimānam*) (donor: Mr. Venkatadari Apparao); evening: elephant vehicle (donor: Mr. E. S. Chetty Charity)
12	24	Tues.		Pūrāṭam	7th day of Great Festival: morning car festival (donors: ex-trustee V. Veeraraghavachariar and Mr. Rangi Raghavachariar Trust); evening: holy bath in a garden (donor: Mr. M. Ranganatham Chetty)
13	25	Wed.		Uttirāṭam	8th day of Great Festival: palanquin with deity decorated as child Krishna (donor: Mr. K. Devaperumal Ayya Char-

Table 1 (*cont.*)

Tamil date	English date	Day	Lunar phase	Lunar asterism	Festival details/donors
					ity); evening: horse vehicle (donor: Mr. M. Sudarshanam Ayyangar Trust)
14	26	Thurs.		Tiruvōṇam	9th (and most important) day of Great Festival: palanquin with small human figures representing human carriers (T. K. K. N. N. Vaisya Charity); evening: glass palanquin (Mr. M. Venkatakrishna Chetty); lowering of the flag (donor: T. K. K. N. N. Vaisya Charity)
15	27	Fri.		Aviṭṭam	10th day of Great Festival: palanquin with screen of cooling roots (*veṭṭivērta tiruttēr*) (donor: Mr. T. Baluchettiyar), Festival of Srī Rāmānujā, 1st day: morning: palanquin (donors: Mr. M. R. Sampath Kumaran and Mr. M. C. Krishnan); evening: palanquin borne on human shoulders (*tōḷukkiṉiyān*) (donors: Mr. S. V. Vittoba Naidu and Mr. S. Balakrishnan)
16	28	Sat.		Cataiyam	*Viṭāyatti* (Festival of Rest for Śri Pārtasārati Svāmi): 1st day (donor: Sri P. Kuppuswami Chetty Trust/Mr. R. Krishnamachariar); *Maṇṭakappaṭi* (subritual) at the temple office (donor: Mrs. P. Kannambal Trust); Pēyāḻvār; Festival of Rāmānujā, 2nd day: morning: palanquin and evening *tōḷukkiṉiyān* (donor: Mr. Nathella Sampath Chetty)
17	29	Sun.	Ekātaci	Puraṭṭāci	2nd day of Festival of Rest (donor: Mrs. Vimala Narasimhulu Naidu); 3rd day of

Table 1 (*cont.*)

Tamil date	English date	Day	Lunar phase	Lunar asterism	Festival details/donors
					Festival of Rāmānujā: morning: palanquin (donor: Yatava Kamalammal Trust); evening: *tōḷukkiṉiyāṉ* (donor: Mrs. K. P. Tayarammal Trust)
18	30	Mon.	Tvātaci	Uttiraṭati	3rd day of Festival of Rest (donor: Mr. T. Krishnaswamy Chettiyar); 4th day of Festival of Rāmānujā: morning: palanquin and evening: *tōḷukkiṉiyāṉ* (donor: Mrs. Tēsukkanammal); recitation of 1,008 names of the deity (*sakasranāma arccanai*) (donor: V. C. Sriramulu Chētty Trust)
19	May 1	Tues.		Rēvati	4th day of Festival of Rest (donor: Mr. R. N. Damodaram Naidu); 5th day of Festival of Rāmānujā; morning: palanquin (donor: Jivaratnammal Trust); evening: Sri R. Rangaswami Chettiyar)
20	2	Wed.	Amāvāciya	Aṣviṉi	5th day of Festival of Rest (donor: Elchur Udayavarlu Chetty); 6th day of Festival of Rāmānujā: morning: horse vehicle; evening: *tōḷukkiniyān* (Disciples of the Ethiraja Jīyar Mutt)
21	3	Thurs.		Paraṇi	6th day of Festival of Rest (donor: Messrs. Doraiswami Mudaliar & Sons); 7th day of Festival of Rāmānujā: morning: palanquin; evening: flower palanquin (T. K. K. N. N. Vaisya Charity)
22	4	Fri.		Tirukarttikai	7th day of Festival of Rest (donor: Mrs. Amartavalli Thayarammal); 8th day of Festival of Rāmānujā: morning: palanquin; evening: elephant vehicle (donor: M. V.

Table 1 (*cont.*)

Tamil date	English date	Day	Lunar phase	Lunar asterism	Festival details/donors
					Kannaiya Chetty Charity); Tirumankai Āḻvār
23	5	Sat.		Rōhiṇi	8th day of Festival of Rest (donor: V. P. Rangaswami Ayyangar and Party); 9th day of Festival of Rāmānujā; evening: car festival (donor: Ashtagothram S. R. Srinivasa Ayyangar); Tiruppan Āḻvār
24	6	Sun.		Mirukacīru Tiruvāti	9th day of Festival of Rest (donor: Mr. Gopalachari); conclusion of Festival of Rāmānujā (donor: Triplicane Sri Attanki Swamy); Tirukkachchi Nampikaḷ
25	7	Mon.		Puṉarvacu	Conclusion of Festival of Rest (donor: Mrs. C. S. Annammal); Festival of Mutaliyāṇṭān (donor: S. V. Chetty Charity); Kulasēkara Āḻvār, Empār; Festival of Rest for Rāmānujā: 1st day (donor: Mr. V. K. Krishnamachariar)
26	8	Tues.		Puṣyam	Festival of Rest for Rāmānujā, 2nd day (donor: Mr. G. A. Singamayyangar)
27	9	Wed.		Āyilyam	Conclusion of Festival of Rest for Rāmānujā (donor: Mr. M. S. Chetty Charity)
28	10	Thurs.		Makam	Tīrumaḻicai Āḻvār
29	11	Fri.		Pūram	Āṇṭāḷ; Friday Procession for Vetavaḷḷi Tāyār (donor: Sri Ayya Pillay Charity)
30	12	Sat.		Uttiram	Procession for Vētavaḷḷi Tāyār (donor: Sri Attanki Swami)
31	13	Sun.	Ēkātaci	Aṣtam	Procession of Lord Śrī Pārtasārati Svāmi (donor: Mr. V. Narasimhachari); Kūrattāḻvar

groups in subsidizing portions of the overall ritual calendar? To answer this question, it is necessary to view worship as a redistributive process.

Worship, redistribution, and honor

From one point of view, temple worship in South India based on the *pūjā* model reflects an extremely complex process of religious evolution in India, starting from the Vedic sacrificial system, complicated by the developments of the Puranic or Hinduistic period and increasingly embellished with Tantric elements.[36] In both lexical and structural terms, *pūjā* retains key elements of the Vedic sacrifice.[37] However, in trying to understand the essential structural *contrast* between the Vedic sacrifice and temple worship (*pūjā*), it might be useful to consider the contrast, in the language of economic anthropology, between "reciprocity" and "redistribution" as types of economic transaction. Marshall Sahlins provides the following version of the contrast:

> True, pooling (i.e., redistribution) and reciprocity may occur in the same social contexts – the same close kinsmen that pool their resources in household commensality, for instance, also as individuals share things with one another – but the precise social relations of pooling and reciprocity are not the same. Pooling is socially a *within* relation, the collective action of a group. Reciprocity is a *between* relation, the action and reaction of two parties. Thus pooling is the complement of social unity and, in Polanyi's term, "centricity"; whereas, reciprocity is social duality and "symmetry." Pooling stipulates a social center where goods meet and thence flow outwards, and a social boundary too, within which persons (or subgroups) are cooperatively related. But reciprocity stipulates two sides, two distinct socio-economic interests. Reciprocity can establish solidary relations, insofar as the material flow suggests assistance or mutual benefit, yet the social fact of sides is inescapable.[38]

This view of "reciprocity" fits very well with the classic analysis of Hubert and Mauss, who explain the particular features of religious sacrifice:

> In any sacrifice there is an act of abnegation since the sacrificer deprives himself and gives. Often this abnegation is even imposed upon him as a duty. For sacrifice is not always optional; the gods demand it. As the Hebrew ritual declares, worship and service is owed them; as the Hindus

[36] Gonda, *Visnuism and Sivaism*, p. 85.

[37] Ibid., Chap. 4, passim; also, P. V. Kane, *History of Dharmaśāstra*, 2nd ed., 5 vols. (Poona, 1941), 2: Pt. 2, Chap. 19, passim, particularly p. 714.

[38] Marshall Sahlins, *Stone Age Economics* (Chicago, 1972), pp. 188–9.

say, their share is owed them. But abnegation and submission are not without their selfish aspect. The sacrificer gives up something of himself but he does not give himself. Prudently, he sets himself aside. This is because if he gives, it is partly in order to receive. Thus sacrifice shows itself in a dual light; it is a useful act and it is an obligation. Disinterestedness is mingled with self-interest. That is why it has so frequently been conceived as a form of contract. Fundamentally perhaps there is no sacrifice that has not some contractual element. The two parties present exchange their services and each gets his due. For the gods too have need of the profane . . . In order that the sacred may subsist, its share must be given to it, and it is from the share of the profane that this apportionment is made.[39]

There is no doubt that this model of exchange also has its place in gifting activity to the sovereign deities in South Indian temples. But of greater importance in the South Indian temple is the "redistributive" model of economic relationships. Synthesizing a number of previous formulations concerning "redistribution," Sahlins provides the following analysis:

Rights of call on the produce of the underlying population, as well as obligations of generosity, are everywhere associated with chieftanship. The organized exercise of these rights and obligations is redistribution . . . This . . . takes various forms: subsidizing religious ceremony, social pageantry or war; underwriting craft production, trade, the construction of technical apparatus and of public and religious edifices; redistributing diverse local products; hospitality and succor of the community (in severalty or in general) during shortage. Speaking more broadly, redistribution by powers-that-be serves two purposes, either of which may be dominant in a given instance. The practical, logistic function – redistribution – sustains the community, or community effort, in a material sense. At the same time, or alternatively, it has an instrumental function: as a ritual of communion and of subordination to central authority, redistribution sustains the corporate structure itself, that is in a social sense. The practical benefits may be critical, but, whatever the practical benefits, chiefly pooling generates the spirit of unity and centricity, codifies the structure, stipulates the centralized organization of social order and social action.[40]

This "chiefly" model of redistribution fits the deity of a South Indian temple perfectly. This sharpens the seeming paradox that the chiefly slot is here filled by a deified stone image, which stands at the center of the temple as a set of moral and economic transactions. This paradox becomes muted, however, when we recall that the deity is strictly and literally conceived as a sovereign person. In what cultural terms is this "redistributive" situation conceived and organized?

[39] Henri Hubert and Marcel Mauss, *Sacrifice: Its Nature and Function*, trans. W. D. Halls (Chicago, 1964), p. 100.

[40] Sahlins, *Stone Age Economics*, pp. 189–90.

The gift, which places the donor (*upayakār*) in an active transactional relationship with the deity, initiates a process of redistribution (*viṉiyō-kam*) of a part of the offerings to all those involved in the ritual process: the donor himself, the staff of the temple (*paricaṉaṅkaḷ*, courtiers), and the worshippers (*cēvārtikaḷ*). This is true in the two main forms of worship, *pūjā* and *utsavam*, but in the third form of worship, *arccaṉai*, which fits the "reciprocal" model better, there is no real allocation of shares for either the worshippers or the staff: The offering is simply transvalued by being offered to the deity and returned to the worshipper. But, in the case of *pūjā* and *utsavam*, in which the offering of edible food to the deity is central, shares in the leavings of the deity accrue to all three categories of participants. The largest garland (*mālai*) worn by the deity during a specified ritual period and in some cases the silk vestments of the deity (*parivaṭṭam*) are bestowed on the donor, who is also given a share of the leftover food of the deity (*prasātam*) and priority in drinking the water (*tīrttam*) sanctified by contact with the deity's ablutions or meals.

Similarly, the staff/courtiers of the deity receive a part (*svatantiram*) of the leavings, generally the food leavings, of the deity. And finally, the worshippers receive a share in the sacred water and holy food left over from feeding the deity. This basic apportionment is subject to variation, depending on the particular temple, the particular ritual event, the scale of the celebration, and the largesse of the donor. Although much of the prescription of these shares comes to be customary in particular temples, the role of the donor in initiating the transaction and overseeing the redistribution is, in principle, pivotal. Thus the donor is referred to as *yajamāna* (the Vedic term for the sacrificer) and, in Vaisnava temples at any rate, the share of the worshippers is ascribed to the goodwill of the donor by the term *iṣṭa viṉiyōkam* (the desired redistribution), particularly in processional festivals.

These redistributed leavings of the deity are known as honors (*mariyātai*),[41] and they are subject to variation and fluidity in both their content and their recipients. Recognized sectarian leaders and political figures are often given some prominent combination of

[41] The term *mariyātai* (derived from the Sanskrit *maryāda*) refers to both the feature of persons and offices that is "honorable" and also, in the social/semantic context of temples, to a particular set of transvalued substances that embody and signify such persons. S. Hanchett has pointed out the general importance of this concept in ceremonial competition elsewhere in South India in "Hindu Potlatches: Ceremonial Reciprocity and Prestige in Karnataka," in Helen Ullrich, ed., *Competition and Modernization in South Asia* (New Delhi, 1975), pp. 27–59.

these honors. In Vaisnava temples an important honor is the placing of the *śrī saṭakōpaṉ* (a gold crown symbolizing the feet of Viṣṇu) on the heads of worshippers at the conclusion of *pūjā* and in the course of processionals. Given the public nature of these redistributive acts, the order in which they are distributed among a set of individuals is often as important as their content. Finally, particular days are allocated in the temple calendar to especially honor particular members of the temple staff, such as the priests.

But those honors are not simply denotative emblems of rank or status. They are seen to be the *constitutive features* of culturally privileged roles in relationship to the deity. That is, the receipt of specific honors, in any given context, *renders authoritative* the individual's share (*paṅku*) in the temple conceived as a redistributive process. Such a share would be composed of the right to offer service (*kaiṅkaryam*) to the deity, either through endowment (*upayam*) or through prescribed ritual function; the right to move the resources allocated for the specific ritual event; the right to command the relevant persons involved in the actualization of the given ritual; the right to perform some single part of a complex ritual event; and, finally, the right to worship the deity by simply witnessing the ritual. Depending on whether one was a donor, a temple servant, or a worshipper, and depending on the particular ritual event in question, one's share in the ritual process would have a different concrete content. But the sum total of one's rights, over time, would constitute one's share in the ritual and redistributive process of the temple.

This share is given public expression and authoritative constitution by some combination of the finite set of substances transvalued by association with the deity, which are referred to as honors. This powerful function of honors in the redistributive process of the temple, as well as the actual mechanics of redistribution in this cultural context, can best be appreciated by a representative set of examples of honors issues in the Śrī Pārtasārati Svāmi Temple in this century.

The best example of the constitutive function of honors in respect to the role of donor (*upayakār*) can be seen in the following letter from the descendant of the original donor of a specific trust to the chairman of the board of trustees at the Śrī Pārtasārati Svāmi Temple:

Respected Sir,

Sub: Manavalamamunigal Festival – 9th day morning – Srirangammal Trust – Regarding

I, K. Singarajan, grandson of Srirangammal residing in the above premises, entitled to receive the honours for the above festival and receiving for the past ten years even when my father was alive who was her son entitled for honours. Now I was not informed in the previous year to get the honour and other usual mariadais.

Please let me know in what stage the above said endowment is functioning in this temple and also I request the authorities to investigate the nature of the endowment, the amount invested, and the interest derived.

Thanking you,

Yours faithfully, etc.[42]

That the issue of honors is both the constitutive and the denotative element in a complex orchestration of rights in the redistributive process of the temple is clear. Particularly for donors, the redistributive consequences of their gifts is a serious affair. This can be seen in the following letter of complaint to the trustees from a donor, protesting the misappropriation of some share of sacred food (*prasātam*) generated by his endowment, by the *amīnā* of the temple, the second-in-command of the trustees:

Respected Sirs:

The third day festival of Rapaththu[43] is being conducted through our family by the Reserve Bank of India, Issue Department, Madras, for the last about four decades. On 23-12-1958, 10 Dosais,[44] 10 Vadais,[45] and 10 Laddus[46] were given out for distribution in the Thiruvaymozhi Goshti (Public). Out of that 2 and ¾ of each item was given as Swathanthram[47] according to rules. The balance of 7 and ¼ of each item were intended for distribution among the devotees present, according to the well-established usage prevalent in this Temple. Out of this above portion, which are purely intended for distribution (i.e., 7 and ¼ of each item), 2 Dosais, 2 Vadais, and 2 Laddus were stolen openly and kept separately by the Temple Staff. This was brought to the notice of the Amin, but he refused to take notice. It is pointed out that an ubayakar has every right to see his intention of distribution is properly fulfilled and the trustees are also equally responsible to see that Prasadams are utilised for the purposes for which they are intended.[48]

But it is not simply donors who are concerned about honors and their role in the redistributive process. Members of the temple staff

[42] K. Singarajan to chairman, Board of Trustees, November 5, 1966, Unfiled, Record Room, Śrī Pārtasārati Svāmi Temple, Madras.

[43] This festival is the second half of a 20-day celebration that falls in two segments on either side of Vaikunta Ekātaci, the holiest day of the Vaisnava calendar, and is of particular importance for the remembrance of the sacred poetry of the *āḻvār* poet-saints.

[44] Rice pancakes.

[45] Rice and lentil fritters.

[46] A kind of milk-sweet.

[47] The prescribed share of the temple staff in the leavings of the deity.

[48] C. Singarachary to trustees, December 28, 1958, Record Room, File No. 13, Śrī Pārtasārati Svāmi Temple, Madras.

are also extremely sensitive to this issue, particularly the priests. At the Śrī Pārtasārati Svāmi Temple, the rights of priesthood (*arccakam*) are exercised by two legally divided branches of a single lineage of Vaikānasas, a priestly caste discussed earlier.[49] These priests are today among the most vocal and defensive in asserting their distinct identity and autonomy as against all the other categories of individuals who have some role in temple worship. My main informant, the head of one of these two branches, expressed this feeling of autonomy very clearly. He saw himself as rooted solely in the neo-Vedic texts of the Vaikānasa school and as enjoying a special relationship to the deity. He attributed this special relationship of the priest to the deity to the fact that he was the only one who could do service to the deity involving actual physical contact with it (*toṭṭu kaiṅkaryam*) in those features of worship conventionally hidden from the public, such as bathing and feeding the deity. Thus, he asserted, the honors given to priests, unlike those given to donors and others, are like honors given to God himself.[50]

It is in this context of proud autonomy and distinct identity that we must appreciate the following case, initiated in the High Court of Judicature at Madras by the head of one of the branches of the priesthood at the Śrī Pārtasārati Svāmi Temple in 1933.[51] In his plaint, the priest in question complained about the loss of his appropriate share (*svatantiram*) in the leavings of the deity; his loss of precedence over the other temple servants and worshippers in the receipt of this honor; his loss of income because of the creation of new cashboxes in the temple by the trustees to siphon off public cash contributions that would otherwise come to him; and his loss of the capacity to determine certain ritual matters (*vaitīka vicāraṇai*). In the conclusion to this lengthy legal document,[52] this priest pithily summarized what he conceived to be the damages to his share in the redistributive process of the temple:

The plaintiffs therefore pray for a decree granting:
(a) declaration that the 1st Plaintiff as hereditary Archaka office holder is

[49] For the history of this split in a single priestly lineage, see the documents in Original Suit No. 485 of 1917, City Civil Court of Madras.

[50] For the theoretical/ritual contexts in which the priest is literally identified with the deity, see Diehl, *Instrument and Purpose*, p. 156; this idea, however, has not historically had much consequence on the status of temple priests, who have always been considered Brahmins of low and dubious status. This continues to be so today, where the priests are neither wealthy nor powerful but cling to their special ritual privileges for shreds of status.

[51] C. S. 211 of 1933, High Court of Judicature at Madras.

[52] Para. 16 of the Plaint dated May 14, 1933, in C.S. 241 of 1933, High Court of Judicature at Madras.

entitled according to Vaikhanasa sastras and usage of the institution to receive his Svatantrams first before all other office holders in the temple and distribution to Goshti[53] in every Thaligai[54] offered by Sevarthis and Ubayakars to the various deities in the Plaint temple and shrines attached thereto.

(b) mandatory injunction directing the Defendants (the then Trustees) to give the 1st Plaintiff his Swathantrams first as foresaid.

(c) declaration that the first plaintiff as Mirasi[55] Archaka Office Holder is entitled to "Vaidika Vicharana" in the temple and for an injunction restraining the Defendants from performing religious ceremonies or festivals in the temple except on the date fixed and in the manner settled by the 1st Plaintiff.

(d) mandatory injunction directing the Defendants to remove all hundis introduced by them except the "Para Hundi" and remove the latter from its altered position and locate it at the threshold of the temple and for an injunction restraining the Defendants from introducing hereafter any new hundies in the temple except the said "Para Hundi."

(e) directing the Defendants to pay Plaintiffs Rs. 4850 as damages for loss of reputation, loss of Swathantrams withheld by the Defendants and loss of emoluments owing to the shifting of "Para Hundi" and introduction of new Hundies; also pay 1st Plaintiff at Rs. 50 a month as damages for loss of Swathantrams till they are given first as aforesaid . . .

Memo of Valuation

1. Damages for loss of reputation	Rs. 3000–0–0
2. Damages for loss of emoluments	Rs. 1800–0–0
3. Damages for loss of Swathantrams	Rs. 50–0–0
Total	Rs. 4850–0–0

Submerged in the quaint legalese of the above argument,[56] one can easily see the extremely complicated combination of privileges that this priest sought to defend and the key role in his conception of this package of rights, represented by the honor of priority in the receipt of his share of the divine leavings.

Especially concerned about honors at the Śrī Pārtasārati Svāmi Temple, although they are not strictly speaking part of the temple staff, are a group of Brahmin Vaiṣṇava males known as *attiyāpakās*. They are residents of Triplicane who, by tradition and usage going back at least to the second half of the nineteenth century,[57] monopo-

[53] The term *goshti* (*kōṣti*), which has a wide range of applications, is most closely approximated by the loose and public connotation of the English term *congregation*.

[54] The term *thaligai* (*taḷikai*) refers specifically to some fixed quantity and combination of cooked food offerings to the deity.

[55] For a discussion of the term *mirās*, see Chapter 4.

[56] The origin of this type of legal conception of rights in the temple owes itself to the formative period of interaction between the temple and the English judiciary, which is discussed in Chapter 5.

[57] See Judgment of May 1, 1925, in C.S. 349 of 1923, High Court of Judicature at Madras.

lize the right to recite portions of the Prabandam poetic corpus of the *āḻvār* poet-saints of Vaisnavism at crucial moments both in the daily cycle of *pūjā* worship and during calendrical worship.

Today this group represents the strongest brand of Brahmin adherence to the subsectarian tenets of Teṉkalai Śrī Vaisnavism.[58] They are, as such, fiercely protective of their share in the redistributive process of the temple in relation to the manager/trustees of the temple, the other temple servants (particularly the Vaikānasa priesthood), and other worshippers. In 1923 when all the important groups and individuals involved in the temple were attempting to consolidate their shares in the redistributive process under the judicial aegis of the High Court of Madras,[59] this group made a major bid for formal and legal codification of its rights. The plaint, made by some members of this group against the then trustees of the temple, is a fascinating document, both in illustrating the complex *constitutive* function of honors and in displaying the complex sociopolitical conflicts that tend to express themselves in honors disputes.[60]

Early in the lengthy plaint,[61] it was claimed that "the offices themselves are vested as of right in the sthallatars,[62] above described, and the trustees have no right to exclude any of them from discharging the said duties or claiming their share of the perquisites or emoluments thereof nor have the trustees any right to appoint to the said offices any persons who are not among the sthallatars." The plaintiffs went on to claim that under the direction of two of the trustees, the *amīnā* had withheld the distribution of sacred food due to them, "and made over the entire prasadams to three or four of their own adherents."[63] They also gave a series of other examples of the attempts of the trustees to thwart them in the enjoyment of their proper rights[64] and concluded their plaint with the following prayer to the court (to which lettered cross references to Table 2 have been added):

The plaintiffs therefore pray:

i. for a declaration that the plaintiffs and the other adult male Tengalai Sri Vaishnava residents of Triplicane Sthalathars are entitled to the office of

[58] See Chapter 2 for the history of this ritual element in Vaisnava temples in South India.

[59] The interaction of temple and judiciary in this context is discussed in Chapter 5.

[60] Plaint, April 27, 1923, in C.S. 349 of 1923.

[61] Ibid., para. 6.

[62] The term *stalattar*, which means literally "people of the place," has an archaic semantic reference to the interested local community that had a voice in temple management.

[63] Plaint in C.S. 349 of 1923, para. 13.

[64] Ibid., paras. 14–16.

Adyapakam, Vedaparayanam,[a] Arulapadu,[b] and Puranam Kattiyam[c] in the temple of Sri Parthasarathy Swamy at Triplicane and that the trustees have no right to appoint anybody else to the said offices;

ii. that as holders of the said offices they are entitled to the honors and emoluments set out in Schedule A hereto;

iii. for an injunction restraining the defendants 1 and 2 (two of the trustees) from interfering in any way with the enjoyment of the said offices by the Thengalai Sree Vaishnava Residents of Triplicane or with the performance of the duties and receipt of the emoluments and honors attached to the said offices;

iv. for a decree against the defendants for Rs.200/—being the value of emoluments and honors withheld; and

v. for costs and such other reliefs as this Honorable Court deems fit.

Schedule A.
Perquisites, Emoluments and Honors

1. One-fourth Pongal Thaligai[d] from Dewanum[e] every morning for Kalasanthi[f] service.
2. 1/16 of cooked offerings.
3. 1/30 of Thirupanyarams[g] offered.
4. Iyalpadi[h] two cakes offered at Thiruvandhikappu.[i]
5. Holy water, Sreestagopam,[j] Thulasi,[k] Sandal,[l] Manjal,[m] Garlands, Betel-leaves, Thakshinas,[n] etc., during Tirumanjanam according to the usage of the temple.
6. One torch and one Sannadhi Divatti[o] for each of the Adhyapakam and Vedaparayanam Goshties[p] in procession conducted under torch light.
7. Two umbrellas which usually accompany God in processions to accompany the Adhyapaka Goshti whenever they do not accompany the God in procession.
8. First Thirtham[q] and first Sree Satagopam and first prasadham to be given to the person doing Sadhitharulai[r] service.
9. First Satagopam to the same individual after procession is started and on return to temple.
10. Two viniyogams[s] to Vedaparayanam Swamis.
11. Right of Ishta Viniyogam[t] during monthly and annual festivals of Sree Manavalamamuni.[65]
12. On each of the ten days of the annual festival of Sree Manavalamamuni 30 cakes of Thosai at Dewanam expense to be offered and distributed to Goshti.
13. Distribution of oil on Thirukarthigai,[u] Emberumanar Sathumorai[v] and Oriyadi day.[w]
14. Garland and Sree Satagopam and 1/4 Thaligai and two cakes to Puranam reader.
15. Right to receive Swathantram before similar Swathantram is given to others.
16. Sree Satagopam not to be given to others during Sevakalam[x] in temple both in the temple and during the Friday procession inside the temple.
17. One Thaligai of Sakrapongal[y] on Thirupallandu Thodakkam day.[z]

[65] See Chapter 2, for a discussion of the historical importance of Manavāla Māmuni in the formation of the Teṉkalai subsect.

18. General Vaidika Vicharana of temple matters.
19. Control of distribution of prasadhams and swathantrams in goshti.
20. Right to receive at the seat[aa] of one of the Adhyapakas the following:
    (a) 30 cakes of Thosai on the 5th day of Brahmotsavams at Muchi Mantapam.
    (b) 15 Thosais, 8 Vadais and 8 Appams[bb] on Dwajarohanam[cc] days.
    (c) One pongal Thaligai in the morning and 15 Thosais in the night of Pavithrotsavam day to Vedaparayanam.
    (d) 8 Appams and 8 Vadais in addition on the last day to Vedaparayanam.
21. Offering Thirumankappu[dd] and Srichurnam[ee] to Alwars and Acharyas and distribution of the same to Goshti.
22. Offering Thirumanithadams[ff] and Abayahastams[gg] to Sree Udayavar[hh] and Sree Manavalamamuni on festival days.

Schedule B
Duties

1. Daily service[ii] both morning and evening.
2. Special service during festivals, Thirumanjanams,[jj] Processions, etc.
3. Recital of Stothrapatra Eckrikais[kk] during certain special festivals and processions.
4. Sadhitarulai service by a member of the goshti.
5. Kattiams.
6. Reading Kaisika Puranam[ll] on the Kaisika Dwadhasi day and Sthalapurana[mm] during Pallava Othsavam.
7. Saying Arulapadu.

Sd. etc.

In the final decree by the High Court of Madras, the bulk of the specific demands made by the *attiyāpakās* in the above plaint was upheld.[66] Ever since then the judgment and decree in this case have served as the legal charter of this group, which they evoke whenever they feel their privileges are being threatened. But the most significant fact revealed by this claim is the close way in which honors, emoluments, and duties are tied together in the perception of this group. Second, their insistence on self-government with minimal interference from the trustees or anybody else is demonstrative of an equally fundamental fact about the politics of worship in South Indian temples, namely, the extent to which particular groups and individuals view themselves as subordinate to the deity *alone* and thus as not subject to the control of their fellow worshippers or fellow servants. This point is taken up later in this chapter. Finally, the plaint, at the risk of drowning the reader in a host of details, displays the tremen-

[66] Decree, November 12, 1925, in C.S. 349 of 1923.

Table 2. *Definitions pertaining to prayer to the court*

[a]*vētapārāyaṇam*	Recitation of the Vēdas at fixed ritual times
[b]*arulappāṭu*	Formulaic beginning of the recitation of the Prabandam corpus of the Aḻvārs
[c]*kaṭṭiyam*	Specific formulaic praises of the deity uttered at specific junctures in daily and calendrical worship
[d]*poṅkal Taḷikai*	Sweet cooked rice offerings to the deity
[e]*tīvanum*	Management, from the Arabic *divān*, meaning official/state
[f]*kalāsanti*	The first of the daily cycle of *pūjā*
[g]*tiruppaṇṇiyāram*	Fried foods (cakes, hoppers, etc.) offered to the deity
[h]*iyalpaṭi*	On behalf of those singing the Prabandam
[i]*tiruvantikkāppu*	Rituals for averting evil influences at the end of daily worship or festival
[j]*śrī saṭakōpan*	Metal representation of the feet of Viṣṇu placed on the heads of worshippers at particular points in daily and processional worship
[k]*tuḷaci*	Basil leaves, considered especially sacred in Viṣṇu temples
[l]sandal paste	Part of the adornment of the deity; when redistributed is also considered an honor
[m]*mañcal*	Turmeric paste; similarly, an honor
[n]*takṣiṇā*	From Vēdic usage, meaning fees to the ritual officiant
[o]*caṉṉiti tīvaṭṭi*	Torch used in the sanctum sanctorum
[p]*kōsti*	Used here in a more narrow sense to designate not the general body of worshippers but those entitled to recite the *Prabandams* and the Vēdas
[q]*tīrttam*	Water sanctified by contact with the deity's ablutions or meals
[r]*sātit aruḷā*	"Please begin," the ceremonial beginning of the recitation of the Prabandam in all Vaiṣṇava temples, the right to utter this formula being considered highly prestigious
[s]*viṉiyōkam*	Redistribution; used here in a narrower sense to specify the right of those reciting the Vēdas to receive twice the quantity of that received by the other worshippers
[t]*iṣṭa viṉiyōkam*	Generally refers to the donor's right to allocate the leavings of the deity; here used in the sense of being commandeered by the *attiyāpaka*s
[u]*tirukkārtikai*	Festival on the full-moon day in the month of *Kārttikai*

Table 2 (*cont.*)

[v]*emberumānār sārrumurai*	Conclusion of the annual ten-day festival in honor of Srī Rāmānujā, the great synthesizer of the Srī Vaiṣṇava tradition in South India
[w]*oriyati* day	Unknown
[x]*cēvākālam*	Times when the Prabandam is being recited
[y]*cakkirapponkal*	A type of sweet rice preparation
[z]*tiruppallāntu totakkam*	The commencement of a portion of the *Prabandam* corpus composed by Periyāḻvār
[aa]seat	Used to translate a traditional term for "home"
[bb]*appam*	A type of hopper
[cc]*dvajārohanam*	The ceremony of hoisting the flag*
[dd]*tirumankāppu*	Placing of the sectarian mark on the foreheads of the deities
[ee]*śrīcūraṇam*	A special powder used in making the sectarian mark on the foreheads of the deities
[ff]*thirumanithadam*	Unknown
[gg]*apayahastam*	Sandalwood impression of the right hand of the chief deity
[hh]*Śrī Udayavar*	Another title for Srī Rāmānujā
[ii]service	Used here to mean the recitation of the Prabandam
[jj]*tirumañcanam*	Special baths given to the deity, above and beyond the daily bath
[kk]*stotrapatra Echcharikkai*	A particular type of panygeric formula in reference to important *acāriyas* of the Śrī Vaiṣṇava tradition
[ll]*kaicika purāṇam*	A text recounting the mythic importance of a certain festival day
[mm]*sthalapurāṇam*	The text that recounts the mythic origin and traditions of the temple

*For information on the powerful symbolic role of the flag in Viṣṇu temples, see J. Gonda, *Aspects of Early Visnuism* (Utrecht, 1954), pp. 255–9.

dous density of the interface between the overall ritual process of the temple and the share of a single group in its redistributive process.

Given their indispensability to the contemporary "liturgy" of the Śrī Pārtasārati Svāmi Temple, it is not surprising that the *attiyāpakās* have as high a stake in honors and redistribution as donors, trustees, and temple servants. Worshippers, who have no fixed or enduring ritual role in the "liturgy" (narrowly conceived), can also become profoundly involved in the concern over honor and honors at the temple. An important example of this last sort of concern is provided by the activities of some non-Brahmin worshippers at the temple, who began to assert their own claims in the idiom of honor in the 1940s.[67]

Between 1944 and 1968, a number of non-Brahmin groups and individuals protested against certain temple practices, first in letters and petitions to the temple authorities and then in quasi-legal action before the Hindu Religious and Charitable Endowments (Administration) Department.[68] These protesters were not part of a single, organized movement over the entire period. Rather, they viewed themselves self-consciously as expressing a single and continuous set of concerns. They were generally lower-middle-class members of the Naidu caste, loosely affiliated to a small and low-prestige non-Brahmin religious association.[69] They conspicuously lacked power, in both the religious and bureaucratic hierarchy of the temple and the larger arenas of Madras politics and society.

Their protests consistently focused on three practices at crucial points during temple services[70] that they viewed as inequitable: (1) Whereas the *tīrttam* (holy water) was given to the Brahmin males in the congregation in one vessel (*vaṭṭil*), it was given to the non-Brahmin portion of the congregation in another; (2) whereas the entire congregation was obliged to remain standing while the Brahmins received the *tīrttam* and *śrī saṭakōpaṉ* honors, the Brahmins immediately sat down to receive the *prasātam* (sacred food) while the non-Brahmins were still standing to receive the *tīrttam*; (3) the non-Brahmins rarely received the *śrī saṭakōpaṉ* honor at all and certainly not "immediately after and in continuation with the Brahmin

[67] I have described these protests, their context and consequences in "Protest and Participation: Non-Brahmins in a South Indian Temple." Paper delivered at the Twenty-seventh Annual Meeting of the Association for Asian Studies, San Francisco, March 24–26, 1975.

[68] My sources for this movement are a Tamil pamphlet, *Tiruvallikkēni Tivyatēsa Ūlalkal (Akramaṅkaḷ)* [*Decadences and irregularities in the Triplicane temple*] (Madras, 1944), by K. Ramanuja Dasan and others; interviews with Mr. and Mrs. T. K. Ramanujadoss in Madras, October–December 1973, and some official correspondence cited later.

[69] The 1944 pamphlet was published by an association called the Rāmānujā Tivyājnā Paripālana Sapai (Society for the Protection of Rāmānujā's Code). In the 1960s, T. K. Ramanujadoss, the principal force behind the protests and my main informant on this movement, received moral, not financial, support from a predominantly non-Brahmin religious organization, the Nampillai Sapai, in which he was involved.

[70] In addition to the 1944 pamphlet, see correspondence between T. K. Ramanujadoss, temple trustees, and HRCE Dept. from 1960–1, in the possession of the former; correspondence between A. Ilayalwar Naidu, temple trustees, HREB, and *attiyāpakās* in 1948–9, Record Room, Śrī Pārtasārati Svāmi Temple, Madras.

devotees at the congregation."[71] Those core complaints were also accompanied by descriptions of the derogatory and careless manner in which these honors were given to non-Brahmins, treating them as if they were "dogs and cattle."[72]

Throughout their protests, these non-Brahmins nowhere challenged the monopoly of the first honors, at crucial moments, by the Brahmin *attiyāpakās*. Rather, the non-Brahmins wished to highlight two implications of these inequitable practices: (1) that these malpractices caused them *avamāṉam*[73] (dishonor; this term not only captures the sense of public degradation felt by the non-Brahmins but also tersely expresses their feeling that by manipulating the honors appropriate to non-Brahmins, Brahmins degrade them in the royal presence of the deity); (2) the deeper and subtler implication of the non-Brahmin protests was that the effect and intent of these malpractices was to sever the bond uniting Brahmins and non-Brahmins in a single community organized by service to a single sovereign deity. For Brahmins to receive *tīrttam* in a separate vessel, for them to deny to non-Brahmins the *śrī saṭakōpaṉ* in continuity with them was, from the non-Brahmin point of view, to deny their share in the divine leavings, their appropriate role in this divine polity. And finally, Mr. T. K. Ramanujadoss and his wife, who spoke to me eloquently about the history of their struggle in this matter, were fully conscious of how much their aspirations were a reaffirmation of the role of non-Brahmins in medieval Śrī Vaisnavism of the Teṉkalai subtradition.[74]

The several cases of conflicts over honors that I have cited are, in fact, conflicts over the shares of persons and groups, embodied in condensed cultural forms, in the redistributive process of the temple. Whether they involve donors, trustees, temple servants, or worshippers, they involve, in common, issues raised by the relationship of service (*kaiṅkaryam*) to the sovereign duty. The most important fact about these various forms of service is that they are all relatively autonomous forms of participation in the overall ritual and redistributive process of the temple. Each person or group involved in service of any kind thus possesses an inalienable and privileged relationship to the sovereign deity concretized in some sort of "share"

[71] Memo from T. K. Ramanujadoss to temple trustees, 1961.
[72] Ibid.
[73] Ramanuja Dasan, *Decadences and Irregularities*, p. 3.
[74] For a discussion of the role of non-Brahmins in medieval Śrī Vaisnavism, see Chapter 2.

(*panku*), and embodied and rendered authoritative by some sort of honor.

What holds these various "servants" together is not a simple hierarchy of functions, no single pyramid of authority, but rather (1) their shared orientation to, and dependence on, the sovereignty of the deity they serve and (2) the sheer logic of functional interdependence, without which the ritual process would break down. Even the managerial roles, such as that of trustee and that of *amīnā*, are not conceived to be superordinate in any clear hierarchical way. They are authoritative only insofar as they do not disturb any one of the shares that they must orchestrate to keep the moral and economic cycle of temple ritual going.

This should not imply, however, that the temple is an ill-disciplined collection of independent agents. Particular chains of command do exist, as well as particular norms that govern these chains. But these norms, which vary from temple to temple, are legitimated by a shared idea of the past, of hallowed convention, which is based on a fragile consensus. Thus changes in the social and political environment of the temple tend to fragment this delicate consensus fairly easily.

At the best of times, the boundaries within which orders can be given and be expected to be obeyed are tightly defined. When these boundaries are overlooked, and the share of some individual or group is seen to be threatened, conflict erupts. It is at these moments of conflict that we can most clearly observe that the many groups and individuals who possess shares of some kind in the temple recognize their privileged interaction with the deity as the only really authoritative relationship.

Thus, the problem arises of how to arbitrate conflicts that arise at any of the complex interphases of these shares: conflicts most often expressed in the idiom of honor. South Indians have answered this problem by invoking another relationship to the deity, the relationship of "protection" (Sanskrit, *paripālana*; Tamil, *kāppāṟṟutal*). This "protective" function is today exercised by three trustees, appointed by the Hindu Religious and Charitable Endowments (Administration) Department, a part of the government bureaucracy of Madras, and by an executive officer who is a career officer in this bureaucracy assigned temporarily to a particular temple. The executive officer has a clerical staff of about ten individuals.

Before going on to explore the ideas underlying the relationship of "protection" and its tension with the relationship of "service," it

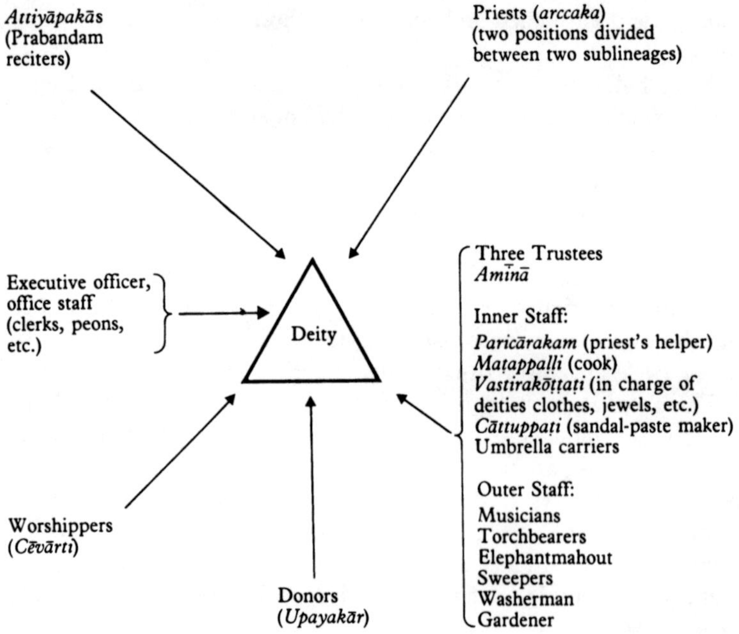

Figure 5. Functional roles in the temple

might be useful to chart all the individuals and groups who *today* play some part in the redistributive process of the temple (Figure 5).

The actual number of people involved today in the temple, apart from the mass of worshippers and the great multiplicity of donors (see Table 1), is greater than it appears on this chart. Although there are only two priestly "offices," each of which is controlled by one segment of the same Vaikānasa lineage, the two officeholders in question employ, between them, approximately twelve assistants because the number of subshrines and the density of the ritual calendar would make it impossible for two persons to handle its demands. Similarly, the *attiyāpakās*, who are a self-governing and self-recruiting group, number, at most times, about thirty males. Similarly, if we total the inner and outer staff, there are twenty-two incumbents, although there are only ten slots. Finally, the clerical staff under the executive officer numbers about ten.

In principle, today, the functional division of labor among all these co-sharers in the redistributive system of the temple is clear. The liturgy, narrowly conceived, is monopolized by the priests, who perform worship according to the texts of Vaikānasa Āgama, and by the *attiyāpakā*s, whose recitation of the Prabandam of the *āḻvār*s is now a rigorously fixed and fiercely maintained portion of daily services, both within the sanctum and in the processionals outside the temple. They are assisted in this by the incumbents in all the positions I have labeled "inner" and "outer" staff, who fulfill key roles in the actualization of daily and processional worship.

The trustees, who are generally prestigious members of the Teṉkalai community of Madras, are the overseers of the ritual process. The *amīnā* is the day-to-day supervisor of the ritual process, ensuring cooperation, planning ahead, and communicating the wishes of the trustees and the executive officer to the various ritual officiants. The executive officer, with his supporting clerical staff, oversees the relationship of the temple to the outside world: the proper filing, recording, investment, and allocation of the material resources of endowments; the conduct of lawsuits by and against the temple; and the logistical functions of stores, accounts, and salaries. The donors provide the economic backbone of this ongoing ritual process. The worshippers are its active witnesses.

Not all the co-sharers in the temple, however, participate in its redistributive process in the same way. The bureaucratic staff under the executive officer have no traditional share in the divine leavings of the deity but are today salaried employees of the government. However, both the executive officer and his immediate subordinate, the superintendent of the temple office (also a civil servant), are often honored during festivals by receiving *tīrttam*, garland (*mālai*), and *śrī saṭakōpaṉ* honors immediately after the main donor of the ritual. In the crowded, intensely dramatic setting of many of these celebrations, these honors serve to relate the temple officers prominently with the deity. The trustees, who are generally men of substance in their own right, are unpaid in any form, but they too receive honors at crucial times, which demarcate their important *protective* role.

Worshippers and donors receive all the above honors as well as shares in the cooked food leavings of the deity, but given the nature of their roles, these shares are occasional and not regular or continuous. The other co-sharers, the *amīnā*, the *attiyāpakā*s, the priests, and the members of the "inner" and "outer" staffs, have regular and fixed shares in the cooked food offerings of the deity as well as "special" combinations of the more dramatic public honors at particular times. Today, the *amīnā* and the members of the inner and outer staffs also receive small cash salaries in addition to their regular shares in the cooked rice leavings of the deity. In the cases of conflicts over honors that have been cited, an attempt has been made to show that, in the twentieth century, consensus around participation in the ritual/distributive process is fragile. Given the organizational and cultural complexity of the process, therefore, some agency is required to oversee it, or in South Indian cultural terms, to "protect" it. In what does "protection" consist?

Protecting the temple

In pre-British South India, and to a considerable extent today, the role of the king (*aracaṉ*) is understood to entail the protection of the temple. Although this concept has taken different concrete expressions at different times, which will be discussed in detail in the next three chapters, it also has a common meaning over time. This enduring meaning and the symbiosis between king and deity that it suggests are a product of my own interpretation. It is nowhere asserted in the general terms in which it will be presented here. It is supported, however, by a mass of specifics, which are contained throughout the body of the study. For heuristic purposes, therefore, it is baldly asserted here, but the remainder of this study provides its empirical justification.

To protect the temple means to ensure that the services, resources, and rules that define the redistributive process of any given temple are shared, allocated, and defined so that conflict does not arise and disharmony does not set in. The kingly role of protection stands in a delicate relationship to the temple, for the king cannot *rule* the temple. He himself is the servant (*cēvārti*) of the deity and indeed the human agent of the divine sovereignty enshrined in the deity.[75] But because the deity cannot, by its very nature, arbitrate conflict among its servants, the human king is necessary to fulfill this function.

In fulfilling this royal function of "protection," the king is only the ultimate recourse. Conflicts may be solved locally and amiably by

[75] According to indigenous accounts, the Kings Hariharā and Bukka, cofounders of the Vijayanagara Empire in South India, handed over their kingdom, via a sectarian leader, to the deity Virūpāksa at Hampi and subsequently ruled their kingdom on his behalf; a similar set of circumstances obtained under the Gajapati rulers of Orissa; around A.D. 1750 the Mahāraja of Travancore in South India surrendered his kingdom to the deity Śrī Padmanābhasvāmi: After Indian independence in 1947, he refused to take an oath as head of the integrated states of Travancore–Cochin because he had been ruling on behalf of, and as a servant of, the deity (see Sontheimer, "Religious Endowments," pp. 75–6, for sources).

local assemblies. Nor is the protective function of the king in reference to the deity monopolistic. All organized relationships to the deity, relationships of systematic service, are seen to be, in a sense, protective, insofar as they safeguard, maintain, and nurture some aspect, however finite, of the redistributive process centered on the deity. Thus "protection" and "service" are the two extreme (ideal-typical) poles of all relationships to the deity. Just as the "protective" function of the king is only the highest human expression of service to the deity, so even the most humble form of service to the deity shares some of the prestigious, authoritative, and superordinate texture of the protective role of the king. In this sense, though separated by many other features, the king and the elephant man are together servant/protectors of the sovereign deity.

In purely cultural terms, therefore, we can see in the relationship of human kings to temple deities in South India an elegant and symbiotic division of sovereignty. The sovereign deity is the paradigm of royal authority. By serving this deity, in the form of elaborate gifts that generate special "royal" honors, and by protecting the redistributive process of the temple, human kings share in this paradigmatic royalty.[76] By being the greatest servant of the sovereign deity, the human king sustains and displays his rule over men.

But in operational and empirical situations, this cultural model can become problematic, for it does not clearly specify the *boundaries* of the temple, both as a political and administrative institution and as a ritual process. In short, it does not provide a set of rules for temple control. By temple control is meant the acknowledged competence of an individual or an agency to authoritatively allocate the roles, rights, and resources involved in the ongoing maintenance of worship. Not even the protective mandate of kings can abrogate what are perceived to be appropriate shares in relation to the sovereign deity.

Human kings are obliged to interact with temples. This is partly because, in enshrining the deity, temples are repositories of kingship, in its paradigmatic sense, and linked to this fact, they are also concentrations of economic, political, and cultural resources for the hinterlands they dominate. But the prerogatives of kings as "protectors" are always *potentially* subject to challenge from other "servants" of the deity, who perceive their rights and shares as independently derived from the sovereign deity. To a considerable

[76] These activities of South Indian kings are described in detail in Chapter 2.

extent, conflicts concerning shares and rights, often expressed in the language of honor (*mariyātai*), derive from this structural aspect of the shared sovereignty of human kings and temple deities.

But particularly traceable to this source are contemporary conflicts between the state and local temple servants and/or worshippers. In the pre-British period a complex and dynamic pattern of relationships existed between kings and temples, which preempted the occurrence of this fundamental conflict.[77] But since the arrival of the British, and the impact of their institutions, the symptoms of this structural problem have been stronger. The necessity for conceiving this structural problem in historical terms can best be appreciated by looking at the most recent expressions of the tension between state and locality at the Śrī Pārtasārati Svāmi Temple.

State versus sect at the Śrī Pārtasārati Svāmi Temple

Today, the government of the state of Tamilnātu, through the Hindu Religious and Charitable Endowments (Administration) Department, legally exercises administrative control over a vast number of temples in the state, among them the Śrī Pārtasārati Svāmi Temple. This large and powerful arm of the executive branch of government exercises such control over temples in the state by virtue of a direct process of legal and institutional evolution that began in 1925. By the passage of Act I of 1925, the Legislative Assembly of Madras presidency created a central authority to administer the affairs of temples in the presidency.[78] Under this act, the newly created Hindu Religious Endowments Board (HREB) was answerable to the legislature, and its actions were subject to appeal in the courts of law. It stood at the apex of a relatively decentralized system of administration, whose lower levels included temple committees, which were elected bodies at the district level, created by Act XX of 1863;[79] the trustees of particular temples; and the priests and other servants of the given temple.[80]

The powers of this board were, in principle, very elaborate and included supervision to ensure the proper application of the endow-

[77] Chapter 2.

[78] Chandra Y. Mudaliar, *The Secular State and Religious Institutions in India: A Study of the Administration of Hindu Public Religious Trusts in Madras* (Wiesbaden, 1974), describes the debates that prefaced the passing of this act, pp. 47–51.

[79] Ibid., pp. 26–31, for an analysis of this act and its provisions.

[80] Ibid., p. 77.

ments of religious institutions; inspection and investigation of income and expenditure; administration in respect to the salaries of its subordinate staff; the appointment and suspension of all but a few kinds of trustees; the sale of temple properties; and the rectification of situations of misappropriation or maladministration by administrative orders. As a tribunal invested with discretionary powers in relation to Hindu religious endowments, the board also had judicial prerogatives, which were expressed in its power to hear appeals and settle conflicts at any of the subordinate levels of the structure. Finally, it had quasi-legislative powers relating to the framing of rules and bylaws, subject to review by the local government.

Between 1925, when the board was first formed, and 1951, when it was abolished, there were a number of fresh pieces of legislation, which increased the centralized powers of the board and correspondingly diminished the powers of the local temple committees and trustees, the former of which were abolished in 1944.[81] The temples in Madras city had been exempted from this supervision until 1946, but by Act X of 1946, they too fell under the purview of this burgeoning centralized bureaucracy.

Because it was in Madras city, the Śrī Pārtasārati Svāmi Temple fell under the jurisdiction of the HREB after 1946. But it was not until 1951 that the enhanced role of the state ran up against local resistance at Triplicane. Act XIX of 1951 was the first act relating to religious endowments in Madras after India gained its independence in 1947. By this act, the HREB was abolished and a separate department of the government, the Hindu Religious and Charitable Endowments (Administration) Department (HRCE Department) was created with an even more extensive mandate than its predecessor.[82]

This department was to assume immediate powers of general superintendence over 184 major monasteries, 114 minor monasteries, 12,232 major temples, and 16,257 minor temples.[83] Both in the public and parliamentary debates prior to the passage of this act, and in the criticisms and court cases after its passage, it is clear that the act contravened the perceived rights and freedoms of numerous individuals and communities.[84] By and large, these objections to the powers of the HRCE Department were phrased in the language of

[81] This process is documented and analyzed in ibid., pp. 85–103.
[82] Ibid., pp. 146–8.
[83] Ibid., p. 152.
[84] Ibid., pp. 161–202.

the Constitution of independent India and focused on the contradiction between the immense powers of this department and the religious freedoms essential to the maintenance of a secular state. Some of these objections, and the legal decisions generated by them, necessitated modifications in the act, which were promulgated in the Madras Act XXII of 1959.[85]

Although this act did introduce some legal and administrative refinements[86] it did not in any fundamental way restrict the immense powers of this branch of the government over Hindu religious institutions in the state. To understand local resistance to this Leviathan, let us turn now to the concrete details of the primarily legal battle between the HRCE Department and the members of the Teṉkalai subsect of Śrī Vaisnavas in Triplicane from 1951 to 1968.

On October 19, 1951, the commissioner of the HRCE Department, in an unprecedented administrative order,[87] appointed a trustee for the Śrī Pārtasārati Svāmi Temple to fill a vacancy created by the efflux of time. This act was contested by members of the Teṉkalai sect at Triplicane, who claimed that filling appointments to this office was their legal and historical prerogative. The conflict was taken to the High Court of Judicature at Madras, which, through a judgment of its appellate side, upheld the claims of the Triplicane Teṉkalai community and quashed the commissioner's order.[88] The government, in turn, made an appeal against this order, and a tribunal of the appellate side of the High Court, including its then chief justice, reversed the previous decision, allowed the appeal, and thus reestablished the legality of the original administrative action by the state.[89]

In an elaborate petition filed on October 14, 1957, the legal representatives of the Teṉkalai community of Triplicane appealed to the High Court of Madras for permission to take the matter to the Supreme Court of India, on the grounds that it raised some fundamental constitutional issues.[90] On April 17, 1958, the Madras High

[85] For a discussion of some of these issues, see J. D. M. Derrett, "Religious Endowments, Public and Private," in J. D. M. Derrett, ed., *Religion, Law and the State in India* (London, 1968), pp. 482–512.

[86] Mudaliar, *Secular State*, pp. 214–15.

[87] Order No. 8 of the commissioner, October 19, 1951, HRCE.

[88] Order, September 17, 1952, in Writ Petition 840 of 1951, High Court of Judicature at Madras.

[89] Order, April 12, 1957, in Writ Appeal 17 of 1953 against Writ Petition 840 of 1951.

[90] Memorandum, October 14, 1957, in S.C.C.M.P. 8032 of 1957 in Writ Appeal 17 of 1953.

Court acceded to this petition and the case moved to the Supreme Court of India in New Delhi.[91] However, the case was dismissed on September 12, 1964, by the Supreme Court on a technicality (the death of one of the respondents), and the appeal was not considered on its merits.[92] Thus, finally, the state managed to uphold its original administrative order against the efforts of the Teṉkalai community of Triplicane to contest it.

Meanwhile, even before the state had won its de facto victory in the matter of appointment of trustees, it began proceedings to make fundamental alterations in the scheme of management of the temple. Starting in 1951, the deputy commissioner of the HRCE Department began proceedings for a major alteration in the scheme governing the temple, which had been framed by the High Court of Madras in C.S. 524 of 1924.[93] This modified scheme, which was created through the quasi-judicial powers of the HRCE Department, radically extended the role and powers of the state in respect to the temple. Although the protests made against the draft of the new scheme by the members of the Teṉkalai community were vociferous, only one alteration was made in the final scheme: The draft scheme, which proposed that members of other Vaisnava communities could be appointed in the absence of appropriate candidates for the trusteeship from the Teṉkalai community of Madras, was amended to restrict the trusteeship to members of the Teṉkalai community of Madras. For the rest, the far-reaching alterations of the 1925 scheme were retained, and they deserve to be noted.[94]

First, the right of the Teṉkalai community of Triplicane to elect the trustees of the temple, already eroded by the governmental appointment of a trustee in 1951, was formally abrogated, and it was decreed that trustees would henceforth be appointed by the commissioner of the HRCE Department.[95] Second, an executive officer was to be appointed, a salaried government servant whose powers at the temple were wide-ranging. No person other than the executive officer was to receive the income of the temple or to make any disbursements from its funds.[96] This officer was also to be responsible for

[91] Order, April 17, 1958, in S.C.C.M.P. 8032 of 1957.

[92] See Plaint, para. 10, in O.S. 2910 of 1968, City Civil Court of Madras.

[93] For the interaction between temple and court over a forty-year period, which resulted in the formation of this scheme, see Chapter 5.

[94] Draft of Modified Scheme, attached to Notice in O.A. 55 of 1961, drafted May 20, 1963, HRCE.

[95] Ibid., para. 4.

[96] Ibid., para. 10.

"the performance of the daily services and the periodical festivals according to usage and customs in the temple."[97] He was also to have custody of the records, accounts, and other movables of the temple,[98] with the exception of the jewels, vessels, and other valuables, over which he would share custody with the chairman of the board of trustees.[99] It was, in addition, decreed that "the servants of the temple shall work under the immediate control and supervision of the Executive Officer."[100] In the matters of temple budgets, leases, and auctions of temple property, legal suits on behalf of the temple, and the *tiṭṭam* (scale of expenditure for ritual), the executive officer was to have the primary responsibility, and the trustees were assigned a role that was, at best, consultative.[101] There were serious protests against this massive expansion of the powers of the HRCE Department by members of the Teṉkalai community of Triplicane, both in quasi-judicial proceedings before the commissioner of the HRCE Department and in legal action in the court.[102] But all these protests met with failure.

Thus, ever since the late 1960s the power of the state at the Śrī Pārtasārati Svāmi Temple has been immense. Through the HRCE Department, the state appoints the temple trustees and the executive officer, who effectively runs the temple, and the Teṉkalai community of Triplicane no longer exercises any *collective* rights of control over the temple.[103] This was the result of a process that took almost two decades. In the course of the various legal and quasi-legal battles that took place between the two sides over this period, each couched its case in a number of substantive arguments that it is useful to consider.

Let us consider first the arguments made in behalf of the state. The general framework within which the specific arguments on behalf of the state were couched was clearly stated in the debates in the Legislative Assembly that preceded the passage of Act XIX of

[97] Ibid., para. 11.
[98] Ibid., para. 13.
[99] Ibid., para. 14.
[100] Ibid., para. 17.
[101] Ibid., paras. 20, 22, 23, 25.
[102] O.S. 2910 of 1968, City Civil Court of Madras.
[103] This does not mean, however, that particular Teṉkalais or groups of Teṉkalais, such as the *attiyāpakās*, donors, worshippers, etc., lost particular rights; similarly, the ritual rules, subject to the conservative dictum of "custom and usage," cannot be easily altered; lastly, the trustees are from the Teṉkalai community of Madras. What was lost was the corporate and collective right of the Teṉkalai community to manage themselves.

1951. The act was introduced in 1949 by the Honorable T. S. S. Rajan, who recounted many instances in the past – under Hindu rulers, under the East India Company, and under the rule of the English crown – that provided ample justification for the interference of the government in order to protect the properties of religious institutions.[104] In response to the question of the legality of such interference in a secular state, which India claimed to be, he replied: "We have examined the question and we have been assured that we have been within our rights to handle religious institutions and endowments . . . The fear of interfering with religious institutions has always been there with an alien government but with us it is very different. Ours may be called a secular government, and so it is. But it does not absolve us from *protecting* the funds of the institutions which are meant for the service of the people" (emphasis added).[105]

A week later, after considerable debate, this protective mandate of the state was put in even more colorful and radical terms by the Honorable O. P. Ramaswamy Reddiar: "The regulation of Hindu temples and *maths* [monasteries] is the regulation of the community's life and conduct; the revival of our temples is the revival of our people. The temple is the invaluable link between Men and God, between society and religion, between public morality and private morality . . . If we do not make our temples a positive force, radiating a healthy, progressive, social and cultural outlook, we will be playing into the hands of the surging Godless crowd."[106]

It is this variant of the indigenous belief in royal protection of temples that provides the broad basis for the specific arguments of the HRCE Department in its conflict with the Teṉkalai community of Triplicane. In an elaborate affidavit filed before the High Court of Madras in March 1952, the HRCE Department defended its appointment of a trustee to the Śrī Pārtasārati Svāmi Temple on a number of grounds.[107]

The HRCE Department argued, first, that it was not true that the Teṉkalai Vaisnavite residents of Triplicane had been in charge of the general administration of the temple and had appointed or nominated trustees: "There is no valid usage regarding the selection

[104] *Madras Legislative Assembly Debates*, February 4, 1949, 17:677–9, quoted in Mudaliar, *Secular State*, p. 149.

[105] Ibid.

[106] *Madras Legislative Assembly Debates*, February 10, 1949, 17:973, quoted in Mudaliar, *Secular State*, p. 163.

[107] Counter affidavit of first respondent in Writ Petition 840 of 1951.

of the trustee. Before 1843 the temple was managed by a trustee appointed by the government."[108] Second, the HRCE Department denied that the provisions in the High Court scheme of 1925, which referred to lists of voters for the election of trustees, were in pursuance of "immemorial usage": "The right to vote was given by the scheme decree. The right of election of the trustees is not traceable to any usage apart from the scheme."[109] Third, according to the legal representative of the HRCE Department, the administration of the temple "did not vest in the Thengalai residents but in the trustees of the temple."[110]

Finally, it was asserted that the temple was neither owned nor maintained by the Teṉkalais: "It is an ancient and historic shrine resorted to by vast numbers of Hindu worshippers and several non-Thengalai Hindus have made large and substantial endowments to the temple."[111] Essentially on the basis of these four arguments, the court deemed it appropriate for the commissioner of the HRCE Department to appoint a trustee to the Śrī Pārtasārati Svāmi Temple. In a later appeal, when an adverse decision was being contested, the representatives of the state argued that even "on the footing that the Thengalai community have the right by usage to nominate or elect trustees, that power stood transferred to the appropriate authorities under the Act [Act XIX of 1951]."[112]

The hard legal core of the position of the state was founded on Sections 39(I) and 42 of Act XIX of 1951.[113] In upholding the position of the state, the Madras High Court[114] explicated these sections of the act in relation to the court scheme of the temple (the bedrock of the Teṉkalai argument) as follows.[115] The upshot of the judge's analysis was that the provisions of the 1924 scheme could be overridden by the HRCE commissioner, fully justifying the HRCE appointment of trustees, unless temple trustees could be proven to be hereditary officeholders. However, and ironically, it was the very scheme framed by the High Court in 1925 that prevented the Teṉkalais from making an argument for the hereditary nature of the trusteeship. As the judge who passed the final order pointed out, the

[108] Ibid., para. 3.
[109] Ibid., para. 7.
[110] Ibid., para. 9.
[111] Ibid., para. 10.
[112] Memorandum of Grounds, October 31, 1952, in Writ Appeal 17 of 1953 against Writ Petition 840 of 1951, para. 12.
[113] These sections pertain to the appointment of temple trustees by the state.
[114] Order, April 12, 1957, in Writ Appeal 17 of 1953.
[115] C.S. 527 of 1924, High Court of Judicature at Madras.

hereditary argument could be made only in terms of "usage," but "it cannot be said succession continued to be governed by usage when the fact is that it was governed by the provisions of the scheme."[116] The Teṉkalais were thus hoisted on their own petard. The very document that was the foundation of their argument against the state (the scheme in C.S. 527 of 1924) was also the instrument of the sabotage of their claims.

In summary, the arguments advanced either by, or in behalf of, the HRCE Department had four components: (1) at the most tacit level, underlying Act XIX of 1951, was the classic protective mandate of the king with respect to the temple; (2) the sheer legislative fiat represented by Sections 39(I) and 42 of Act XIX of 1951, which permitted the appointment of trustees by the state to all temples except those that had "hereditary trustees" (this was the coup de grace for such schemes for temple self-government as that created by C.S. 527 of 1924 for the Śrī Pārtasārati Svāmi Temple); (3) the argument in regard to "hereditary trustees" was aborted by the proposition that schemes framed by the court for the governance of temples superseded the usages on which they might be based, thus becoming autonomous legal entities and subject, therefore, to legislative modification or veto; and (4) it was argued that "prior to 1843" the government had appointed the trustees to the temple.

The arguments of the Teṉkalai community against the incursions of the state can now be anticipated to some extent, but their specifics are important. The essentials of the Teṉkalai argument are present[117] in a lengthy affidavit filed by M. Ramakrishna Naidu on behalf of the Teṉkalai community of Triplicane in the legal battle against the state in the early 1950s. This document began with a detailed summary of the 1924 court scheme, which had heretofore governed the temple and according to which the Teṉkalai community of Triplicane had been organized into an electoral polity, which controlled the appointment of trustees to the temple.[118] After noting that this scheme was itself only the last in a series of court-framed schemes going back to 1885, the petitioner went farther back in history to bolster the Teṉkalai argument:

> 3. Such schemes were based upon the ancient and immemorial usage of this institution relating to the nomination of Dharmakarthas as stated in the

[116] Writ Appeal 17 of 1953.

[117] Affidavit of first petitioner, December 7, 1951, in Writ Petition 840 of 1951, High Court of Judicature at Madras.

[118] Ibid., para. 2.

minutes of consultation dated 29–4-1843, namely the nomination of one or more Dharmakarthas should be left hereafter on the occurrence of a vacancy to the suffrage of the Thengalai sect as has heretofore been customary.

4. As in all ancient temples the origin of this temple is only traditional but the usage relating to the same as to the selection of a Dharmakartha is that when a vacancy arises it should be left to the suffrage of the Thengalai sect living within a specified boundary in the locality of Triplicane. Such a right has been recognized by the ancient records of the Government dating so far back as 1836, 1843 onwards.

5. It was this usage and right of the Thengalai voters of the Triplicane village or town that was re-recognized and established in the various schemes from 1878 onwards. The administration of the temple and its affairs have gone on under the scheme of C.S. 527 of 1924, till about 1946, when by Act X of 1946, Act II of 1927, the Madras Hindu Religious Endowments Act was extended and made applicable to religious institutions in the City as well.

6. In or about 1947 under the amended Act of the Hindu Religious Endowments Board superseded the Board of Supervision that existed under the said scheme. That was the first inroad into the provisions of the scheme by the Hindu Religious Endowments Board under Act II of 1927.[119]

After connecting this historiography to the most recent order of the commissioner of the HRCE Department, as the culmination of a gradual process of incursion, the petitioner argued that it was illegal, primarily on the grounds that these legal schemes only *recognized*, but did not replace, "immemorial usage."[120] Thus, he argued, even given the tricky provisions of Sections 39(I) and 42 of Act XIX of 1951, there was no way that the immemorial rights of the Teṉkalai community could be abrogated: "Thus, even if the office be regarded as nonhereditary, the Commissioner cannot exercise the powers under Section 42, with regard to this temple."[121] In a later petition, the Teṉkalais argued that "the rights of the specific sect of voters to appoint or elect trustees is a right to administer the temple and its properties and the same cannot be taken away by Act XIX of 1951 and to that extent the provisions of the Act are *ultra vires*,[122] and invalid."[123] Thus, the Teṉkalais rested their case on the primacy of usage over law.

[119] Ibid., paras. 3–6.

[120] Affidavit of first petitioner, December 7, 1951, para. 9(iv).

[121] Ibid.

[122] The doctrine of *ultra vires*, which comes out of English law, asserts that "the Courts will interfere with the exercise of public power if it is arbitrary." For a discussion of the historical and technical difficulties of this doctrine, see A. T. Markose, *Judicial Control of Administrative Action in India* (Madras, 1956), pp. 43–7.

[123] Memorandum, October 14, 1957, in S.C.C.M.P. 8032 of 1957.

In their last organized legal attempt to resist the incursion of the state, the Teṉkalai argument took its strongest form. In their plaint in *Srinivasachariar v. The Commissioner H.R. and C.E.*, the Teṉkalais reviewed the entire history of the interaction between state and sect up to 1967 and concluded from this review that "every time there was a threat to the rights of the Thengalai denomination or community of Triplicane, steps were taken to prevent the same and so far there has been *a measure of protection*" (emphasis added).[124] Finally, it was argued by the Teṉkalai community that the rights that were theirs by immemorial usage were also those that were protected by the Constitution of independent India in its provision concerning religious denominations.[125]

Thus, we can see that the arguments of the Teṉkalai community of Triplicane, like those of the state, refer to a past that is held to vindicate their *exclusive* right to manage the temple. This past, enshrined as "usage," is perceived to be superordinate to the legal and administrative history of the past century and a half, although this latter history is cited in support of the antiquity of "usage." Finally, although the Teṉkalai argument appears to exclude the state from any direct role in the affairs of the Śrī Pārtasārati Svāmi Temple, the wish of the Teṉkalai petitioners for "a measure of protection" reveals the difficulty of asserting rights in relation to a sovereign deity that cannot, in a practical sense, "protect" the rights of its worshippers. Ironically, from the point of view of the Teṉkalai community today, the agency that has always been called upon to protect their rights, the state, is also the Leviathan that has all but abolished them. In the language of Louis Dumont, the state has concretely "encompassed" the sect.

This situation is partly the outcome of a set of cultural and structural facts that I have analyzed in the course of this chapter. Put simply, this set of facts can be summarized as follows: The *shared sovereignty* of royal deity and human king governs the redistributive process of the temple; this fact, as well as the multiplicity of donors who confuse the boundaries between the temple and its social environment, results in a situation in which the day-to-day management of the temple is not a simple matter of a hierarchical pyramid of authority but rather involves the orchestration of a complicated set of "honorable" shares in the divine polity of the deity. This complex

124 Plaint, June 1968, in O.S. 2910 of 1968, City Civil Court of Madras, para. 11.
125 Ibid., para. 14.

orchestration, under the aegis of a shared sovereignty, is necessarily fragile, and conflicts around "honor" and "honors" in the temple are the clearest symptoms of friction.

But this structural situation and the cultural propositions on which it is founded do not provide an exhaustive explanation of the recent conflict between state and sect at the Śrī Pārtasārati Svāmi Temple in Triplicane. It is equally the outcome of the impact of colonial ideas and institutions on an institution based on these ideas. The remainder of this study is concerned with the elucidation of this historical process. Accordingly, the following chapter establishes the pre-British paradigm of relations between kings and temples in the Vijayanagara period. Subsequent chapters explore the impact of British administrative and legal institutions on the temple.

The purpose of the following four chapters, therefore, is twofold: (1) to explore the historical roots of the contemporary conflict between state and sect at the Śrī Pārtasārati Svāmi Temple in Triplicane, and (2) to provide evidence for the persistence of certain features, both cultural and structural, of the redistributive process which is the heart of the South Indian temple.

2

KINGS, SECTS, AND TEMPLES: SOUTH INDIAN ŚRĪ VAISNAVISM, 1350–1700

The primary concern of this chapter is to place the Śrī Pārtasārati Svāmi Temple in the ethnohistorical context of South Indian society from 1350 to 1700.[1] This task entails two separate, though interlinked, kinds of analyses. The first, of a general and schematic sort, presents a general model of the ways in which kings interacted with temples in this period, with some historical examples. The second function of this chapter is to account, within this general ethnosociological framework, for the sectarian development that ultimately affected the politics of the Śrī Pārtasārati Svāmi Temple.

The general framework that underpinned the relationship of kings, sects, and temples during this period can be described in terms of four propositions:

1. Temples were ritually essential to the maintenance of kingship.
2. Dynamic sectarian leaders provided the links between kings and temples.
3. Although the day-to-day management of temples was left in the hands of local (generally sectarian) groups, the responsibility for solving temple conflicts that resisted local resolutions was vested clearly in the human sovereign.
4. In a particular ethnosociological sense, kingly action regarding temple conflict was not *legislative*, but *administrative*.

Temples and kingship

In classical Indian thought, generosity to Brahmins, codified in the "law of the gift" (*tānatarmam*), was an important element of the role of kings.[2] It has recently been carefully demonstrated that in South India, under Pallava rule, in the late seventh and eighth centuries a fundamental change occurred in the conception of what constitutes

[1] A slightly condensed version of this chapter was published as an essay, "Kings, Sects and Temples in South India, 1350–1700 A.D.," *Indian Economic and Social History Review* 14, No. 1 (January–March 1977): 47–73, and was reprinted in Burton Stein, ed., *South Indian Temples: An Analytical Reconsideration* (New Delhi, 1978).

[2] Marcel Mauss, *The Gift* (New York, 1967), pp. 53–9; V. R. R. Dikshitar, *Hindu Administrative Institutions* (Madras, 1929), pp. 102–4.

sovereignty: The giving of gifts, which was previously only one element of the basic definition of kings as *sacrificers*, now became the central constituent of sovereignty.[3] This shift during Pallava rule coincides with the beginnings of temple building associated with Puranic deities, such as Viṣṇu and Sivā. During the next period of South Indian history, when the Cōḻa house dominated the South (ca. A.D. 900 to 1200), this model of kingly generosity was the basis for a generous royal endowment of temples, as well as for the establishment and subsidy of *brahmadēya*s (settlements of learned Brahmins, with highly favorable tax assessments). However, in the articulation and public display of sovereignty, even in the Cōḻa period, it appears that temple construction had begun to play a peculiar and powerful role.[4]

Starting from about A.D. 1350, and during the next three centuries of Vijayanagara rule, there was a serious decline in the status of *brahmadēya*s and a concomitant growth and expansion of temples in South India.[5] Royal endowments to temples became a major means for the redistributive activities of Vijayanagara sovereigns, which played an important role in agrarian development in this period.[6] At the same time, temple endowment was a major technique for the extension of royal control into new areas, and transactions involving both material resources and temple honors permitted the absorption of new local constituencies into Vijayanagara rule. This latter process is documented in this chapter.

Sectarian leaders as mediators

Even before the commencement of the Vijayanagara period, the relationship of sovereigns to their predominantly agrarian localities

[3] Nicholas B. Dirks, "Political Authority and Structural Change in Early South Indian History," *Indian Economic and Social History Review* 13, No. 2 (1976): 125–58.

[4] George W. Spencer, "Religious Networks and Royal Influence in Eleventh Century South India," *Journal of the Economic and Social History of the Orient* 12 (January 1969): 42–56, Pt. 1, and "Royal Initiative Under Rajaraja I," *Indian Economic and Social History Review* 7, No. 4 (December 1970): 431–42.

[5] Burton Stein, "Integration of the Agrarian System of South India," in R. E. Frykenberg, ed., *Land Control and Social Structure in Indian History* (Madison, Wisc., 1969), pp. 191–4, and "Temples in Tamil Country, 1300–1750 A.D.," in Stein, ed., *South Indian Temples*. K. Sundaram, *Studies in Economic and Social Conditions in Medieval Andhra (A.D. 1000–1600)* (Madras, 1968), passim, but especially Chap. 5; A. Krishnaswami, *The Tamil Country Under Vijayanagara* (Annamalainagar, India, 1964), pp. 98–105.

[6] Burton Stein, "The Economic Function of a Medieval South Indian Temple," *Journal of Asian Studies* 19, No. 2 (1960):163–76.

was mediated by a host of powerful local personages and groups.[7] This continued to be so, although in rather different ways, in the Vijayanagara period. The relationship of kings to temples in the Vijayanagara period cannot be understood without taking into account the wide variety of local corporate groups and local leaders who were responsible for the management of temples.[8] But of all these groups and persons, increased prominence was gained by local sectarian assemblies and mobile sectarian leaders. The function of these sectarian leaders and the local sectarian constituencies they represented in facilitating the linkage of sovereigns to temples is dealt with in detail later in this chapter.

Local management and royal intervention

Although royal figures conducted extensive and elaborate relationships with temples, by the building of new temples and by the extension and enrichment of old ones, the day-to-day management of temples remained in the hands of local notables.[9] Nevertheless, it is clear that Vijayanagara kings and their agents played an active role in the supervision of these increasingly complex religio-urban centers. This supervisory role, which is demonstrated in the increased participation of royal agents in all sorts of local decisions,[10] was activated primarily in contexts where the locality was unable to internally resolve temple conflicts. These situations of royal intervention give us an important perspective on the relationships of sovereigns to temples. Hence, it is worth considering some of these situations in detail.

The following example of royal arbitration in temple affairs is provided by B. A. Saletore:

> Thus in A.D. 1363 in the reign of Bukka Oḍeyar, a grave dispute was amicably settled in the Araga-rājya which was ruled over by Virūpaṇṇa Odeyar. The people of Heddūrnāḍ and the temple āchāyas disputed with the Sūris as to the boundaries of the land belonging to the Pārsvadēva temple of Taḍatāḷa in Heddūr-nād, in the Tīrthahaḷḷi tāluka. The great

[7] Burton Stein, "The Segmentary State in South Indian History," in Richard G. Fox, ed., *Realm and Region in Traditional India* (Durham, N.C., 1977), pp. 3–51.

[8] T. V. Mahalingam, *South Indian Polity* (Madras, 1967), pp. 386–9.

[9] Ibid.; see also B. A. Saletore, "The Sthānikas and Their Historical Importance," *Journal of the University of Bombay* 7 (July 1938):29–93, Pt. 1.

[10] See, for example, *Epigraphia Carnatica*, IV, Ch. 113, 15, quoted in B. A. Saletore, *Social and Political Life in the Vijayanagara Empire, 1346–1646* 2 vols. (Madras, 1934), 2:355.

minister Nāgaṇṇa and various important officials like *Pradhāni* Dēvarasa, along with other *arasus* or lords, and the Jaina Mallappa summoned the elders of the three cities and the Eighteen Kaṃpaṇas, and held an enquiry in the Araga-*chāvaḍi* or hall. "And having made the nāḍ agree, they fixed the boundaries (specified) according to the former custom as those of the temple endowment of Parsvadēva."[11]

The next example comes from T. V. Mahalingam's *South Indian Polity*:

The manner in which a dispute was settled in the Tiruvoṟṟiyūr temple was decided in the fourteenth century by one Viṭṭappar of Anegondi, who was appointed the king's officer in the temple, is interesting. As soon as he took charge of his office "he found that the *padiyilār*, the *Iṣabbattaḷiyilār* and the *Dēvaraḍiyār* had struck work in that temple and that two previous attempts at reconciling their differences in the fifth year of Rājanārāyaṇan Sambuvarāyan by the *Mudaliyār* of Perumbaṟṟappuliyūr (Cidambaram) and subsequently by the trustees, had proved abortive. Viṭṭappar now enquired of the *Vīrasōḷa-aṇukkar* and the *Kaikkoḷar* for the cause of this strike, and having called together a meeting of the Srirudras, *Srimahēsvaras* the *Isabbattaḷiyilār* and the *Dēvaraḍiyār* in the *Vyākaraṇadāna maṇḍapa* of the Tirrvoṟṟiyūr temple, settled a procedure in the matter of the order to be followed in regard to temple service. It appears, however, that the matter was not finally settled even then; for, three years later (in S. 1293) under orders of Kaṃpaṇa Udaiyār these had to meet in the same *maṇḍapa* presided over this time by the officer Tuṇaiyirundanambi Kongarāyar. More representatives than on the previous occasion had gathered including the trustees and the district representatives (*Nāṭṭār*) and the question was decided not only as between the *Isabbattaliyilār* and the *Dēvaraḍiyār*, but concerned also indirectly *Sokkattaḷiyilār*, *Muttukkārar*, *Viranukkar* (*Vīrasōḷa-aṇukkar* mentioned earlier) and the *Kaikkōḷar* all of whom must have been servants of the Tiruvoṟṟiyūr temple in one capacity or another. The points settled were many, and involved several details which it is unnecessary to repeat. In effect, the *Isabbattaḷiyilār* were required to serve in the shrine of the God and the *Dēvaraḍiyār* in that of the Goddess on festive occasions within the temple, and when the Gods were carried in procession outside the temple through the streets, to *maṇḍapas*, gardens, tanks, and other sanctified spots, and when minor deities,including the image of the sage Tiruvādavūr Nāyānār (Māṇikka-Vāsagar) on the occasion of his hearing the *Tiruvembāvai*, were paraded, the procedure was to be somewhat different.[12]

Similarly, Saletore reports the following example from the second half of the fifteenth century:

An inscription dated only in the cyclic year *Raktākshi*, *Kārttigai*, 27th day, but assigned to the times of Virūpāksa II, son of Harihara II, gives us the

[11] Ibid., 1:371.

[12] *Annual Report on South Indian Epigraphy*, 1913, para. 51, reported in Mahalingam, *South Indian Polity*, pp. 225–6.

details of the settlement of the question of the right (*kāni*) of worship in the Aragaḷūr temple, Salem district. The judgment was given by Tirumalli Nāyaka, who was evidently an officer placed over the district or deputed for the purpose. The dispute was between the *sthānikas* or temple managers themselves of the Kāmēsvara temple at Aragalūr. The judgement of Tirumalli Nāyaka contains among other things, the following: "(1) A has been enjoying for a long time the privilege of worshipping all the thirty days of the month in the temple, while actually only fifteen days belong to him by right, and fifteen days belong to another person named B; (2) the privilege of B thus enjoyed by A without proper authority, requires settlement; (3) in support of the latter part of the statement made in (1), there are records in the temple to prove that fifteen days of B (now abandoned by him and enjoyed by A) have under orders been counted as unclaimed (*irangal*); (4) of this privilege of fifteen days so declared unclaimed, you have sold on your own responsibility seven and a half days to a third person C and given him a sale-deed; (5) by so doing you have deprived the acquired right of A enjoyed by him for the last eight or ten generations; (6) at this stage, the *nāṭṭār* (the representatives of *nāḍu*) appeared to have volunterred to settle the question of enjoyment – A being found issueless(?) – and to have called the parties to present themselves before them together with A; (7) you – the managers – were also required (under my orders) to be present on the occasion, to hear the case, and to carry out the decision arrived at by the *nāṭṭār* and to have, in the meantime, during this period of hearing (by the *nāṭṭār*), the worship of the temple performed by outsiders, on payment; (8) A having then appealed to me while I happened to be present at Aragalūr, to hear the case personally and give a just decision, I and the *nāṭṭār* together advised the parties to put their case before the *mahājanas* and issued an order to this effect; (9) in obedience to our order the *mahājanas* of the *agrahāra* of Kuḷattūr, Alambaḷam, Saḍaiyanpaṭṭu and Maṭṭiyākurichchi met together, heard both sides and decided that although A may have been the hereditary holder of only fifteen days of the privilege it was not fair to sell a part of the disputed portion there to an outsider like C while the right to purchase (in virtue of long enjoyment) primarily rested in A; (10) accordingly, therefore, to this decision of the *mahājanas* we order that A must continue to enjoy the full thirty days as before and that the sale-deed you have given to C should be cancelled."[13]

The final example, dated A.D. 1555, also comes from Saletore:

Words having arisen between all the (?) cultivators and the Paṇchāḷas (or artisans) in the place belonging to (the god) Chennigarāya of Bēlūr – according to the decision formerly given by Rāma-Rājayya-Tirumala-Rājayya regarding the caste observances of the Paṇchāḷas, fixing the southern street of Bēlūr for them, the stones were put up at the four boundaries (specified) within which the Paṇchāḷas might erect rows of houses, carry on their caste observances and make jewellery, enjoying in the temple of Chennigarāya the same privileges and positions as were granted to the

[13] *Annual Report on South Indian Epigraphy*, 1914, pp. 96–7, reported in Saletore, *Social and Political Life*, 1:375–6.

Paṇchāḷas at the car-festival in Vidyānagara. Such is the sāsana granted to the Paṇchāḷas, in accordance with the order of Rāma-Rājayya-Tirumala-Rājayya, by us – the Vēdanti Rāmarajayyapa, the eighty-eight Srī Vaishṇava Brahmins, Banadarasayya, agent for the affairs of Rāma-Rājayya-Tirumala-Rājayya, and Senabova Seṭṭi, agent for the affairs of Rāmapayya.[14]

In analyzing these authoritative settlements of temple disputes, it is important to notice that they are neither vertical administrative fiats nor pieces of royal legislation but are, rather, administrative commands (*rāja cācanam*) of an arbitrative sort. These publicly and communally arrived at decisions must be understood as *vyavastā*s (regulations) among members of local corporate groups, which were rendered authoritative by the participation of the king or his agents. In this context, the *rāja cācanam* (royal command) was "the act by which the king sanctions a collective regulation."[15] Such *Rājā cācanam*s, which rendered local regulations authoritative, were widespread in middle-period South India:

In the South of India in particular, a number of these *vyavasthās* sanctioned by the king survive to this day. They are not confined to conventions between the inhabitants of a locality or region, but also include accords concerning colonies of Brahmins, guilds, or corporations of tradesmen, which show that the custom of having these compacts confirmed by the king was very widespread. The majority are concerned with the maintenance of a temple, the celebration of a cult, the division of taxation amongst members, the making of a dam or a reservoir. But we also find provisions dealing with the law of succession, the forms of marriage, the penalties applicable in those guilty of certain crimes, which are certainly within the domain of the *sāstras*.[16]

Kingship as administration, not legislation

This species of royal intervention presumes a model of the king as an *administrator* rather than a *legislator*, following Lingat's brilliant distinction.[17] This contrast is important in two senses. First, it suggests that the commands of Hindu kings were administrative, in the sense that they were addressed to specific individuals and groups, were not of general applicability, and were subject to alteration or repeal according to the pragmatic needs of kingship.[18] On the other hand, legislative power would imply "a right attributed to a constitution-

[14] *Epigraphia Carnatica*, 5:45, quoted in Saletore, *Social and Political Life*, 2:200.
[15] Robert Lingat, *The Classical Law of India* (New Delhi, 1973), p. 229, fn. 54.
[16] Ibid., p. 227.
[17] Ibid., p. 228.
[18] Ibid., pp. 224–32.

ally competent authority to pronounce rules having a general application and possessing, in principle, a permanent character."[19] The most important consequence of this contrast is that royal judgments were only orders, which could not fix the law or even strictly serve as an illustration: "Although the intervention of the king in judicial matters may be decisive, it brings no new element to interpretation. In settling disputes between his subjects, the king merely does his duty, which is to secure order and peace in his realm. This is the office of an administrator and not a legislator."[20]

The most important implication of this view, which is dealt with at length in Chapter 5, is that it clarifies the enormous change imposed by British notions of law and legality, wherein all judgments became themselves legal rules, hence precedents:

> Whilst, in the classical system, the judgement had no other object but to put an end to a dispute brought before the judge, it now began to constitute a precedent upon which the rule of *stare decisis* conferred the status of a source of law. Thus law-in-action, which had not existed except potentially in the *sāstras* and treatises, henceforward became extracted and fixed in the case law of these new courts.[21]

The second important consequence of the distinction between the administrative orders of the Hindu king and the judicial decisions of the British courts was that, in the former case, the orders were context specific and context bound,[22] whereas in the latter case, the case law generated by legal decisions, as well as the legislation on which such decisions were based, created rules and precedents of general applicability, so that decisions made in one context had, under certain conditions, automatic application in other contexts.

But the orders of Hindu kings in reference to "regulations" concerning temples were "administrative" only in a special ethnohistorical sense. The administrative actions of the king, in this context, did not imply a centralized bureaucratic staff on the Weberian model of legal-bureaucratic authority.[23] As in the validity of royal commands, as well as in the machinery for making such decisions, context sensitivity was the rule. In the examples cited of royal intervention,

[19] Ibid., p. 224.

[20] Ibid., p. 256.

[21] Ibid., pp. 263–4.

[22] For the general idea of "context-sensitivity" as a feature of "rules" in many domains of traditional Indian culture, I am indebted to Professor A. K. Ramanujan, University of Chicago, who in several conversations, lectures, and unpublished works has identified and defined this stimulating feature of Indian thought.

[23] Max Weber, *The Theory of Social and Economic Organization* (New York, 1964), pp. 329–36.

the "staff" that makes the decision is a complex and contextually variable nesting of individuals and corporate groups forming a single, unique interlocking system, linking the king, his agents, local assemblies, sectarian groups and leaders, temple functionaries, and, in some cases,[24] local worshippers. There was, thus, no single, centralized, permanent, bureaucratic organization but a temporary affiliation of a number of local groups, authoritatively constituted by, or in the name of, the king, making public decisions on specific matters.[25] Here again, the British bureaucracy in the nineteenth century, because of its centralized and permanent character, was unable to preserve the balance between the royal "protection" of temples and their direct and systematic subordination to the centralized bureaucracy of the state.[26]

In classical Indian thought, the distinctive function of the king is expressed in the formula *prajānām paripālanam*, which means protection of his subjects,[27] or in some other variant formulaic expression of the same idea. In respect to temples in South India, the central aspect of this royal function was the responsibility of the king to maintain peace between his subjects and order in his realm.[28] However, given the spatial and temporal variability in the set of "staffs" through which kings did actually arbitrate temple disputes, they could only stimulate, ratify, and render authoritative reasonable local agreements. The actual day-to-day maintenance of these royally sanctioned regulations was necessarily the responsibility of authoritative local groups. Thus, we find in the bulk of the inscriptions from temples in middle-period South India a stylized conclusion whereby the protection (*rakṣai*) of these regulations was entrusted to local sectarian groups. In the inscriptions of the Tirupati Temple, for example, the stylized formula is "Śrī Vaiṣṇava Rakṣai."[29]

The second aspect of the kingly role, the lavish endowment of temples, did not by itself distinguish kings, because temple donors in the middle period came from a wide cross section of society.[30] In relation to temples, the distinctive function of royalty was the com-

24 See the Triplicane cases discussed at the end of this chapter.

25 This argument is an extension of the argument in Stein, "Segmentary State in South Indian History."

26 See Chapters 3 and 4.

27 Lingat, *Classical Law of India*, p. 222.

28 Ibid., p. 223.

29 *Tirumalai-Tirupati Devastanam Epigraphical Series*, 6 vols. (Madras, 1931–8), passim.

30 See, for example, ibid., Vol. 6, Pt. 2, *Epigraphical Glossary*, Section III, "List of Donors for the Temples at Triumalai and Tirupati."

bination of generous endowment with the task of "protection" (paradigmatically: dispute arbitration). It was this second aspect of the kingly role that formally distinguished it from other social roles, and thus we have a record of a sixteenth-century dialogue between a Paṇdya ruler and the learned Brahmins at his court as to which was preferable, donation or protection. They declared protection to be superior, saying: "Render thou protection which is purifying."[31]

Hindu kings in middle-period South India thus had two sorts of relationships to temple deities: endowment and protection. The latter aspect of their role, however, did not connote a capacity to legislate in the modern Western sense, nor did it imply centralized bureaucratic management of temple affairs. The effective bearers of royal commands, and thus of the "protective" function, were local, generally sectarian groups and leaders. *Without endowment*, the king would cease to place himself in an active relationship with the redistributive powers of the deity and thus would fail to acquire the honor constitutive of sovereignty. *Without protection*, that is, without the authoritative ratification of local regulations by royal edicts (*rāja cācanam*), the king would have abnegated his fundamental duty toward his subjects. In South India, between 1350 and 1700, this cultural model formed the basis for a dynamic set of relationships between warrior-kings, sectarian leaders, and temples, which had important consequences for Vaisnava sectarian development.

Kings and temples: a transactional framework

Toward the middle of the fourteenth century, certain scholastic disputes within the Śrī Vaisnava community in South India had divided its leadership into two schools. By the end of the seventeenth century, this rift had become the intellectual expression of a complex social phenomenon, namely, the division of the community into two antagonistic subsects, which were beginning to compete, pan-regionally, for control of Vaisnava temples. To account for this fundamental alteration in the structure of the sect, it is necessary to appreciate a certain set of relationships that lay at the core of sectarian activity in this period. The method of the following section is first to schematically describe this set of relationships and then its empirical manifes-

[31] *Travancore Archaeological Series* (Trivandrum, India, 1930), 1:108–9 and 113, cited in Chandra Y. Mudaliar, *The Secular State and Religious Institutions in India: A Study of the Administration of Hindu Public Religious Trusts in Madras* (Wiesbaden, 1974), p. 1.

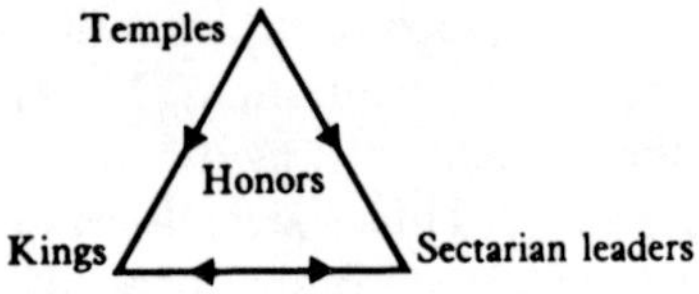

Figure 6. Medium of honors

tations and transformations over the entire period, thus accounting for the ultimate shape of South Indian Śrī Vaisnavism at the beginning of the eighteenth century.

In analyzing sectarian activities (whether Vaisnava or not) in this period, a three-way transactional system emerges from the evidence. This set of transactions links political rulers, sectarian leaders, and temples in a complex triangular set of exchanges. Although honors and material endowments in the South Indian temple represent two aspects of a single redistributive process,[32] it is analytically possible to separate them. So separated, it is possible to see two parallel, but distinct, levels of transaction that link kings, sectarian leaders, and temples, one involving transfers of honor, the other involving transfers of endowed material resources.

In the medium of honors, it is possible to see four kinds of transaction during this period. Temples confer honors on political rulers; political rulers confer honors on sectarian leaders; temples confer honors on sectarian leaders; and sectarian leaders confer honors on political rulers. This level of transaction can be schematized as seen in Figure 6.

In the medium of endowed material resources, a different set of transactions obtains. Political rulers transfer material resources (most often shares in the agrarian produce of specified villages) to temples; political rulers also transfer such material resources to sectarian leaders; and sectarian leaders, in their own capacity, also endow temples. This transactional level can be schematized as seen in Figure 7. If these two transactional levels are visually juxtaposed, the complexity of the relationships between these three loci becomes obvious (see Figure 8).

The juxtaposition of these two diagrams raises a problem. Except in one transactional case, the relationships between any two of these units is symmetrical and involves the exchange of honors for material resources. The only problematic, and seemingly gratuitous, relationship is the conferral of honors by political rulers on sectarian leaders.

[32] The analysis of this redistributive process is the subject of Chapter 1.

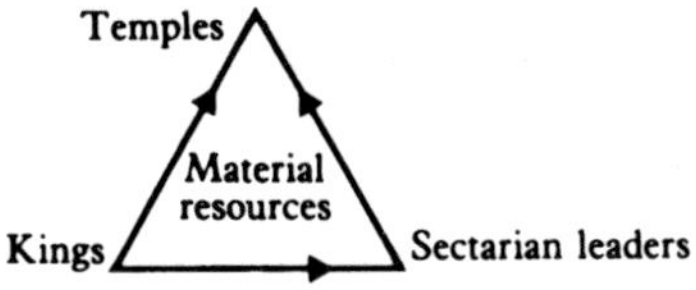

Figure 7. Medium of endowed material resources

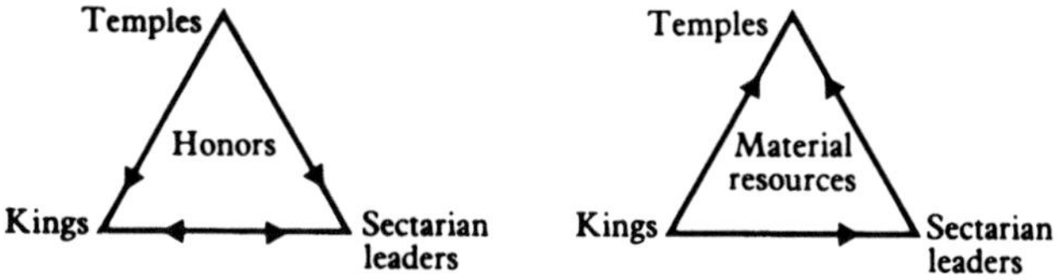

Figure 8. Exchange of honors and resources

That is to say, the relationship between political rulers and sectarian leaders, conceived in terms of honors and material resources, is asymmetrical. Political rulers confer honors as well as material resources on sectarian leaders, whereas sectarian leaders seem to repay this only in part (i.e., by the conferral of honors on political leaders).

Is this asymmetry a real one? Although this question can be posed in schematic terms, it can be answered only empirically and historically. The following hypothesis concerning the relationship between political rulers and sectarian leaders during this period gives empirical flesh to the above scheme and also suggests that sectarian leaders did indeed repay the endowments given to them by political leaders in a cognate medium. Specifically, it is argued that in the sociopolitical context of the period from 1350 to 1700 sectarian leaders were crucial intermediaries for the introduction, extension, and institutionalization of warrior control over constituencies and regions that might otherwise have proved refractory. This intermediary role of sectarian leaders, which rendered control by conquest into appropriate (and thus stable) rule, was effected primarily in, and through, sectarian control of the redistributive capacities of the temples. Thus sectarian leaders permitted Telugu warriors to render their military expansion culturally appropriate by "gifting" activity and its main product; temple honor.

Put differently, it might be said that the ceremonial exchanges of honor between warrior-kings and sectarian leaders rendered public, stable, and culturally appropriate an exchange at the level of politics and economics. These warrior-kings bartered the control of agrarian resources gained by military prowess for access to the redistributive processes of temples, which were controlled by sectarian leaders. Conversely, in their own struggles with each other, and their own local and regional efforts to consolidate their control over temples, sectarian leaders found the support of these warrior-kings timely and profitable. Empirically, and diachronically, this relationship between warrior-kings and sectarian leaders is neither simple nor transparent. It is a complex symbiosis in which mobile figures of both types augmented and sustained each other. How did this relationship come to apply to Śrī Vaisnava institutions?

Scholastic fission: Śrī Vaisnavism, A.D. 1137–1350

The schismatic tendencies in the Śrī Vaisnava movement after A.D. 1350 can be traced back in part to the complex and uneasy synthesis of diverse religious, social, and philosophical elements achieved by Rāmānujā in the eleventh and twelfth centuries. The greatest strictly intellectual work of Rāmānujā was his *Śrī Bhāṣya* on the *Vēdānta-Sūtra* of Vyāsa. This work is the cornerstone of the philosophy of *visiṣṭ-advaita* (qualified monism) and was a calculated riposte to the rigorous *advaita* philosophy of Samkara. Although it is couched in the precise language of logic and metaphysics, this work, like the rest of Rāmānujā's corpus, shows distinct traces of the kind of poetry and paradox that characterized the Prabandam (devotional poetic compositions) of the *āḻvār* poet-saints of the early medieval period.[33] Rāmānujā replaced the impersonal Godhead of Saṃkara with the personal God Nārāyaṇā (Viṣṇu), gave high recognition to the technique of devotion for the achievement of *mōkṣa* (liberation), and insisted on the reality of phenomenal existence (*vyavahāra*).[34] In these senses, the popular devotionalism of the Prabandam poems was brought into synthesis with the Vēdas, the *Upanisads*, and the *Bhagavad-Gīta*.

Second, Rāmānujā actualized the views of his predecessor Yamunācāryā, who, in his *Āgamaprāmaṇya*,[35] established the orthodoxy of the Pāñcarātra Agamic school, whose adherents in South India had placed great emphasis on *arccavatāra* (the presence

[33] John B. Carman, *The Theology of Rāmānujā* (New Haven, Conn., 1974), p. 211.

[34] V. Rangachari, "Historical Evolution of Sri Vaishnavism in South India," in H. Bhattacharya, ed., *The Cultural Heritage of India*, 4 vols. (Calcutta, 1956), 4:175.

[35] On the cultural and historical context of this work, see J. A. B. van Buitenen, "On the Archaism of the *Bhāgavata Purāna*," in M. Singer, ed., *Krishna: Myths, Rites and Attitudes* (Chicago, 1968), pp. 23, 40.

of god in images) and thereby concentrated their brand of devotionalism on temple ritual.[36] Rāmānujā is believed, according to some sectarian traditions, to have favored the Pāñcarātra mode of worship and to have introduced it in several Vaisnava temples in South India, sometimes ousting priests of the older Vaikānasa school.[37] If this is true, Rāmānujā not only extended the concerns of his predecessors in reconciling temple worship with orthodox Vedic praxis, which is basically domestic and aniconic, but specifically displayed his orientation toward the elaboration and popularization of temple worship. For the priests of the Vaikānasa school, certainly up to the medieval period, appear to have practiced a rather spare, severe, and simple form of temple worship, not responsive to the increased medieval wish to deify the *āḻvār* poet-saints and the *ācāriyas* (sectarian leaders/apostolic heads). Nor were Vaikānasa priests enthusiastic about the elaboration of the temple calendar with costly and pompous celebrations. In short, their preferences were inimical to the expansion of temple activity to include broader social groups and interests.[38] The priests of the Pāñcarātra Agamic school, by contrast, seem to have been more open to the elaboration of the festival calendar, less rigorous in their recruitment patterns than the strictly endogamous Vaikānasas, and in general more open to popular, multi-caste participation in temple affairs.[39]

Third, Rāmānujā's career was peripatetic and involved teaching as well as organizational activity all over South India.[40] Among these organizational activities, the most important was the establishment of seventy-four *simhāsinātipati*s, or *ācāriyapuruṣa*s, selected from prominent Śrī Vaisnava families throughout South India, who were to be the pillars of the Śrī Vaisnava faith and the leaders of the Śrī Vaisnava community.[41] This organization extended the already formed "Acarya Cult" that existed before Rāmānujā.[42] The descendants of these seventy-four individuals formed the skeletal structure of the leadership of the Śrī Vaisnava community in later periods. But the major organizational aspect of Rāmānujā's activity was his work in temples, which involved the systematization of temple worship, the

[36] V. Rangachari, "Historical Evolution," pp. 164, 173.

[37] V. N. Hari Rao, ed., *Kōil Oḻugu* (Madras, 1961), pp. 45–6.

[38] T. K. T. Viraraghavacharya, *History of Tirupati*, 2 vols. (Tirupati, 1953–4), 1:516–26.

[39] Ibid.; see also K. R. Venkataraman, "The Vaikhānasas," in Bhattacharya, ed., *Cultural Heritage of India*, 4:160–2.

[40] Carman, *Theology of Rāmānujā*, pp. 43–4.

[41] V. Rangachari, "Historical Evolution," p. 176.

[42] Ibid., p. 172.

sanctification of the recitation of the Prabandam as a formal part of it, and the allocation of duties and corresponding honors to all those regularly involved in temple service.

It is not clear to what extent this blueprint was carried out in all the Vaisnava temples of South India. What is clear is that the great temple at Śrīrangam was intended by Rāmānujā to be the cultural and organizational model for all other Vaisnava temples. The *Kōil-Olugu*, which describes Rāmānujā's code (*uṭaiyavar tiṭṭam*) for the Śrīrangam temple, is an extraordinary document. The structure it ascribes to the genius of Rāmānujā is an extremely complex web of duties and honors, attached to a highly specialized division of labor and involving the most intricate possible interdependence between various groups of functionaries, both Brahmin and non-Brahmin.[43]

Two points emerge from this organizational picture, which is said to have held good until the "Muslim invasion" (until the first half of the fourteenth century): first, the delicate empirical line between "duties" and "honors" for any one group of functionaries, and second, the extraordinarily delicate dependence of the "honors" of some groups of temple functionaries on the "duties" of other groups. This structure, although complex, was also necessarily fragile, because it is clear that functional considerations were overriden by Rāmānujā's wish to incorporate a maximum number of types of followers into the temple organization and by his personal fiat.[44] This became evident after A.D. 1350.

But the most important aspect of Rāmānujā's heritage, particularly at Śrīrangam, for the later history of Śrī Vaisnavism is the decisive link that was established between temple control, primarily at Śrīrangam, and sectarian leadership in the form of the role of the *ācāriya*, or preceptor.[45] The first of the great Vaisnava *ācāriyas*, Nāta Muni (A.D. 824–924), was the early model for this structural synthesis. Rāmānujā, as the greatest of the *ācāriyas* and the undisputed controller of the Śrīrangam Temple, was its historical paradigm.[46] By the twelfth century, the role of the *ācāriya*, which combines in practice the meanings of preceptor, mediator (between man and God), and sectarian leader, had achieved its centrality in Vaisnava praxis.

43 Hari Rao, *Kōil Olugu*, pp. 48–100.
44 Carman, *Theology of Rāmānujā*, pp. 34–7.
45 V. Rangachari, "Historical Evolution," p. 172.
46 Carman, *Theology of Rāmānujā*, pp. 37–8.

The essence of the *ācāriya's* role was the initiation (*tīkṣai*) of outsiders into the Śrī Vaisnava sect. This was done by the fivefold procedure known as *pāñca-samskāra* (five sacraments): (1) the *tapās*, or the *ācāriya's* branding of the initiate's shoulders with the symbols of Viṣṇu, the conch and the discus; (2) the *puṇṭaram*, or initiation into wearing the sect mark (*nāmam*), the symbol of the Lord's feet; (3) the giving of a divine name to the initiate, namely, Nārāyaṇatāsa; (4) the imparting of certain sacred utterances, or *mantirattrāyam*; and (5) the handing over of a *cāḷakkirāmam* (black fossil ammonite stone) or similar object for daily worship.[47] This *pāñca-samskāra* ritual became the formal process for initiation into the Śrī Vaisnava community. Its monopoly by recognized *ācāriyā*s was the sign of their privilege of recruiting new members to the community, members who accepted the absolute authority of the *ācāriya* in sectarian matters.

In associating this authoritative role with temple control, in the person of Rāmānujā, a link was established between *recruitment* to the sect and the *rewards* for new recruits in the form of shares of some sort of temple service and temple honors. Even if new converts were not rewarded with some share in temple activity, the role of the *ācāriya* was clearly defined by the interdependence, in his person, of the dual function of sectarian recruitment and temple control. The two tasks supported one another. The recruitment function of these leaders enhanced their claim to the control of sectarian resources, of which the temple is the primary example. Conversely, the control of sectarian temples increased the worldly powers of these preceptors and made them more attractive to potential initiates.

By the time of the death of Rāmānujā, therefore, it looked as if Śrī Vaisnavism had made a firm start in South India and laid the foundations for a complex synthesis between a number of disparate traditions and groups: between the Sanskrit texts of the North and the Tamil Prabandam; between the largely domestic and aniconic ritual injunctions of the Vedic tradition and the idol-centered rituals of the Agamic tradition; between the impersonal, metaphysical severity of the *Advaita-Vēdānta* and the personal, emotional intensity of popular devotionalism in South India; and between the varna basis of the Vedic tradition and the sect-centered basis of bhakti devotionalism in South India.[48] The two interlinked institutions that

[47] V. Rangachari, "Historical Evolution," pp. 172–3.

[48] Carman, *Theology of Rāmānujā*, Chap. 2, passim; see also N. Jagadeesan,

expressed these reconciliations were that of the sectarian leader and the complex reorganization of sectarian temples, paradigmatically at Śrīrangam. After Rāmānujā's death, traditionally dated in A.D. 1137, the weak institutionalization of this gigantic mosaic became apparent and fissures began to appear in the intellectual basis of Śrī Vaisnavism.

It has rightly been observed that the two centuries following the death of Rāmānujā were "an age of growing party spirit, and not of actual party split."[49] Modern Vaisnava historiography attributes the formal division of Śrī Vaisnavism into two schools (*kalais*) to the leadership and activities of Vēdānta Dēsika (A.D. 1269–1369), who is considered the founder of the Northern (Vaṭakalai) school, and Piḷḷai Lōkācārya (A.D. 1213–1327), who is considered the founder of the Southern (Teṉkalai) school.

The overall issue that divided Rāmānujā's followers was the question of whether the Sanskrit tradition, represented at its peak in Rāmānujā's *Śrī Bhāṣya*, or the Tamil Prabandam devotional poetry of the *āḻvār* poet-saints was to be the focus of religious study, exposition, and sectarian missionary activity.[50] This issue, in part, had tremendous significance as a linguistic question, because the choice of Tamil over Sanskrit as a religious language automatically ensured a wider audience in South India, greater popularity for its proponent *ācāriya*s, and most important, the accessibility of the greatest religious truths to all four varnas of society. Emphasis on Sanskrit, on the contrary, implied a socially and historically conservative position, retaining a relatively Brahmin-exclusive mode of religious discourse, which was certainly closed to Sūdra participation and closely linked to the varna scheme as a system of mutually exclusive roles and duties. The question of which language (and therefore which set of texts) was to be the preferred center of dogmatic attention, Sanskrit or Tamil, was, in fact, the linguistic expression of a considerably wider set of issues that divided the followers of Rāmānujā.

The primary doctrinal extension of the division of the followers of Rāmānujā into Sanskrit (or Bhasyic) and Tamil (or Prabandic)

"History of Śrī Vaiṣṇavism in the Tamil Country (Post-Rāmānujā)" (Ph.D. diss., University of Madras, 1967), p. 60.

49 V. Rangachari, "The Successors of Rāmānujā and the Growth of Sectarianism among the Śrī-Vaishnavas," *Journal of the Bombay Branch of the Royal Asiatic Society* 24 (1914–17):103.

50 Ibid., pp. 127–8.

camps was a subtle but profound scholastic division on the issue of *prapatti*, or self-surrender.[51] In the Prabandam poetic corpus of the *āḻvārs*, the idea of bhakti had been extended to the more extreme doctrine of *prapatti*. The *āḻvārs* replaced the path of devotion with the path of self-surrender, because the Vedantic ideal of bhakti still involved, to some extent, the strict performance of certain coded actions (*karma*) and the acquisition of the knowledge of God (*jnāna*).

Prapatti, as a technique for salvation in the poetry of the *āḻvārs*, severs itself radically from *karma* and *jnāna*. Instead, it lays a radical and exclusive emphasis on the attitude of total helplessness and surrender before God. Followers of both the Sanskrit and the Tamil schools, after Rāmānujā, accepted the importance of the technique of *prapatti*, but the Sanskrit school nevertheless hedged the idea of *prapatti* with a number of constraints, largely of a practical sort. These practical constraints were expressed in the elaborate preconditions for the recourse to *prapatti*, the actual ritual process of becoming a *prapaṉṉan* (one who has surrendered), and the obligations incumbent upon such a person. This reflected the more Vedantic and bhakti-oriented interpretation of *prapatti* by the Sanskrit school. The Tamil school, on the other hand, retained the radical emotional heritage of the *āḻvārs* and insisted that no complex set of practical prerequisites and consequences was entailed by the attitude of *prapatti*. All that was required was an unconditional surrender to divine grace and a completely passive dependence on it for salvation.

This difference of opinion on the question of *prapatti* was subsequently crudely characterized by the analogy of the "cat" and the "monkey" to express the divergence between the two schools: The Tamil school compared divine grace to the activity of the cat, which protects its young even though they are helpless and utterly passive; the Sanskrit school, on the other hand, preferred the analogy of the monkey, whose young cling to their mothers and are thus safeguarded, in part, because of their own active efforts. The remaining differences between the two schools, which gradually took on more and more contrastive social and ritual forms,[52] are less important than this one.

[51] A. Govindacarya, "The Astadasa-Bhedas, or the Eighteen Points of Doctrinal Differences between the Tengalais (Southerners) and the Vadagalais (Northerners) of the Visistadvaita Vaishnava School, South India," *Journal of the Royal Asiatic Society of Great Britain and Ireland*, 1910, pp. 1103–12.

[52] K. Rangachari, *The Sri Vaishnava Brahmins* (Madras, 1931), pp. 46–8; also see his discussion of the sectarian split, ibid., pp. 37–45.

The elaboration of these doctrinal differences took place largely at Śrīrangam during the two centuries after the death of Rāmānujā. But during the lifetime of Varadācārya (ca. A.D. 1200) of the Northern school, a native of Kāñcīpuram, the center of the Northern school shifted from Śrīrangam to Kāñcīpuram.[53] After this period, Śrīrangam was increasingly the stronghold of the Tamil school and Kāñcīpuram of the Northern school. It is for this reason that the two schools became known as the Vaṭakalai (Northern) and Teṉkalai (Southern) schools, respectively.[54] It was in the first half of the thirteenth century, when the focus of the Sanskrit school shifted to Kāñcīpuram, under the leadership of Varadācārya, that the Tamil/Prabandic school, under the leadership of Nampiḷḷai, took shape at Śrīrangam. Nampiḷḷai's lectures, according to sectarian tradition, were extremely popular, "based as they were on the superiority of creed over caste, of the Prabandhas over the Vedas, of Tamil over Sanskrit, of Prapatti over Bhakti, and so on."[55] From this time onward, Śrīrangam and Kāñcīpuram became the respective loci of the two schools.

But it was during the lifetimes of Vēdānta Dēsika and Piḷḷai Lōkācārya that the scholastic positions of the two schools received their most elaborate formulations. Vēdānta Dēsika was born at Tuppiḷ (near Kāñcīpuram) in A.D. 1269 and died at Śrīrangam in A.D. 1369. He is the acknowledged founder of the Northern school. He lived a peripatetic life, residing at various points at Kāñcīpuram (Chingleput District), Tiruvahīndirapuram (South Arcot District), Śrīrangam (Trichinopoly District), and Satyamaṅkaḷam (Mysore), in addition to pilgrimage tours both to various temple centers in South India, such as Tirupati and Tirunārāyaṇapuram, and to sacred centers in North India as well.[56] His departure from Śrīrangam, about A.D. 1320, seems to have been a concession to the local power of the Tamil school and the difficulties of conducting the Bhasyic enterprise there.[57] Vēdānta Dēsika produced more than one hundred and twenty works, and although he was the acknowledged leader of the Sanskrit school, and thus the focus of considerable controversy, he took a liberal and tolerant approach to

[53] V. Rangachari, "Successors of Rāmānujā," p. 107.

[54] A. Govindacarya, "Tengalai and Vadagalai," *Journal of the Royal Asiatic Society of Great Britain and Ireland*, (1912), pp. 714–17.

[55] V. Rangachari, "Successors of Rāmānujā," p. 118.

[56] V. Rangachari, "The Life and Times of Srī-Vēdānta-Dēsika," *Journal of the Bombay Branch of the Royal Asiatic Society* 24:277–312.

[57] Ibid., pp. 301–2.

his Tamil school opponents. In his view, the growing conflicts in Śrī Vaisnavism were not matters to celebrate. In fact, he considered them to be strictly scholastic arguments, rooted in differing emphases rather than radical variations in belief.[58]

During the lifetime of Vēdānta Dēsika, the philosophical basis of the Southern school was laid by Piḷḷai Lōkācārya with the help of his brother Aḻakiya Maṇavāḷa Perumāḷ Nāyinār.[59] The eighteen treatises composed by Piḷḷai Lōkācārya, subsequently termed the *Aṣṭātacarahasyam*, undoubtedly form the philosophical basis of what later came to be called the Teṉkalai sect. The most important of these works is the *Śrīvacana Pūśaṇam*, a treatise on the doctrine of *prapatti*, in which great emphasis is laid on *ācāriyapimānam*, or respect for the preceptor.[60] In fact, it is this text that lays the foundations of the most crucial link in Teṉkalai thought, between the idea of *prapatti* (absolute surrender to divine grace) and the crucial necessity of mediatorship by an authoritative intercessor, the *ācāriya*.[61] It is important to note that these two ideas are common to both schools.[62] But the Tamil school, especially under the leadership of Piḷḷai Lōkācārya, made the logical connection of the two ideas a cornerstone of their sectarian beliefs.

The Vaṭakalai view of *prapatti*, because it retained some of the Vedantic leanings of bhakti, did not render the individual's efforts for salvation dispensable. Thus, although the idea of respect for, and submission to, sectarian leaders was important for the Sanskrit school, it never became crucial to it, because *intercession* by an authoritative figure was to some extent rendered dispensable by the individual's personal strivings for salvation. The Tamil school, by contrast, interpreted the idea of *prapatti* so that it rendered the individual utterly helpless in the search for salvation. Their insistence on the importance of intercession, therefore, rendered the *ācāriya*'s power of guidance much more central at the same time that his authority was made absolute.

[58] Govindacarya, "Tengalai and Vadagalai," p. 716.

[59] V. Rangachari, "Successors of Rāmānujā," pp. 124–5.

[60] T. K. Nārāyaṇasāmi Nāyaṭu, ed., *Srī Piḷḷai Lōkācāriyār Srī Vacana Pūcanam Manavāla Māmunikal Viyākkiyānam: Tamil Ākkam* (Madras, 1970); see, for example, Sūtra No. 450 (p. 660): "ācāriyā apimānamē uttārakam" ("honoring the *ācāriyā* is verily the means of salvation").

[61] A. Govindacarya and G. A. Grierson, "The Artha-Panchaka of Pillai Lokacarya," *Journal of the Royal Asiatic Society of Great Britain and Ireland*, 1910, p. 567.

[62] Govindacarya, "Tengalai and Vadagalai," p. 716.

It has often been noted that the Tamil school's interpretation of *prapatti*, and its reliance on the Tamil Prabandam rather than the Sanskrit Vēda, made it much more flexible and open to the participation of Sūdras.[63] This is undoubtedly true. But what is of greater long-term significance is that in connecting recruitment and sectarian authority and in relating individual helplessness to the need for an absolutely authoritative sectarian leadership, the Tamil school made a much more imaginative intellectual leap. Thus, they could not only recruit wider portions of the population, but, in principle, they could submit them more radically to the authority of sectarian leaders.

By the first half of the fourteenth century, therefore, South Indian Śrī Vaisnavism was an intellectually divided community. This intellectual division had created two lines of succession in sect leadership (*guruparamparai*), which were to provide the skeleton for the affiliation of Vaisnava leaders all over South India. But the active scholastic wrangling and the incipient competition for constituencies and patrons had so far been restricted to Śrīrangam, although Kāñcīpuram had emerged already as a potential base for the Sanskrit school. Furthermore, the battle was still largely scholastic.[64] Its primary sociological expression, conflict over temple control, had not yet begun, even at Śrīrangam, where, on the whole, Rāmānujā's arrangements remained stable. It was only after the second half of the fourteenth century that these tensions exploded out of textual and rhetorical arenas to the primary political arenas of temple and royal court.

Telugu control and temple politics: A.D. 1350–1500

The growth of Śrī Vaisnava sectarian activity in the century and a half after A.D. 1350 had for its context a transitional political environment. It was during this period that the Telugu warrior-

[63] Burton Stein, "Social Mobility and Medieval South Indian Hindu Sects," in J. Silverberg, ed., *Social Mobility in the Caste System in India: An Interdisciplinary Symposium* (Paris, 1968), pp. 78–94.

[64] This is not to imply that before the fourteenth century, the growth of Śrī Vaisnavism was a quiet textual affair. Rāmānujā's own activities at Śrīrangam, to take only one example, did meet with vigorous opposition from various entrenched interests in the temple (see Carman, *Theology of Rāmānujā*, pp. 35–6). The point, however, is that these, and other, battles over institutional control during Rāmānujā's life and in the two centuries following it did not come out of the scholastic issues that have been described.

founders of the Vijayanagara Empire consolidated their control over South India. The first fifty years of this period, especially in the Tamil country, illuminate the process by which this Telugu penetration was achieved.

Indigenous sources, both inscriptional and sectarian, describe this process in a remarkably unified stylistic code, of which the primary elements are: (1) the defeat of the "Muslim invaders" of the Tamil country by Telugu warriors; (2) the "restoration," by these warriors, of temple worship alleged to have been interrupted or destroyed by the Muslims; and (3) the establishment of new political order by these Telugu warriors. A typical example of this stylized description is an inscription from Tirukkalākuṭi in the Ramnad district, which states that "the times were Tulukkan [Muhammedan] times and [that] Kampana-Odeyar came on his southerly compaign, destroyed the Muhammedans, established orderly government throughout the country and appointed many nāyakkaṉmār [officials] for inspection and supervision in order that the worship in all temples might be revived and conducted regularly as of old."[65]

The first thirty years of the Saṅkama dynasty (the first dynasty) of Vijayanagara are characterized by a number of inscriptions that adhere to this code. Several of these inscriptions involve Kōpaṇṇa, a Brahmin minister-general of Kampana Uṭaiyār II of the Saṅkama dynasty, who seems to have been the model for Telugu penetration of Tamil country through the "restoration" of temples. The inscriptional evidence shows that Kampana's conquest of the Tamil country and his defeat of the Muslims was followed by extensive involvement in temple endowment in the districts of South Arcot,[66] Trichinopoly,[67] Chingleput,[68] and Madura.[69] Kōpaṇṇa, his minister-general, seems to have been one of the main agents of Kampana Uṭaiyār II in this institutional penetration of the Tamil country.[70]

[65] A.R. 34 of 1916, in para. 33, *Annual Reports on South Indian Epigraphy for 1916.* (In the rest of this chapter, this numbered series of inscriptions will be prefaced by the initials A.R. The text of these reports will be referred to as *Annual Reports.*) For an excellent sample of the indigenous sources that adhere to this code, see V. N. Hari Rao, "A History of Trichinopoly and Srirangam," (Ph.D. diss., University of Madras, 1948), pp. 299–307.

[66] A.R. 159 and 163 of 1904.

[67] A.R. 282 of 1903.

[68] V. Rangachari, "The History of the Naik Kingdom of Madura," *Indian Antiquary* 43 (1914):7.

[69] A.R. 111 of 1903.

[70] E. Hultzsch, "Ranganatha Inscription of Goppanna: Saka-Samvat 1293," *Epigraphia Indica* 6 (1900–1):322–30.

Three inscriptions from Kāñcīpuram[71] in the Kailāsanāta Temple give us an idea of the nature of this Telugu involvement in Tamil temples. The first, dated A.D. 1364, comes from the Rājasimhavarmēsvaran shrine and testifies to the restoration of temple lands and worship by the order of Kōpaṇṇa.[72] The second inscription, also dated A.D. 1364, is from the same temple but is far more detailed and interesting.[73] It describes Kōpaṇṇa's order to the temple authorities ratifying the sale of some temple property to a community of weavers and their leaders (*mutali*), with the right to mortgage and sell this property. Along with this property, however, they were to be free to mortgage and sell their "honors" as well: their precedence (*mutalmai*) in the receipt of the betel-nut honor (*aṭaippam*), their service of the deity (*tēvar aṭimai*), and their proper place in rank (*aṭaivu*).

The third inscription, dated A.D. 1369, refers to the establishment of a *maṭam* (monastery) and the allotment of some property in return for the job of sharing in the recitation of sacred hymns before the deity, to the religious preceptor of a chieftain in a town in South Arcot.[74] This last inscription indicates that one function of the allocation of temple privileges by Telugu warriors was to ease their ties with Tamil rulers. In this case, Kōpaṇṇa appears to have done this by allocating a specialized ritual role in a temple in Chingleput District to the *ācāriya* of a chieftain in South Arcot.

Taken together, these three inscriptions from Kāñcīpuram suggest that the initial penetration of Tamil country by Telugu warrior-chiefs was not simply pillage. It involved inroads into some core Tamil institutions, whose function was revived or extended and whose resources were reallocated to individuals or groups favored by these warriors. The result of these inroads was not only to establish constituencies (such as the weavers) beholden to them; they might also have established links between these warriors and indigenous rulers. In establishing such linkages, sectarian leaders were of considerable importance.[75] This linkage can be observed most directly in the case of Vaisnava temples after A.D. 1350, particularly at Śrīrangam. In this general atmosphere of intensification of royal

[71] A.R. 27, 28, and 29 of 1888.
[72] See E. Hultzsch, ed., *South Indian Inscriptions* (Madras, 1890–), 1:120.
[73] Ibid., p. 122.
[74] Ibid., 1:123–5.
[75] A.R. 56 of 1900, V. Rangacharya, *A Topographical List of the Inscriptions of the Madras Presidency*, 3 vols. (Madras, 1919),1:57; see also, T. Gopinatha Rao, "Soraikkavur Plates of Virupāksha: Saka Samvat 1308," *Epigraphia Indica* 3 (1905–6):298–306.

involvement in temples, Vaisnava sectarian leaders, particularly of the Prabandic (Southern) school, made spectacular progress.

Telugu warrior-kings and Prabandic Śrī Vaisnavism, A.D. 1350–1500

The first signs of institutionalization of the Southern school are expressed in the formation of the Śrīranganārāyaṇa Jīyar Ātīnam (monastic organization) at Śrīrangam. Although traditional hagiologies vary about the date of the establishment of this Prabandic institution, it seems safe to assign it to the first quarter of the fourteenth century.[76] Kūranārāyaṇa Jīyar, the first occupant of this seat, appears to have been an outsider, but one who gained immense popularity at Śrīrangam. As a response to his popular status, the temple servants, lead by Periya Āyī,[77] installed him in this institution and also gave him several duties and privileges in the temple.[78] The honors and duties that were allocated to this Jīyar[79] indicate the growing power of the Prabandic school. In the course of time, the honors allotted to the incumbent of this position increased and came to be on a par with the other prominent *ācāriyapuruṣa* families at Śrīrangam. Later incumbents of this position enhanced their power by offering discipleships to the Sūdra servants of the temple.[80]

The primary index of the growing importance of this subsectarian institution was the nature of the honors given to its head: precedence in the receipt of *prasātam* (sacred remnants of the food consumed by the deity) in certain ritual contexts; exclusive receipt of the *prasātam* in certain physical areas of the temple; the periodical receipt of certain insignia from the temple servants to indicate his fitness for this pontifical seat; the receipt of *tīrttam* (sacred water left over from the deity's meals or his bath), *parivaṭṭam* (the silk turban first worn by the deity), and a garland, also previously worn by the deity.[81]

It appears, moreover, that the entry of this popular sectarian leader into the redistributive process defined by temple honors was

[76] Hari Rao, "History of Trichinopoly," p. 295.

[77] The grandson of Mutali Āṇṭān, to whom Rāmānujā had assigned the *śrīkāriyam* (management) of the temple.

[78] Hari Rao, *Kōil Oḻugu*, pp. 121–2.

[79] This term indicates a sectarian leader who also has a fixed role in temple management and goes back, according to sectarian tradition, to Rāmānujā's organizational activities all over South India.

[80] Hari Rao, *Kōil Oḻugu*, p. 124.

[81] Ibid., pp. 122–5.

not automatic. It was resisted by the members of the Kantāṭai family, who had been powerful in temple affairs since the time of Rāmānujā. They eventually accommodated the Jīyar and offered him an important share in these honors in deference to his popularity.[82] This monastic seat was subsequently to become one of the most important loci of Teṉkalai sectarianism.[83] To understand this process, however, it is necessary to take a lengthy detour and to examine in detail the impact of Vijayanagara rule on Śrīrangam in the period from A.D. 1350 to 1500.

The Śrīrangam Temple was a major example of the process by which Telugu warrior-chiefs "restored" Tamil temples after Muslim rule. Both Kōpaṇṇa and Sāḷuva Kuṇṭa, generals under Kampana II, were major benefactors of the temple after A.D. 1371. But their endowments were not made directly: They were made through sectarian notables. Kōpaṇṇa, for example, is believed to have donated fifty-two villages to the temple through Periya Kriṣṇarāya Uttamanambi.[84]

The rise to power of several sectarian leaders and the involvement of Telugu warrior-kings in temple honors disputes are carefully recounted in the *Kōil Oḻugu.*[85] According to this narrative, Sāḷuva Kuṇṭa appointed a certain Uttamarkōyil Śrīrangarājan to be the fifth head of the Śrīranganārāyaṇa Jīyar Ātīnam and established for him certain honors in the temple. The members of the Kantāṭai family took umbrage at this, seeing in it a reduction of their own status, and appealed to Kōpaṇṇa, the other Telugu general involved in the affairs of the temple. But, we are told, "since that Durgātipati patronized the Jīyar, he overlooked it."[86] At this point, the Kantāṭai family appealed to Periya Kriṣṇarāya Uttamanambi, who was already rising in power as an agent for Vijayanagara interests in the temple. Uttamanambi is said to have proceeded to Vijayanagara in A.D. 1372 to lay these problems before the *rāya* (king). Although the outcome of this dispute is not known, it certainly heralds the rise of the Śrīranganārāyaṇa Jīyar Ātīnam as a base for Prabandic Vaisnavism, as well as the beginnings of a long and fruitful relationship

[82] Ibid., pp. 121–2.
[83] V. N. Hari Rao, "Vaishnavism in South India in the Modern Period," in O. P. Bhatnagar, ed., *Studies in Social History (Modern India)* (Allahabad, 1964), pp. 129–30.
[84] Hari Rao, *Kōil Oḻugu*, p. 135.
[85] Ibid., pp. 136–8.
[86] Ibid., p. 136.

between members of the Uttamanambi family and the Vijayanagara court.

The Uttamanambi family claim descent from Periya Āḻvār, who migrated to Śrīrangam from Śrīvilliputtūr.[87] Their rise to power began in the lifetime of Periya Krișṇarāya Uttamanambi. He appears to have received cash grants from Kampana II, as well as from Kōpaṇṇa and Virupaṇṇa Uṭaiyār, which he converted to land grants to the temple.[88] He apparently also used this cash to make various kinds of gifts to the temple such as ornaments, utensils, pillared halls adjoining shrines, towers on temple structures, and processional vehicles for the deity.[89] These endowments were sometimes explicitly in behalf of patron-kings,[90] but they were sometimes apparently wholly personal acts by this sectarian figure. This Uttamanambi made another trip to Vijayanagara in about A.D. 1375 and was commanded by Virupaṇṇa, one of the brothers of Kampana II, to build a special type of hall. Subsequently, this chieftain came to Śrīrangam and performed a special ceremony there: the *tulapuruṣa* ceremony.[91] According to the *Kōil Oḻugu*, Periya Krișṇarāya Uttamanambi visited Vijayanagara several times and obtained land grants from a number of highly placed warriors in the Vijayanagara alliance, many of which he converted to specific ornamental and architectural additions to the temple in the names of these warrior-chiefs.[92]

Between A.D. 1397 and 1419, fresh complications arose in the arena of temple control and temple honors because of the rise to power of Vēdācārya Paṭṭar, a member of another *ācāriyapuruṣa* family. Vēdācārya Paṭṭar is believed to have usurped some privileges belonging to the Kantāṭai family, which was temporarily in eclipse. This generated honors disputes in the temple.[93] These disputes were settled by Mai-Nilai-Yiṭṭa Uttamanambi, who appears to have effected a compromise in A.D. 1418 whereby the powers of Vēdācārya Paṭṭar were diminished and those of the Kantāṭai family revived. This settlement was made in the authoritative pres-

[87] Hari Rao, "History of Trichinopoly," p. 307.

[88] Ibid., pp. 307–8.

[89] Ibid., pp. 307–10; Hari Rao, *Kōil Oḻugu*, pp. 142–3; T. N. Subramanian, ed., *South Indian Temple Inscriptions* (Madras, 1957), 3:1300, Pt. 2.

[90] Hari Rao, *Kōil Oḻugu*, p. 143.

[91] Ibid., p. 138; on the role of the *tulapuruṣa* ceremony in the fulfillment of the sovereign function, see Mahalingam, *South Indian Polity*, pp. 26–7.

[92] Hari Rao, *Kōil Oḻugu*, pp. 142–3.

[93] Ibid., p. 144.

ence of an agent of the Vijayanagara ruler as well as agents of the Śrīranganārāyaṇa Jīyar.[94]

During the reigns of Dēvarāya I and Dēvarāya II (A.D. 1406–1449), two brothers of the Uttamanambi family of sectarian leaders became all-powerful in the Śrīrangam Temple.[95] Various lands, whose supervision and application to specific purposes was entrusted to these sectarian leaders,[96] were endowed by these rulers to the temple, thus linking the Uttamanambi brothers and the rulers. These land grants permitted the Uttamanambis to associate themselves prominently with the construction of new shrines, the installation of new deities, the building of *maṇṭapam*s, and the gifting of ornaments to the deity, all activities bound to increase their share in the redistributive process of the temple.[97]

For the Vijayanagara rulers, this relationship ensured the application of these resources to the proper ends and ensured as well that they would be recognized as the benefactors of the temple. Indeed, the relationship must have been profitable for the Vijayanagara rulers, because an inscription of Dēvarāya II states that Uttamanambi was the recipient of several royal honors such as a pearl umbrella, a pair of *kāhaḷam*s (musical instruments), two lamps, a golden vessel, and an ivory shield from Dēvarāya II, along with other royal emblems.[98] In this intricate set of transactions between Vijayanagara warrior-kings and the Uttamanambi family of sectarian leaders, the working out of a complex process may be observed: The Telugu warriors linked themselves to the temple as a source of honor through the patronage of sectarian leaders and the reallocation of land and cash to these sectarian figures. At the same time they associated these sectarian leaders with their own kingship by investing them with royal honors. This increased the local authority of these sect leaders at the same time that it made Vijayanagara rule locally honorable.

This fruitful and symbiotic relationship between Vijayanagara rulers and the descendants of Periya Kriṣṇarāya Uttamanambi continued throughout the fifteenth century: Tirumalaināta Uttamanambi had a similar relationship with Mallikkarjunā (A.D.

[94] Ibid., p. 145.

[95] Hari Rao, "History of Trichinopoly," pp. 310–15.

[96] Ibid.; see also *Annual Reports* (1937–8), para. 63; *Epigraphia Indica* 16:222–3 and 18:138 ff.

[97] Hari Rao, *Kōil Oḻugu*, pp. 146–58; *Annual Reports* (1937–8).

[98] A.R. 84 of 1937–8 (see Subramanian, *South Indian Temple Inscriptions*, 3:1298–9, Pt. 2). This inscription partly verifies the indigenous account in Hari Rao, *Kōil Oḻugu*, pp. 146–7, which describes the quasi-royal status of these brothers in Śrīrangam.

1449–1465).[99] Similarly, Krisnarāya Uttamanambi, in A.D. 1487, mediated the endowments of Erramanci Timmappā Nāyakar to the temple.[100]

The last decades of the fourteenth century witnessed the breakdown of the First Dynasty of Vijayanagara and the concomitant rise of the Sāḷuva dynasty. This turbulent political shift had its effects on temple politics at Śrīrangam. The Uttamanambi family appears to have retained much of its power in this transitional period,[101] but it did have to make one major accommodation to the new rulers of Vijayanagara. The Uttamanambis conceded considerable status to a foreign (*tēcāntari*) sectarian leader called Kantāṭai Rāmānujatāsar. This particular individual is a model of the social and geographical mobility of sectarian leaders during this period and of their close links with kings. Kantāṭai Rāmānujatāsar is best known for his activities at Tirupati as the agent of Sāḷuva Narasimha, a subject that is dealt with later in this chapter.

The available evidence makes it difficult to identify this person.[102] But it seems fairly certain that he rose from obscurity to prominence by the appropriate manipulation of his "discipleship" to prominent sectarian leaders and his trading of this credential for political currency under the Sāḷuvas at Tirupati. He arrived at Śrīrangam after having established his credentials as the agent of Sāḷuva Narasimha at Tirupati between A.D. 1456 and 1489. He seems to have entered the highest levels of the sectarian hierarchy at Śrīrangam by becoming the disciple (*siṣya*) of Kantāṭai Aṇṇan. He then gained the privilege of the *tēcāntari muttirai* (a seal that gives certain rights to prominent visiting sectarian figures). This privilege seems to have been his sumptuary instrument for gaining a wedge into temple affairs and for appropriating certain honors in precedence over a member of the powerful Uttamanambi family.[103]

Kantāṭai Rāmānujatāsar also seems to have expanded his powers in the temple by associating himself with Narasa Nāyaka, a general of Sāḷuva Narasimha. Narasa Nāyaka's defeat of the provincial chief Kōnēri Rājā, the semi-independent representative of the previous dynasty in this region, signaled the establishment of

[99] Hari Rao, *Kōil Oḻugu*, pp. 158–61.
[100] Ibid., pp. 161–3; Hari Rao, "History of Trichinopoly," p. 331.
[101] Hari Rao, "History of Trichinopoly," p. 336.
[102] Ibid.; T. K. T. Viraraghavacharya, *History of Tirupati*, 2 vols. (Tirupati, 1953–4), 2:582–3.
[103] Hari Rao, *Kōil Oḻugu*, pp. 165–6.

Sāḷuva rule in this region.[104] The *Kōil Oḻugu*, in fact, ascribes Narasa Nāyaka's defeat of Kōnēri Rājā to the repeated requests of Kantāṭai Rāmānujatāsar for relief from the depredations of the latter.[105] The role of sectarian intermediary for Narasa Nāyaka at Śrīrangam seems to have been as fruitful for Rāmānujatāsar as his relationship to Sāḷuva Narasimha had been at Tirupati. He managed Narasa Nāyaka's endowments, made some endowments himself, and as a consequence gained a significant share in temple honors.[106] He also seems to have had a cordial relationship with the Śrīranganārāyaṇa Jīyar Ātīnam.[107] Kantāṭai Rāmānujatāsar's activities at Śrīrangam testify to the close connection of sectarian intermediaries to warrior-rulers during this period, a connection that was pivotal to the rise of these leaders and to the penetration of the institutional structures of Tamil country by these warriors.

It was in this environment that Prabandic Vaisnavism at Śrīrangam received its institutional form under the leadership of Manavāḷa Māmuni (A.D. 1370–1445). During the lifetime of Manavāḷa Māmuni, Prabandic Vaisnavism became the dominant sect of the southern parts of the Tamil country. It made inroads as well into the northern parts and marginally into the Telugu and Kannaḍa countries. Manavāḷa Māmuni's activities involved a judicious combination of five kinds of strategies: (1) the enhancement of the Prabandam as an authoritative doctrinal source; (2) the elaboration of the importance of radical submission to the *ācāriya*; (3) the creation of subsectarian networks organized around "discipleship," which spanned most of Tamil country; (4) the use of royal patronage, on a disaggregated local basis, to provide both material resources and royal honors for sectarian leaders in specific localities; and (5) the specific linkage of subsectarian affiliations to temple control. The interdependent and synthetic use of the fivefold strategy by Manavāḷa Māmuni specifically ensured Teṉkalai control over a number of temples in South India. How was this strategy historically realized?

Manavāḷa Māmuni was a native of Āḻvār Tirunagari (Tinnevelly District), which had become the stronghold of Prabandic Vaisnavism by the time of his birth in A.D. 1370. After becoming the major Vaisnava figure in Āḻvār Tirunagari, he proceeded to Śrīrangam, the heart of Vaisnava sectarian activities. In Śrīrangam, early in the

[104] Hari Rao, "History of Trichinopoly," pp. 338–43.
[105] Hari Rao, *Kōil Oḻugu*, pp. 166–7.
[106] A.R. 13 of 1939, and Hari Rao, *Kōil Oḻugu*, pp. 169–70.
[107] Hari Rao, "History of Trichinopoly," p. 342.

fifteenth century, he appears to have gained control of a monastery in Śrīrangam and some share in temple honors through the Kantāṭai family.[108] He then went to Kāñcīpuram, where he pursued Bhasyic studies for some time, but returned to Śrīrangam in A.D. 1425.[109] It was between A.D. 1425 and 1432 that he seems to have become a decisive power at Śrīrangam and to have acquired the title of Periya Jīyar.

Manavāḷa Māmuni's major achievement was the conversion to discipleship of the powerful Kōyil Kantāṭai family. He also converted to discipleship the current head of the Uttamanambi family,[110] Prativāti Payaṅkaram Aṇṇāṉ (a native of Kāñcīpuram and previously a strong adherent of the Sanskrit school), Erumpi Appa, Emperumāṉār Jīyar, Paṭṭar Pirāṉ, Appiḷḷai, and Appiḷḷāṉ. These seven individuals, along with Rāmāṉuja Jīyar, who had been his disciple and lieutenant (originally at Āḻvār Tirunagari), came to be known as the *aṣṭa-tikkaja*s, or the eight pillars of the faith. After the death of Māmuni, these eight individuals carried on and consolidated the Prabandic enterprise all over South India:

> He authorized Aṇṇa and Aṇṇan to carry on his lectures in the Bhasya and Bhagavadvishaya. He sent Tōḷappa to Tirunarayanapuram to carry on his work there. He appointed Ramanuja Jiyar the guardian of his creed in the South, and Bhattar Piram Jiyar at Srirangam. He dispatched Erumbi Appa to his native place . . . He appointed Appillai, Appillan on similar missions. All these who formed the *Ashta-diggajas* popularized the creed of their teacher, thanks to the support of stray kings and chiefs, and thus introduced a socio-religious change which was of a revolutionary nature.[111]

These individuals provided the institutional basis of Teṉkalai Vaisnavism in South India in the centuries that followed Māmuni's death. During Manavāḷa Māmuni's own proselytizing period at Śrīrangam and in his travels all over South India, he seems to have benefitted from the patronage of local princes to assist his own activities. He converted a local chief called Saṭakōpa-tāca and was his intermediary for the construction of various pillared halls in the Śrīrangam Temple.[112] He also appointed a Jīyar in Tirupati and converted a Tuḷuva prince under the name of Rāmānujatāsar.[113]

[108] V. Rangachari, "The History of Sri Vaishnavism," *Quarterly Journal of the Mythic Society* 7, No. 2 (January 1917):197–8.
[109] Ibid., p. 118.
[110] Hari Rao, *Kōil Oḻugu*, pp. 150–1.
[111] V. Rangachari, "History of Sri Vaishnavism," p. 206.
[112] Ibid., p. 201.
[113] Ibid., p. 206.

Similarly, in the Madurai/Ramnad region, he gained the discipleship of a king called Mahāpalivāṇaṭa Rāya, "who not only received the *pāñcasamskāram* from the teacher, but gave him all royal paraphernalia, lifted his palanquin and endowed the village of 'Muttarasan' or Aḻakiya Maṇavāḷanallūr."[114] Finally, he managed to establish his second-in-command at the Vānāmamalai Maṭam in Tinnevelly, which is today the single most important base for Teṉkalai sectarian activity in South India.[115]

When Māmuni returned to Śrīrangam after his last triumphal tour of the South, his decisive role in relating royal figures to his sect is noted in a traditional biography called the *Yatīndrapravaṇaprapāvam*, which points out that "the *jīyar* brought with him costly jewels, umbrellas of silk, *chāmaras* [fly whisks], flags and colours, carpets, cushions and quilts of silk, and presented these to the deity, and how the temple authorities honoured him by escorting him in pomp to his *maṭha*."[116]

But it was not simply to the politics of conversion that Manavāḷa Māmuni devoted himself. He wrote a number of works. Most were of the nature of commentaries on the works of his predecessors.[117] The most important of these was his commentary on the *Śrīvacana Pūśaṇam* of Piḷḷai Lōkācārya, which gave Māmuni further opportunity to clarify and elaborate the related Teṉkalai doctrines of *prapatti* and absolute dependence on an *ācāriya*.[118] But his most important intellectual and rhetorical act was the series of year-long lectures on the sacred Prabandam that he gave at Śrīrangam between A.D. 1432 and 1444.[119] These lectures, which have a very special place in Teṉkalai historiography, were given at the peak of Manavāḻa Māmuni's powers. They symbolized the centrality of the Prabandam to all future Teṉkalai activity and affiliation.

Thus, by the time of Māmuni's death in A.D. 1445, Prabandic Vaisnavism, through its subsectarian proponents, had achieved considerable success, measured by royal patronage and temple control, in Tamil country, principally at Śrīrangam but also in numerous other temple centers. It also had made some minor headway at Kāñcīpuram. This headway was negligible. In Tirupati, although

114 Ibid.

115 For a detailed description of this process and its consequences, see D. Ramaswamy Tatachar, *The Vanamamalai Temple and Mutt* (Tinnevelly, India, 1937).

116 V. Rangachari, "History of Sri Vaishnavism," p. 204.

117 Ibid., p. 203.

118 See earlier in this chapter.

119 V. Rangachari, "History of Sri Vaishnavism," p. 205.

representatives of the Prabandic school had achieved some success, they by no means controlled the temple. This consolidation of much of Tamil country by this Vaisnava subsect was doctrinally associated with the emphasis on the Tamil Prabandam and with the skilled intermediary functions of sectarian leaders who, by linking royal patronage and temple honor, managed to become powerful religious chiefs themselves by A.D. 1500. It is after A.D. 1500 that members of the Sanskrit school began to consolidate their own institutional bases along similar lines and by similar strategies. To understand this transition, however, it is necessary to consider the nature of sectarian politics at Tirupati, the great "Northern" (in Tamil country) center of Śrī Vaisnavism.

The temple complex at Tirupati evolved during the Vijayanagara period in three major ways that distinguished it from its structure in earlier periods: (1) the embellishment of the ritual calendar with a vast number of new festivals, supported by many architectural/iconic additions;[120] (2) the shift in the nature of endowments from an emphasis on things, like the burning of perpetual lamps, to an emphasis on food offerings,[121] which formed, along with their redistribution as *prasātam*, the core of temple economics in the Vijayanagara period;[122] and (3) the increased importance of the recitation of the Vēdas and the Prabandam by Brahmin and non-Brahmin devotees.[123] These three interlinked developments in the period from A.D. 1350 to 1650 transformed this temple complex from a small set of shrines, dominated by the simple rituals of the Vaikānasa priesthood,[124] to a vast socioreligious center. This center attracted lavish endowments from rulers and merchants, involving the creation of numerous sectarian establishments and the organization of numerous institutional structures, managed by sectarian leaders, for the housing and feeding of Śrī Vaisnava pilgrims from all over South India. This transformation was effected by the penetration of the temple by Tamil Śrī Vaisnava leaders and their disciples and their fruitful mediation of royal (and non-royal) endowments to the temple.[125]

[120] S. Subrahmanya Sastry, *Report on the Inscriptions of the Devastanam Collection with Illustrations* (Madras, 1930), passim.
[121] Viraraghavacharya, *History of Tirupati*, 2:v.
[122] Stein, "Economic Function," passim.
[123] Viraraghavacharya, *History of Tirupati*, 2:vi.
[124] Ibid., 1:517–19. See also earlier in this chapter.
[125] Viraraghavacharya, *History of Triupati*, 1:519–41.

It was in the fifteenth and sixteenth centuries that Śrī Vaisnava, primarily Tamil, sectarian leaders helped in the growth of popular and royal support for the Tirupati complex. This was used to extend Vaisnava sectarian activity into Telugu and Kannada country. The model for the symbiotic relationship between rulers and sectarian leaders is the relationship between Kantāṭai Rāmānuja Aiyaṅkār (whose activities at Śrīrangam have already been noted) and Sāḷuva Narasimha, the king of Vijayanagara.[126] It is worth investigating this relationship in some detail, because it casts light on matters that are pertinent to all such relationships.

Kantāṭai Rāmānuja Aiyaṅkār was the agent through whom, starting in A.D. 1456,[127] Sāḷuva Narasimba linked himself to the redistributive cycle of the Tirupati Temple and publicly established his patronage of non-Brahmin worshippers there. He did this by allocating taxes from some villages for some food offerings to the deity. He allocated the "donor's share"[128] of the *prasātam* to the *Rāmānujakūṭam*[129] that he established at Tirupati, which was to be managed by Rāmānuja Aiyaṅkār. In this case, the *Rāmānujakūṭam* managed by Rāmānuja Aiyaṅkār was for the benefit of non-Brahmin Śrī Vaisnavas, a group of whom were his disciples.[130] It was the non-Brahmin constituency that benefited from the "donor's share" of the *prasātam* created by Sāḷuva Narasimha's endowment. Between A.D. 1456 and 1473, Rāmānuja Aiyaṅkār was the intermediary between this non-Brahmin constituency and the sanctified products of royal endowments,[131] as well as endowments by other land controllers.[132]

Kantāṭai Rāmānuja Aiyaṅkār was originally commissioned to simply oversee his royal patron's endowments and their proper redistribution to his non-Brahmin disciples of the *Rāmānujakūṭam*. But he appears to have used his status to give these non-Brahmins some important roles in temple worship and thus in temple honors.[133] In the period between A.D. 1467 and 1476 he apparently used his influence with the Sāḷuva emperor to make crucial alterations in

126 Stein, "Social Mobility," and Viraraghavacharya, *History of Tirupati*, 2:557–601.
127 *Tirumalai-Tirupati Devasthanam Epigraphical Series*, Vol. II, No. 4.
128 Stein, "Economic Function," discusses this term.
129 This term designates a free feeding house for Śrī Vaisnavas, often non-Brahmin pilgrims and devotees at a sacred center.
130 Viraraghavacharya, *History of Tirupati*, 2:591.
131 *Tirumalai-Tirupati Devasthanam Epigraphical Series*, Vol. II, Nos. 23, 31, 50.
132 Ibid., Vol. II, Nos. 64, 67, 68.
133 Ibid., Vol. II, Nos. 22, 31, 38, 50, 68, 81, 135.

the redistributive cycle of the temple. He made an agreement with some Paḷḷis who had rights over some temple lands to pay them a fixed rent and to give to his *Rāmānujakūṭam* the benefits of extra productivity created by building channels on the land.[134] In 1467 he made an agreement with the *stāṉattār* (temple managers) to create an offering to the deity, the "donor's share" of the *prasātam* being allocated to his non-Brahmin constituency by the investment of his own capital in the agrarian development of some temple land.[135] In November 1468 he persuaded the temple managers to allot some temple land for worship to an image of Kulacēkara Āḻvār, which he had installed in Tirupati.[136] Between A.D. 1469 and 1470 Rāmānuja Aiyaṅkār made six arrangements with the temple managers to develop temple land, endow additional temple ritual by the additional agrarian product so generated, and allocate the "donor's share" of the resulting *prasātam* to his non-Brahmin constituency.[137] In one of these cases, he explicitly recognized his dependence on his royal patron by describing the offering as being for "the merit of Narasiṃharāja-Uḍaiyar."[138]

The most interesting example of Rāmānuja Aiyaṅkār's influence and his use of it to generate additional honor, in the form of *prasātam*, for his own non-Brahmin following is seen in a 1496 inscription.[139] In this case, Rāmānuja Aiyaṅkār seems to have been the intermediary for the endowment of a large sum of cash to the temple by a local Śrī Vaisnava devotee. This sum was to be invested in agrarian development by the temple managers, and from the resulting agrarian surplus a number of ritual events were to be subsidized. But among these ritual events were two important innovations: the celebration of the natal stars (*tirunakṣattiram*) of all twelve *āḻvār*s in front of the shrine of Rāmānujā and the singing of the Prabandam by Brahmin and non-Brahmin devotees *together* in the same shrine.[140] The achievement of these innovations was made possible by embedding them in a complex scheme of allocation of resources for various items of worship and an equally disaggregated allocation of *prasātam*

[134] Ibid., Vol. II, No. 24.
[135] Ibid., Vol. II, No. 26.
[136] Ibid., Vol. II, No. 36.
[137] Ibid., Vol. II, Nos. 38, 40, 44, 45, 47.
[138] Ibid., Vol. II, No. 45.
[139] Ibid., Vol. II, No. 68.
[140] Viraraghavacharya discusses the potential resistance on the part of the Vaikānasa priests in *History of Tirupati*, 1:241–5 and 2:590–1.

honors for various temple functionaries as an inseparable part of this overall package.

Kantāṭai Rāmānuja Aiyaṅkār served a crucial intermediary function linking outside endowers, temple officials, and local Śrī Vaisnava constituencies eager for shares in the honors represented in the leavings of the deity. Such intermediaries were numerous at Tirupati. It is precisely their large number that is an index of the wide range and large quantity of endowments (particularly land) that were gifted to the deity, transformed into *prasātam*, and distributed according to the constituencies and ideas favored by the donor.

Although attempts were made by Śrī Vaisnavas of the Tamil school to give the recitation of the Prabandam a regular role in the ritual of Tirupati even as early as A.D. 1253,[141] it was not until A.D. 1468, under the aegis of Rāmānuja Aiyaṅkār, that this was achieved. From this time onward, the recital of the Prabandam hymns began increasingly to attract donors, who allocated a share of their *prasātam* to the reciters of the Prabandam.[142] In the first quarter of the fifteenth century, the increasing popularity of Prabandam recital among donors led to rivalry among the various sectarian leaders of the two schools at Tirupati for the management and control of this aspect of temple ritual.[143] Starting in A.D. 1516,[144] one of the major leaders of Sanskrit persuasion, the *Jīyar* of the Van Saṭakōpaṉ Maṭam, made endowments in which there was a conspicuous absence of any part in the "donor's share" of the *prasātam* for the Prabandam reciters.

Between A.D. 1520 and 1528, some inscriptions reveal a change in the relationship between this *Jīyar* and the Kōyil Kēḷvi *Jīyars*, who were of the Prabandic school.[145] During this decade the individuals to whom these sectarian leaders allotted their shares in the *prasātam* were increasingly united by their common subsectarian preferences.[146] By A.D. 1530, therefore, it is possible to infer that the increasing prestige of Prabandic Vaisnavism at Tirupati had hardened the divisions between sectarian leaders of the two schools and provided the motive for at least one set of leaders of the Sanskrit school, the *Jīyars* of the Ahōbila Maṭam, to seek opportunities for

[141] Ibid., 2:1016.
[142] Ibid., pp. 1031–46.
[143] Ibid., pp. 1046–55.
[144] *Tirumalai-Tirupati Devasthanam Epigraphical Series*, Vol. III, Nos. 110, 114.
[145] Ibid., Vol. III, Nos. 143, 173, 178; Viraraghavacharya, *History of Tirupati*, 2:1055–7.
[146] Viraraghavacharya, *History of Tirupati*, 2:1055–7.

their own subsectarian beliefs elsewhere (this will be discussed in detail later).

On the whole, by the early part of the fifteenth century the activities of sectarian leaders of the Prabandic school, given an organizational and ideological basis by Manavāḷa Māmuni and his network of disciples, had ensured that most of the Vaisnava temples in Tamil country, with the exception of some in the Chingleput district, were controlled by sectarian leaders of the Tamil school.

Warrior-kings and the Sanskrit school, A.D. 1500–1700

Sectarian leaders of the Sanskrit school were involved in temple-related activities before A.D. 1500. But it was only after A.D. 1500 that they created a counterstructure of an institutional sort by linking themselves to Vijayanagara kings. Given the establishment, by this time, of Prabandic Vaisnavism in most of Tamil country, it is not surprising that these leaders looked for new areas in which to promulgate and institutionalize their beliefs. They succeeded in setting up bases in the Kannada and Telugu areas and in some temple centers in the northernmost parts of Tamil country. Three sets of sectarian leaders were responsible for the major part of this activity: the *Jīyar*s of the Ahōbila Maṭam in the Kurnool district; members of the Tātācārya family of *ācāriyapuruṣa*s, who spread through the Telugu districts in the sixteenth century; and the *maṭātipati*s (monastic heads) of the Brahmatantra Parakāla Tantra Svāmi Maṭam in Mysore. Let us consider briefly these three institutional bases of Sanskrit school activity.

The heads of the Ahōbila Maṭam in Kurmool district were the successors of the *Jīyars* of the Van Saṭakōpaṉ Maṭam in Tirupati, where they conducted intermediary functions for some Telugu chiefs even after the headquarters of the *maṭam* had shifted to Kurnool.[147] As we have already noted, there is some evidence that the shift of this set of Sanskrit school sectarian leaders to Kurnool from Tirupati was probably linked to the increasing prestige of Prabandic Vaisnavism at Tirupati. In the period between A.D. 1554 and 1584 the heads of this *maṭam* established in Kurnool a complex set of temple-centered relationships with Vijayanagara chiefs.[148] By this time these sectarian leaders must have gained sufficient control of the local Narasimhasvāmi

[147] *Tirumalai-Tirupati Devasthanam Epigraphical Series*, Vol. II, No. 101.
[148] Rangacharya, *Topographical List* 2:970–4.

Temple, for their transactions with representatives of the Vijayanagara kingdom show them to have been at the center of various land transactions involving these chiefs, linked directly to temple ritual as well as to agrarian development.[149] For example, in A.D. 1544 –55, an inscription reports that "the Vaishnava teacher Parāṇkusa-Van-Sathagōpa Jiyamgāru, the trustee of the Ahobala temple and the agent of Aḷiya Rāmapayyadēva-Mahārāja, granted a *dasavana-mānya* to Avubalarāja, son of Kōnēti Rājayya and grandson of Rāmarāja-Peda-Kondayadēva-Maharājā of Atrēya gōtra and the lunar race, for having built at Alamuru, which was village of the temple (*tiruvaḷayāṭu*), the tank Kōnasamudram, otherwise called Nārāyaṇasamudram."[150] Also, these sectarian leaders reallocated land, originally granted to them by Telugu warrior-chiefs, to specific ritual purposes in the local temple. An inscription of A.D. 1563 deals with "a gift of land in the village China-Komerḷa in the Ghaṇḍikōṭasīma, by Vaṇ Saṭhagōpa-Jiyyamgāru, to Ahōbalēsvara for providing offerings of rice-cakes on specified festivals in the *maṇṭapa* in front of the *maṭha* which he had constructed . . . The village China-Komerḷa was a gift made to the Jīyyaṃgāru by the chief Krishṇamarāja, son of Nandēla China-Obaṇṇamgāru."[151] At the same time, these sectarian leaders cooperated with warrior-chiefs in the management of royal endowments.[152] In the period A.D. 1578–84, they appear to have invited Vijayanagara's aid in ousting hostile Muslim forces from the locality. Subsequently, they granted temple honors to the warriors responsible for this victory.[153] Thus, by the end of the sixteenth century, the Ahōbila Maṭam had become a major base for the sectarian activities of the Sanskrit school in Telugu country.

The second set of leaders of the Sanskrit school was provided by the Tātācārya family of *ācāriyapuruṣas*, who, in the second half of the fourteenth century, settled in Eṭṭūr (Kistna district). They appear to have spread their activities through large parts of Telugu country, as well as in the northernmost parts of Tamil country.[154]

149 Ibid., A.R. 65, 69, and 79 of 1915.

150 Ibid., A.R. 65 of 1916.

151 Ibid., A.R. 82 of 1915.

152 Ibid., A.R. 76 of 1915.

153 Ibid., A.R. 70 of 1915; see also, "Ahobalam Inscription of Śrī Rangarāya," in V. R. R. Dikshitar, ed., *Selected South Indian Inscriptions* (Madras, 1952), pp. 327–31.

154 S. Vijayaraghavachari, "A Few Inscriptions of Laksmikumara Tatacharya," in *Journal of Indian History* 25 (April 1947):121–31, Pt. 1; see also, Viraraghavacharya, *History of Tirupati*, 2:760–1 for a genealogy of this family.

Sectarian tradition links them with the Vijayanagara court and its increasing preference for Śrī Vaisnavism, starting during the reign of Vīrupāksa I (A.D. 1354–78).[155] Pancamatapanjanam Tātācārya was the *rājakuru* (royal preceptor) of Satāsiva Rāya and his minister Aḷiya Rāmarāya.[156] It is also interesting that this Tātācārya was the nephew of Paraṅkusa Van Saṭakōpa Jīyar, the sixth head of the Ahōbila Maṭam, thus indicating kin-based connections within the leadership of the Sanskrit school.[157]

But it was during the rule of the Araviṭu dynasty of Vijayanagara in the sixteenth century that the royal patronage of the Tātācāryas reached its zenith. This royal patronage was displayed in the massive control of temples by them. Lakṣmikumāra Tātācārya, the adopted son of Pancamatapanjanam Tātācārya, achieved great influence over his patron, Venkata I of the Araviṭu dynasty. Both sectarian sources as well as inscriptions placed great emphasis on the coronation of Venkata I by a Tātācārya, although there is some question as to which of these two individuals was the sectarian leader in question.[158] Although inscriptions suggest that Lakṣmikumāra Tātācārya was in charge of all the temples in the kingdom, he seems to have concentrated his activities in the Chingleput district, to some extent in the Śrīperuṃbudūr and Tiruppukuḻi temples but primarily in the Varadarāja Svāmi Temple in Kāñcīpuram.[159] In this last temple it is clear that the power of Ladṣmikumāra Tātācārya was great, over land, ritual, and the functionaries involved in the transformation of the one into the other.[160] In the 1660s, reflecting the decline of the Vijayanagara Empire and the growth of independent kingships all over South India, Venkata Varadācārya, Lakṣmikumāra Tātācārya's son, migrated to Mysore and associated himself with the growing sovereignty of the Woṭeyār kings of Mysore.[161]

It was probably at this very time in Mysore, during the reign of Dēvarāja Woṭeyār (A.D. 1659–73), that the nucleus of the third

[155] Vijayaraghavachari, "Few Inscriptions," p. 124; see also T. A. Gopinatha Rao, "Daḷavāy-Agrahātram Plates of Venkatapatidēva Mahārāya I: Saka-Samvat 1508," *Epigraphia Indica* 12 (1913–14):162–3.

[156] H. Heras, *The Aravidu Dynasty of Vijayanagara* (Madras, 1927), pp. 301–6.

[157] Rangacharya, *Topographical List*, 2:971.

[158] Heras, *Aravidu Dynasty*, p. 302; Vijayaraghavachari, "Few Inscriptions," pp. 126–7.

[159] Heras, *Aravidu Dynasty*, p. 305; Vijayaraghavachari, "Few Inscriptions," pp. 130–1; *Annual Reports* (1920), pp. 115–16.

[160] A.R. 383 of 1919; *Annual Reports*, p. 115.

[161] C. Hayavadana Rao, *History of Mysore*, 4 vols. (Bangalore, 1943–6) 1:247.

base of Sanskrit school leadership, the Brahmatantra Parakāla Tantra Svāmi Maṭha, was laid.[162] This *maṭam* was founded in Kāñcīpuram in the fourteenth century by a disciple of Vēdānta Dēsika, the revered figure of the Vaṭakalai tradition, through the support of an unknown royal patron.[163] The *maṭam* subsequently shifted to Tirupati, where its heads appear to have been intermediaries for the benefactions of the Mysore chiefs.[164] During the reign of Dēvarāja Woṭeyār, the then head of the *maṭam* shifted its headquarters to Mysore.[165] This was not unnatural, because the rulers of Mysore had publicly displayed their commitment to Śrī Vaisnavism from early in the seventeenth century. They did this by taking the rites of initiation from the *svāmi*s of the Parakāla Maṭam, by using the *varāha muttirai* (boar seal) in their documents,[166] and by the building and endowment of Vaisnava temples.[167] The foundation of this relationship of mutual benefaction between this *maṭam* and the Mysore royal court was probably laid during the reign of Periya Parakāla Svāmi (A.D. 1677–1738).[168] This enterprising leader, who was probably responsible for the beginnings of the pan-regional Vaṭakalai movement for temple control, seems to have had the support of his royal patrons for his scheme.

A Kannada *nirūpa* (order), probably dated in A.D. 1709, during the reign of Kāntirāva Narasarāja Woḍeyār, King of Mysore, contains a royal edict to the effect that "the practice of using *tanian* (invocatory verse) Rāmānuja Dayāpātra in sacred places like the Tirunārāyaṇasvāmi temple at Mēlukōte on the occasion of reciting Prabandas which was in vogue from the time of Rājā Woḍeyār, King of Mysore, up to the reign of Kāntirava Narasarāja Vodeyar, shall continue in the future also in the same manner."[169]

This royal order represents the beginnings of self-conscious pan-regional conflict for temple control between the two schools of South Indian Śrī Vaisnavism. Throughout the eighteenth and nineteenth centuries, and to some extent in the twentieth century, attempts were made by individuals and groups of the Sanskrit school to

162 Ibid.
163 A.R. 574 of 1919; see also N. Desikacharya, *The Origin and Growth of Śrī Brahmatantra Parakāla Mutt* (Bangalore, 1949), pp. xii–xv.
164 Ibid., p. 8.
165 Ibid., p. 13.
166 Hayavadana Rao, *History of Mysore*, 1:169–71, 224, 232.
167 Ibid., pp. 166–8, 363–5, 375–7.
168 Desikacharya, *Origin and Growth*, p. 12.
169 *Archaeological Survey of Mysore: Annual Report 1938*; also see Desikacharya, *Origin and Growth*, Appendix VI.

penetrate temples controlled by the Tamil school or to extend their rights in temples where they shared control with members of the Prabandic school. In every such case, the introduction of the "Rāmānuja Dayāpātra" invocatory verse[170] was the first stage in these battles for temple control, wherein the Sanskrit school was united and inspired by the three sets of sectarian leaders previously described.[171]

The Śrī Pārtasārati Svāmi Temple

The richest evidence for the royal and sectarian context of the Śrī Pārtasārati Svāmi Temple in Triplicane, Madras city, comes from the reigns of two monarchs of the Vijayanagara period, Satāsiva Rāya (A.D. 1537–75) and Venkata II (A.D. 1592–1613). Although these inscriptions are in crucial respects faulty and incomplete, they are nevertheless sufficiently detailed to demonstrate that the Śrī Pārtasārati Svāmi Temple was no exception to the dynamic processes that linked kings, sects, and temples in the Vijayanagara period. The six inscriptions that are most relevant follow in rough chronological order, although in some cases there are no specific dates.

An inscription of A.D. 1564, during the reign of Satāsiva Rāya, records an act of donation that must have been the first major expansion of this temple's ritual and economic scope[172] on the contemporary model of Tirupati. This inscription records the following set of benefactions to the temple: the installation of six new deities in one shrine; the installation of five kin deities in the main shrine of Śrī Pārtasārati Svāmi; the installation of a processional idol (*utsavar*) in the shrine of the goddess Vēta Vaḻḻi Nācciyār; the construction of three new shrines, two pillared halls adjoining the main shrine, a sacred kitchen (*tiru-maṭappaḻḻi*), and a compound wall. The donor also presented jewels to some of these deities and granted the villages of Putuppākkam, Veppēri, and Vyācarpaṭi to the deity.

[170] For a discussion of the place of this verse in Vaisnava temple ritual and for a Teṉkalai account of the circumstances of its origin, see P. B. Annangaracharia r, *Rāmānujā Dayāpātrā* (Kancipuram, 1954).

[171] Hari Rao, "Vaishnavism in South India in the Modern Period," pp. 120–5; Jagadeesan, "History of Śrī Vaiṣṇavism," pp. 252–8; K. S. Rangaswami Aiyangar, *A Second Collection of Papers Relating to Sri Ranganadhasvami Temple, Its Management* (Trichinopoly, 1894).

[172] A.R. 239 of 1903; 81(d) of 1967 in *Cennai Mānakara Kalveṭṭikaḷ [Madras City Stone Inscriptions]* (Madras, 1973), hereafter cited as *Madras City Stone Inscriptions*.

The magnificent nature of this endowment suggests that the donor must have been an individual of considerable substance. Unfortunately, we can only make guesses as to his identity. He refers to himself as Tēcāntāri Narasinkatasan, thus suggesting that he must have been a sectarian leader of considerable importance.[173] This supposition is further sustained by the fact that this inscription makes no mention of the temple staff or the local congregation. It presents the endowment as a direct and unmediated transaction between the donor and the deity, who "graciously received" (*koṇṭaruḷinār*) these gifts. Lastly, the sectarian status of the donor is suggested by his capacity to make endowments of agrarian resources, which suggests links to warrior-kings, at least circumstantially.

The second relevant inscription comes from the sixteenth century but is not precisely dateable.[174] This inscription records an agreement among some of the temple staff about their duties in various shrines in the temple and their shares in the leavings of the deity (*svatantiram*). This agreement must have been a response to conflict (possibly a result of the physical and organizational expansion of the temple in the sixteenth century), because the phrase *kuṟai varāmal* (without any shortcomings) recurs in the text. The final inscribed agreement corresponds to the *vyavastā/rāja cācanam* model discussed at the beginning of this chapter, because it begins with an invocation of the supervisory role of a royal agent (*etirāja-nāyakkar pārapattiyattil*), to whom the inscribed decisions are offered as a promissory agreement (*veṇṇi muṟi koṭuttōm*).

An inscription based on the *vyavastā* model is dated A.D. 1599.[175] It describes a decision made jointly by the agent of the king for temple affairs (*śrī kāriya turanturā*) named Cēnai Mutaliyār, the temple managers (*stāṉattār*), another royal official (*atikāri*) named Koppūri Ōparājayya, and the Paṭṭana-Svāmi (chief) of the Ceṭṭi merchants of Mylapore (a village adjoining present-day Triplicane), to endow a large number of elaborate new festivals. The bulk of the inscription concerns the specific provisions for feeding the deities on these newly created festival days. The source of the endowment is the interest on an agrarian investment, but the donor is unclear.

[173] Although the term *tēcāntāri* has the generic meaning of "a stranger or foreigner," its use in Vaisnava practice has the narrower connotation of a pilgrim or foreign visitor to a sacred center. However, when it is used as a title, as in this case, it indicates sectarian importance for its bearer, in addition to indicating his outsider status.

[174] *Madras City Stone Inscriptions*, 81(f) of 1967; also A.R. 243 of 1903.

[175] Ibid., 81(e) of 1967; A.R. 235 of 1903.

In another inscription,[176] from the reign of Venkata II, the same royal official, Koppūri Ōparājayya, appears as the first in a list of decision makers, followed by the temple managers and the local congregation (*stāṉa-camayam*). In accordance with their joint inscribed order (*cilācācanam paṇṇi koṭuttapaṭi*), a stone deity of Rāmānujā was installed and arrangements were made for its periodic feeding (*amutu ceytal*). Shares were allotted to some of the temple functionaries in the maintenance of this food endowment, although here again the donor and the resource base are not clear because of the fragmentary nature of the evidence.

Undated, but also in the reign of Venkata II, an inscription[177] records a royally sanctioned *vyavastā* made jointly by the royal agent Koppūri Ōparājayya (who appears to have moved up from the status of *atikāri* to that of *śrīkāriya turanturā*), the temple managers, and the local congregation. The agreement, in this case, was to install a deity form of Tirukacci Nampi (a revered contemporary of Rāmānujā's) and also to make arrangements for feeding the newly installed (*tiru pratiṣṭai*) deity. Once again, shares in the endowment, expressed in terms of measures of rice, were allotted to various groups of temple functionaries. The donor, in this case, was a local merchant, Tampu Ceṭṭi. The intermediary function linking this merchant and the temple appears to have been fulfilled by a Śrī Vaisnava Brahmin, Cakravarti Timmappayaṅkār, who was entrusted with the donor's share (*viṭṭavaṉ viḷakkāṭu*) of the food offerings, although no evidence is available on the plan for disposing of this share.

The last relevant inscription,[178] dated A.D. 1603, records yet another *vyavastā* made by the joint order of the royal agent Koppūri Ōparājayya, the temple managers, and the local congregation. This order established the installation of a deity form of Tirumaḻicai Āḻvār, who is believed to have said that he did not belong to any of the three castes and, according to sectarian tradition, was a foundling brought up by a hunter.[179] In Vaisnava tradition, he is believed to have once entered an assemblage of Brahmins reciting the Vēdas on a great occasion, and the Brahmins allegedly stopped the recitation because he was not one of the twice-born. When they forgot where they had stopped, it was Tirumaḻicai Āḻvār who told them

176 Ibid., 81(h) of 1967; A.R. 240 of 1903.
177 Ibid., 79 of 1967.
178 Ibid., 81(g) of 1967; also A.R. 236 of 1903.
179 Viraraghavacharya, *History of Tirupati*, 1:60–1.

where to resume.[180] The deification of this *āḻvār* suggests the Prabandic orientation of the community of donors and worshippers interested in this temple. A Telugu inscription from the second half of the seventeenth century[181] confirms that this orientation toward the *āḻvārs* was not isolated, for it establishes food endowments on the *tirunakṣattiram* (natal star) days of all twelve *āḻvārs*. The A.D. 1603 inscription goes on, like the others, to allot shares in the endowment to a wide range of temple functionaries, including the temple managers, the priest's assistants (*paricārakam*), the cook (*svayampāki*), the temple watchman (*tirumēṉi kāval*), the torch-bearers, and the temple priest. The donor in this case appears to have been a sectarian leader, Anumancipallai Emperumānācāriyār, probably of Prabandic persuasion, through his disciple Nārāyaṇa Aiyaṅkār.

In the sixteenth and early seventeenth centuries, therefore, the Śrī Pārtasārati Svāmi Temple in Triplicane, Madras city, was clearly embedded in a complex set of processes involving royal participation as well as sectarian involvement, which framed its transformation into a relatively complex ritual center. Although the evidence is insufficiently strong, the general tenor of temple worship at the Śrī Pārtasārati Svāmi Temple was clearly of a Prabandic, *āḻvār*-oriented sort. However, this was not apparently a focus of controversy. It was not until 1754, when the temple had been under British jurisdiction for a century, that subsectarian conflict arose at Triplicane between Teṉkalais and Vaṭakalais, which will be discussed in the following chapter.

[180] Ibid., p. 65.
[181] A.R. 237 of 1903, in V. R. Chetty, *History of Triplicane and the Temple of Sri Parthasarathi Swamy* (Madras, 1948), pp. 88–9.

3

BRITISH RULE AND TEMPLE POLITICS, 1700–1826

In the case of the Śrī Pārtasārati Svāmi Temple, the shift from a Hindu political context to a British mercantile environment was relatively swift and direct.[1] The English merchants of the East India Company acquired trading rights and some land for their settlement on the Coromandel coast (in what is today Madras city) from a local Hindu ruler in 1639. By 1676 the village of Triplicane, including the Śrī Pārtasārati Svāmi Temple, was confirmed as British territory.[2] The attitude of these English merchants toward this and other temples within their jurisdiction was pragmatic. Ad hoc decisions concerning temples (especially when they involved the economic advantage of the English or when public order was threatened) were made.[3] But for the rest of the seventeenth and most of the eighteenth centuries a clear policy was never formulated.

In spite of certain similarities between the ad hoc and pragmatic approach of the East India Company toward temples and the preexisting Hindu model of king-temple relations, there were three basic contrasts. First, temples were, at no time, fundamental, in a *normative* sense, for the establishment or expansion of British authority in South India. Thus the exchange of honors between king and deity as a basis for political authority largely ceased to exist. *Mutatis mutandis*, the English merchant-rulers, did not transact in any systematic way with sectarian leaders or groups or with local organizations of any traditional sort. Rather, they depended increasingly on the intermediary capacities of natives who were, in any case, pivotal broker figures in their own colonial economy. Later, in the eighteenth and nineteenth centuries, they depended on their own expanding bureaucratic appa-

[1] The impact of the Muslim presence in South India, as a model for British administrators in respect to temples, is difficult to assess and appears to have been very uneven. In general, however, the English seem to have utilized prior Hindu models. In the case of the Śrī Pārtasārati Svāmi Temple, the low impact of the Muslim "interlude" in the seventeenth century is indicated by the records that do exist.

[2] H. D. Love, *Vestiges of Old Madras*, 3 vols. (Madras, 1913), 1:352.

[3] Chandra Y. Mudaliar, *The Secular State and Religious Institutions in India: A Study of the Administration of Hindu Public Religious Trusts in Madras* (Wiesbaden, 1974), p. 6.

ratus. Second, in dealing with temples, the English merchants of the company reversed the emphasis of indigenous sovereigns, who had left day-to-day management of temples in local hands but who had not hesitated to authoritatively resolve local conflicts. The English mercantile authority in South India gradually expanded its day-to-day involvement in temples. At the same time, they were increasingly reluctant to "interfere" in native disputes, particularly those they artificially characterized as "religious." And third, the structure of English colonial institutions as well as English ideology regarding Hindu temples provided a built-in division that at times became a contradiction between the administrative and judicial arms of the state. This division constituted yet another fundamental contrast with previous Hindu sovereigns, who dealt with temples from the point of view of a unified kingly capacity, which was simultaneously judicial and administrative. Taken together, these departures from the previous indigenous structure of relationships created tensions and dialectical pressures that altered temple politics in crucial respects.

During the eighteenth century the major evidence concerning the Śrī Pārtasārati Svāmi Temple in British records concerns the conflict between Vaṭakalis and Teṉkalais over the monopoly of recitation of a particular prayer. Such conflict seems to have begun at this temple in the first quarter of the eighteenth century, but it was not until 1754 that it was brought to the formal attention of the British in a petition from members of the right- and left-hand castes at Triplicane:

> Whereas a dispute hath arisen and long subsisted between the Tengala and Wadagala Bramineys at Triplicane in relation to certain prayers or orations called Sarasayalasa Dayapatram, and Ramanuza Dayapatram . . . the Tengala Bramineys insisting that the Sarasayalasa Dayapatram etc. and the Ramanuza Dayapatram etc. should be said by all Waishnaway Bramineys at the beginning and ending the Probandum and the Wadagala Bramineys, contending that they should not be restrained in this particular but be left at liberty to repeat the Ramanuza Dayapatrem etc. publickily at the beginning and ending the Probandum. And whereas there are two principal pagodas at Triplicane, the one called the Vencatty Kistnah Swamey, the gate where fronts the East, and the other called Tellisinga Swamey, the Gate whereof fronts the West and whereas the Religious Rights and Ceremoneys and all publick Worship at the said Pagodas hath been obstructed by reason of the said dispute, which the Inhabitants in general are desirous should be terminated to the satisfaction of both parties, therefore We the heads and principal persons of the Right and Left Hand Castes, do for ourselves and on Behalf of the rest of the Inhabitants most humbly request the Honble President and Council will be pleased to put an end to the said disputes by

Ordering that in future the Tengala Bramineys shall be at liberty to repeat the Sarasayalasa Dayapatrem etc at the beginning and ending the Probandum in the Pagoda called Vencaty Kistnah Swamy and in all the Chappells and places of worship belonging to the same and that the Wadagala Bramineys shall have the liberty of repeating the Ramanuza Dayapatrem etc. at the beginning and ending the Probandum in the Pagoda called Tellisinga Swamey and in all the places of worship belonging to the same and that neither of the said Bramineys will on any account interfere with or Molest or disturb each other in the performance of their respective Rights in the said Pagodas, Chappells and places of worship in manner aforesaid.[4]

Although the governing council of the English merchant polity agreed that "the said request be granted in all its particulars, and that the order of this Board for that purpose be signified to the contending Bramineys and published by beat of tom-tom,"[5] the dispute arose again in 1780. A Teṉkalai petition to the British suggests the naive and violent way some English administrators had sought to settle the conflict:

Your petitioners most humbly beg to represent unto your Honor etc. that since the Pagoda of Triplicane was built there was but one form of prayer, called Streeshylasha Dyapautram, used in the said Pagoda by Tingalah and Vadagala Braminees, but the latter, Vadagalah Braminees, composed a new form of prayer, called Ramanjaloo Dyapautram, designed to introduce in the said Pagoda; but their efforts proved abortive. While Admiral Boscowen was in this place, a dispute having arisen between Tingalah and Vadagalah Braminies, when they complained the same to Admiral Boscowen, who enquired into the affair, made peace between the two parties, and caused them to read the old prayer as usual . . . Lord Pigot . . . caused the Vadagalah Braminies to read their new invented prayer in the said Pagoda by sending the Town Major with a party of Sepoys, also the Company's and Polligar Peons to assist and proceed forcibly in reading the said new prayer. Accordingly the Town Major and the party of Sepoys etc. went and executed their orders in a most violent manner for about 10 days.[6]

At this point the government decided equally arbitrarily in favor of the Teṉkalais, which resulted in a counterpetition from the Vaṭakalai Brahmins.[7] Mr. Sadleir, a member of the Governor's Council, made the following determination about the problem:

It is said, about 50 or 60 years before Mr. Saunders came to the Government, similar disputes then existed, which rose to such heights the Bramineys were sometimes obliged to suspend their ceremonys. This was the case during the Government of Mr. Pitt, Mr. Benyon and Mr. Morse. When Madras was restored, Admiral Biscawen's Dubash took part with the Tangala

[4] *Diary and Consultation Book, Fort St. George*, (1754), 83:133.
[5] Ibid., p. 124.
[6] Love, *Vestiges*, 3:193.
[7] Ibid., p. 194.

Bramineys and supported them against their competitors, who complained to Mr. Saunders of the Outrage offered to them. Mr. Saunders, I am informed, made a long and strict enquiry into the nature of the dispute, ordered that each sect should have a different place of worship, To Wit, the Pagoda whose gate fronted to the East should be used by the Tangala Bramineys, and the one whose gate fronted to the West to be used by the Wadagala Bramineys. To accommodate the present differences and to establish that order and peace so much to be wished in the religious worship of the Natives, I am clearly of Opinion that the judgement of the Board of date 2nd September 1754 and 23rd May 1776 do stand confirmed, or that neither of the Prayers named Streesyla Diapatrom or Ramanja Diapatrom be allowed to be said in future.[8]

The government then resolved to suspend the use of the prayer in question until further investigations could be made as to which form was the traditional one.[9] Political disturbances in South India, however, caused the matter to be shelved. In 1790 the Vaṭakalais petitioned as follows:

The Humble Representation of Wadagala Braminies of Triplicane Humbly Sheweth That a Dispute hath subsisted between us and Tangala Braminies at Triplicane, concerning certain prayer or Oration to be used in the said Triplicane Pagoda, for a long while . . . That during the revolution of Lord Pigot, Tangala Braminies found means to usurp the Pagoda which hath been allotted to us by the above Decrees and Clandestinely procured an order, during the government of Sir Thomas Rumbold, which mentioned that the ancient Prayer shall be read, not particularly whose prayer was ancient. Wherefore, after Sir Thomas Rumbold's departure, We addressed our case to the Board, who, upon examining the matter, thought fit to suspend the prayer in dispute till further examination, which will also appear to your Honor etc. by the Company's record of 1780. And now, as the Feast of the Pagoda coming on, and the said Tengala Braminies understanding that We have lodged a Petition to your Honor, etc. concerning this business, they without taking leave from your Honor etc. as they use to do every year, gather up a multitude of Braminies, and by force and violence hindered our prayer and turned us out the Pagoda, and have irregularly performed their own prayer . . . We therefore humbly Pray Your Honor etc. that a Tom Tom may be beated at the said place for performing our prayer as usual without the hindrance of any person or Persons whatever.[10]

No record is available of the disposal of this petition, but in 1795 the Vaṭakalais complained that the Teṉkalais had taken control of both shrines. The board, however, declined to interfere and said: "The Board do not think it advisable to interfere in the religious disputes of the natives, lest, by giving a decision on grounds of

[8] Ibid.
[9] Ibid., pp. 388–9.
[10] Ibid., p. 389.

which they are not certain, it might become the cause of decisions serious in their consequences to the peace of the inhabitants."[11]

It seems clear from these petitions that the successful establishment of de facto Teṉkalai control of the Śrī Pārtasārati Svāmi Temple was due to the Teṉkalai sympathies of several powerful native merchants and intermediaries (*dubāshis*) who were granted control of the Triplicane temple as part of the perquisites of their broker offices in the colonial economy. This model of merchant domination of Triplicane was inaugurated in the 1670s when the village was leased to Kāsi Vīraṇṇa, the company's chief native merchant.[12] Throughout the eighteenth century such native figures were pivotal in the affairs of the temple, and it appears that it was, in part, their Teṉkalai affiliations that assured Teṉkalai success.

The most relevant contrast between these intermediary figures and the sectarian intermediaries of the Vijayanagara period is that the consolidation of temple control by the former was achieved in a context of confused arbitration and a passive transactional relationship between the deity and the reigning authorities. In the latter case, sectarian leaders were the instruments and beneficiaries of active transactional relationships between king and deity. The native merchant-brokers of the eighteenth century filled the role created by the eclipse of indigenous royalty and the reluctant and ambiguous "royal" posture of the East India Company.[13] This structural rise of indigenous merchant-broker types in temple affairs in eighteenth-century Madras was short-lived, and starting in the latter part of the eighteenth century the burgeoning bureaucratic center of English rule placed increasing constraints on these men and their successors in temple control.

The formation of the Board of Revenue in 1789 reflected the increasing bureaucratic centralization of the colonial state in South India and marked a major stage in the transformation of the East India Company from a trading power to a political regime in South India, a process that was complete by 1803. In 1796 the government made an important policy decision: The collection as well as the distribution of all temple revenues in the limited territories under their control was centralized.[14] A system of compensatory payments

[11] Ibid., p. 390.
[12] Ibid., 1:352.
[13] For examples, see V. R. R. Dikshitar, "Around the City Pagodas," in *Madras Tercentenary Commemoration Volume* (Madras, 1939).
[14] Mudaliar, *Secular State*, p. 8.

was also initiated for locality fees traditionally collected by temples, which were abolished. With the theoretical centralization of revenue flows to and from the temple, the natural consequence was the elaboration, at least in principle, of the government's prerogative to audit the use of these funds by temple authorities. Similarly, bureaucratic control over temple managers, who were to execute a bond "binding themselves to the due appropriation of the Church funds and to submit to any enquiry the Board may order relative thereto," was systematized.[15]

In reality, as will be shown in the case of the Śrī Pārtasārati Svāmi Temple after 1800, these policy orientations were only gradually and haphazardly put into practice. But the basis for increased bureaucratic involvement in temple affairs had been laid by 1800. At the core of the English orientation lay two tendencies that were the reverse of the relationship of indigenous, premodern sovereigns to temples: (1) Where the temple had been largely self-sufficient in its day-to-day management (in the systematic appropriation of endowments to ritual purposes), it was made increasingly dependent on a genuinely centralized bureaucracy, rather than a locality-based, context-sensitive administrative "staff." (2) When the temple was in need of external intervention in situations of conflict, it was faced with English reluctance to arbitrate temple disputes, especially those defined arbitrarily as "religious" disputes. These two policy reversals were themselves consequences of the larger ideological and institutional basis of British rule, as well as of its specific application to temples.

The nature of this process, as well as its context, can best be appreciated by a close scrutiny of the interaction between the temple and the Board of Revenue after 1800. This is so because, given the centrality of revenue collection to British domination, the temple fell directly under the jurisdiction of the Board of Revenue. The temple was under the direct supervision of the collector of Madras, who reported to the Board of Revenue, which was in turn responsible to the chief secretary of the Madras government. The records of the board in this period provide material on a number of interactions between the temple and the colonial administration. The question these records pose is: What was temple conflict about and why did it invite the arbitration of the colonial state?

[15] Board of Revenue Consultations (hereafter BOR Cons.), December 5, 1796, 169:10701, quoted in Mudaliar, *Secular State*, p. 8.

The Board of Revenue and temple conflict, 1800–1820

In 1799 a petition of complaint against the churchwarden (*dharmakarta*, manager) of the temple was received by the board "respecting the administration of the revenues" of the temple.[16] Mr. Read, the official Tamil translator to the board, was ordered to inquire into the allegation. He published a notice, which was affixed to the walls of the temple, summoning all those involved to come to the investigator.[17] Mr. Read questioned all the complainants and sent a report to the board with his analysis of the problem. On the basis of this report, the board ordered the formation of a native committee to decide on the substantive issues involved and commissioned this committee to "resolve on the future regulations to be established for conducting its affairs."[18] Such a body of regulations was produced, ratified by the board, and contractually agreed to by the churchwarden.

From the British point of view, the most serious charge against Narrain Pillay, the churchwarden, was a charge of embezzling the funds of the temple. When the complainants were investigated, however, four of them were found to have given their signatures by proxy. They all disavowed the charges of embezzlement. The only one whose evidence suggested "peculation" was suspect, because he had once been ill-treated by the churchwarden. Mr. Read's report suggested to the board that the accusation of this witness might be "suspected as a return of enmity and malice."[19] The signers of the petition appeared to have been recruited by agents of the main instigator, who had convinced the petitioners that an issue relevant to them was at stake. In one case they approached a complainant and "said there are irregularities in the Church which we must represent to the Governor."[20] In another case a complainant was told that the petition "related to certain infringements of our privileges in the Church."[21]

The accusations of embezzlement, however, were not empty. In fact, the accusations were a convenient code in which to express a considerably more complex complaint involving the rights of the complainants to certain shares in the distributed leavings of the

16 BOR Cons., India Office Library (IOL), May 20, 1799, 12:4367.
17 Ibid., p. 4608.
18 Ibid., June 6, 1799, 13:4999–5000.
19 Ibid., p. 4964.
20 Ibid., p. 4970.
21 Ibid., p. 4976.

deity. It is revealing that the witnesses did not draw any clear semantic distinction between the crime of "embezzlement" and the crime of improper distribution of the central value objects of the temple. The following exchange between one witness and Mr. Read is instructive.

Q: Have you to complain of irregularities against Narrain Pillay as Churchwarden of the Triplicane Pagoda?
A: Yes, he does not allow us the customary share of the holy rice etc. that we formerly had.
Q: Do you know if Narrain Pillay embezzled any of the income of the Church?
A: In consequence of his stopping the daily allowance of rice etc. to the Pagoda, I have reason to conclude he has done so.
Q: Do you know if Narrain Pillay has embezzled the income of the Church?
A: I have no concern with the incomes, my profession being that of reading the Vedas.[22]

In the substantive matter of distributing the holy leavings of the deity, two charges against the churchwarden were made by all the complainants.[23] First, he gave preference to certain foreign Brahmins of the Kantāṭai family in the distribution of holy water and cakes at the festivals and daily offerings at the temple. This preference was an honor legitimately due to them only for the first three days after they arrived at the temple. Second, it was alleged that the *māṉiyakkāraṉ* (treasurer) of the temple (usually the second-in-command of the churchwarden) had been withholding the proportion of the holy rice that the complainants claimed, "by rights a participation grounded on ancient usage."[24] Mr. Read correctly defined these charges as being the real matter under contention, categorized them as a "caste dispute," and recommended their referral to a "committee of the caste." The charges of embezzlement, he argued, were empty. The Rules and Regulations of 1800, formulated by this Native Committee and ratified by the board, provided an extraordinary text of the crucial political issues in the redistributive culture of the temple (Appendix A).

As in the case of witchcraft and sorcery in Africa and elsewhere, it is clear that the accusations of "embezzlement" were only a convenient code in which to express the core structural tensions in the temple and the relationships generated by its central values and symbols. Furthermore, a brief revival of this dispute in 1808–9

[22] Ibid., p. 4972.
[23] Ibid., p. 4964 ff.
[24] Ibid.

revealed that even in the case of the main complainant, who stuck to the strict charge of embezzlement, a more fundamental issue was involved.[25] In this case, the petitioner (also the main witness in 1799–1800) contended that a difference of 500 *pagoda*s between the receipts and disbursements of the temple had been appropriated by the churchwarden himself. Subsequent investigation revealed that the churchwarden had legitimately invested this sum in an interest-bearing bond issued by the East India Company. Even more interesting, however, was the discovery that Appan Iengar, the petitioner, was not really a disinterested critic but had wished to offer the British a better deal:

Q: What did you desire him (the Churchwarden) to write?
A: I desired him first to state the receipts of the Pagoda and to deduct the present charges and then to state that I was willing to pay the Company 500 pagodas per annum.
Q: How did you know that you could defray the expenses and give 500 pagodas to the Company?
A: I proposed to be a contractor and then to give the profit to the Company – amounting to Pagodas 41–30 per month.[26]

Thus, even in this case, the accusation of embezzlement was a linguistic vehicle in a competition for control of the temple, here expressed in the direct idiom of "tax-farming." When looking at temple conflict, therefore, three things may be observed: (1) Because the conflicts concern a redistributive process in which any share entails a measure of control, all conflicts entail the factionalization of the community; (2) the language of factionalization entails accusations of "embezzlement"; and (3) because the issue is one that divides the temple community and challenges its current leadership and also because it is phrased in moral terms that appeal to the English, their arbitration is rendered necessary; it is explicitly invited by one of the factions; and their "interference" is seen as appropriate and necessary by the English themselves. These features of temple conflict remain pertinent throughout the period covered by this study. The role of the colonial state in temple affairs in this period, however, is a peculiar one and can be looked at in several ways.

First, and as a continuation of eighteenth-century norms, the English involved themselves in the ratification of appointments to the churchwardenship, as in the previously mentioned case in 1809.

[25] Ibid., November 17, 1808, 20:10426–8.
[26] Ibid., p. 10429.

Such ratification was seen as appropriate by all concerned. But it was viewed by the English as a minimal regulative task, confined to seeing that appropriate local figures were chosen, without involving positive recruitment or interference on their part. Later in the nineteenth century this ratificatory role became itself another stimulus to the pursuit of factional struggle in the temple.

Second, the English bureaucracy attempted to arbitrate temple conflicts by the invitation of the Hindu constituency of the temple. Viewing the temple as a "trust" in the contemporary Western sense (something that was made explicit later), the English were most sympathetic to charges of embezzlement. But they were simultaneously eager to disassociate themselves from "ritual" questions, which they tried to return to the natives themselves to arbitrate. Even in the latter situations, however, the English bureaucracy did provide a machinery for investigation, a forum for debate, and an authoritative rule-making apparatus, as in the 1799–1800 case.

Third, the colonial state during this period had two kinds of economic relationships with the temple. It exercised its right to audit the accounts of the temple only intermittently and in response to charges of "embezzlement." In general, the maintenance of proper books was left to the churchwarden who, at normal times, ran a fairly autonomous economic enterprise. As for the traditional economic role of the state, namely, subsidizing the temple through endowments, the English continued to do this in an indirect way. They permitted a certain amount of the quitrent (urban land tax) that was due from the residents of the village of Triplicane to be withheld and redirected for the support of the temple. This was done in conscious accord with what was established to be traditional practice.

In a petition sent to the board in June 1804,[27] some of the leading residents of the village of Triplicane deplored the attempt by the then collector of Madras to impose a quitrent on their lands. They based their argument on the grounds that from time immemorial "your petitioners' progenitors as well as your petitioners continue to defray the expenses of the annual solemnities of the Church – in lieu of paying quitrent to the Pagoda – and never hitherto paid anything to the Honourable Company."[28] Arguing that making such contributions to both the temple and the company would tax them excessively, the petitioners requested that the quitrent should be paid only to

[27] Ibid., June 14, 1804, 60:4867.
[28] Ibid.

the temple for the performance of its ceremonies. The board agreed "to authorize the Collector to issue to the inhabitants certificates subject to the usual quitrent and from the amount to pay into the hands of the Churchwarden for the support of the Pagoda a sum equal to the contributions which he shall ascertain to have usually been made towards conducting its ceremonies."[29] By this provision, the colonial administration allowed the temple to continue as a relatively autonomous economic center, although this was complicated by the interposition of the collector's office in the collection of the quitrent.

Finally, two cases illustrate the last function that the state was invited to perform, namely, the "protection" of the rights of the temple with respect to the outside world. In the first case, in 1817, the churchwarden petitioned the collector for help in a problem involving temple land.[30] The land in question was assigned to a dancing girl attached to the temple, who, unable to perform her duty, had sold her land (and her right to a share of the dancing performance) to another dancing girl, who had in turn let the land out to some tenants. These were all seen to be legitimate transactions. But when the second dancing girl wished to build a house on the property and evict the tenants in accordance with the original agreement, the tenants not merely refused but said they had applied for a notice of ejectment to the Supreme Court of Madras, a part of the judicial wing of the colonial state. The churchwarden consequently requested the collector of Madras "to see that the said Periapapal as servant of the Pagoda may receive the assistance necessary from the Company's Solicitor, and that the ground may be restored to her according to the custom of the pagoda."[31] Although the outcome of these legal proceedings was not available in Board Consultations, the board agreed to instruct the law officers of government to defend the suit.

In the second case,[32] in 1818, some land bequeathed by an individual to the temple was contested in the Supreme Court by an adopted grandson. The widow of the dead man, requesting the aid of the collector of Madras, asked him to "accept the garden as per deed of bequest as early as possible and cause the services of God to be performed."[33] As in the previous case, the board recommended that

[29] Ibid., p. 4878.
[30] Ibid., January 9, 1817, 13:807–15.
[31] Ibid., p. 814.
[32] Ibid., May 21, 1818, 66:6050–8.
[33] Ibid., p. 6054.

"the law officers of government may be directed to defend the rights of the Churches in the event of any suit being instituted in the Court on the part of the adopted child."[34] Though the outcome of this suit does not appear to have been recorded in the Consultations of the Board, it is interesting to note that the East India Company conceived of itself as "protecting" the rights of the temple; that it did so *not* by fiat but by the request of the temple itself; and lastly, that the threat to the temple was posed, in part, by the availability, as a separate legal recourse, of the English judicial system to those wishing to contest temple rights.

Thus, by 1818, several factors had emerged that remained central to temple politics in the nineteenth century. First, and continuously with its pre-British cultural history, temple control gave rise to disputes that were not manageable within the confines of the temple itself and consequently required the arbitration of the state. Second, the involvement of the state in temple affairs was *uneven*. In economic matters, its interference was minimal. But in political and legal questions its role was crucial. In neither case, however, was there a systematic state ideology or policy with respect to the temple. There was only an ad hoc administrative style. The cultural role of the state, although marked by several features that were in conscious accord with the policies of previous rulers toward the temple (endowment, dispute-arbitration, and "protection"), was nevertheless not coherent. This was not only a result of the ad hoc style of English administrators but followed also from the primary distinction between early colonial rule and its native predecessors, namely, the desire to separate the executive arm of the government from the judicial arm.[35]

This institutionalized separation of legitimate authority (vested in the courts) from effective power (vested in the executive) had two interrelated consequences. First, it meant that the executive arm of the colonial state had no special legitimacy for the extension or consolidation of its control over South Indian institutions. Thus, its actions were open to challenge by South Indians. Second, an independent and superior moral authority, namely, the judiciary, was available to South Indians as an institutional forum and tool with

[34] Ibid., p. 6057.

[35] For a general discussion of the social and policy context in which the principle of the separation of the executive from the judiciary was instituted, see M. P. Jain, *Outlines of Indian Legal History* (Bombay, 1972), passim; in particular, see Chaps. 11, 12, 13, 15, and 16.

which to actualize such challenges to the effectiveness of British administrative/political control over their institutions. Between 1821 and 1826, just such a challenge was posed to British control over the temple by the then churchwarden, Annaswamy Pillay.

Bureaucratic control and local autonomy, 1821–1826

The single episode of conflict that spans this five-year period is interesting from several angles. It reveals the conflicts between various levels of the British administration, the complexity of temple conflict, and the interaction of these two sets of conflicts in a direct challenge to English control of the temple. The failure of this challenge provides a micro context in which to examine the process by which the colonial state effectively penetrated the temple and thus provided a fresh stimulus to temple conflict. Thus, although the episode under consideration spans only a few years, the structures and processes it reveals remain paradigmatic for the next forty years. It therefore merits the detailed examination that follows, a factual narrative and an analysis of the events of 1821–26.

In May 1821 the board appears to have asked the collector of Madras to withdraw from "interference" with the temples in Madras city.[36] These orders were based on the perception that the Supreme Court of Madras was the local overseeing authority for the temples, according to an opinion expressed by the advocate general for Madras. Although the orders in question were not available to this writer, the collector claimed that the board had asked him to suspend all involvement in the affairs of the Madras temples.[37] This withdrawal of government control, however, resulted in a spate of complaints to the government concerning "embezzlements." Consequently, on January 3, 1822, the board ordered the collector to resume control of the Madras city temples. Their argument was that, "although resort to the Supreme Court might be proper and indeed necessary, in cases involving the recovery of embezzled property or other similar cases, it is desirable that the general protection and patronage of the government through its officers should be exercised in the same manner as heretofore within the limits of the Supreme Court as it is exercised in the Presidency beyond these limits."[38]

[36] See Collector at Madras to BOR, March 20, 1822, in BOR Cons. (IOL), March 21, 1822, 15:2439.
[37] Ibid.
[38] Ibid., January 3, 1822, 10:30.

This was not an arbitrary decision to reestablish control but a direct response to similar petitions to the government such as the one from some temple servants that bemoaned the withdrawal of government control and prayed that "the Collector or some other officer of the government may be authorized to superintend the management and to put a stop to the abuses which at present exist."[39]

In reestablishing control over the temple, the collector attempted to reinstate those temple servants who had been dismissed during the previous year by the churchwarden, principally the *māṉiyakkāraṉ* of the temple. Not only did the churchwarden refuse to reinstate the *māṉiyakkāraṉ* (whom he had replaced with his own candidate), but both he and another local churchwarden went over the collector's head to request from the board copies of the orders on which the collector was alleged to be acting.[40] The board did not provide such copies but merely endorsed these petitions with a vague order to the churchwardens "to conform to such orders as he may receive according to established usage."[41] The collector accelerated the conflict by sending his agents to establish physical control over the movable property of the temple. Physical resistance on the part of the churchwarden's servants resulted, and the criminal case that followed was dismissed by the police superintendent (who was also the magistrate in charge of criminal cases in Madras city) on the grounds that it was a civil and not a criminal case.[42] The collector's attempts to reestablish control over the temple continued to prove futile. His complaints that he was losing all credible authority fell on the conservative and non-supportive ears of the board.

The subsequent arguments between the collector and the board reveal both the confusion of policy that dominated English administrative action and the divergence of views between the collector and his superiors. On March 11, 1822, the collector reported that the churchwarden was taking him to the Supreme Court on grounds of trespass, for having entered the temple and placed seals on the movable property of the temple.[43] In response to the collector's request for governmental aid in his defense, the board indicted the collector for having been put in the role of "defendant" and displayed great reluctance to give him legal support. The collector and

[39] Ibid., August 2, 1821, 88:6964–65.
[40] Ibid., February 11, 1822, 12:1278.
[41] BOR Cons. (Tamilnāṭu Archives, Madras, hereafter TA), February 18, 1822.
[42] BOR Cons. (IOL), February 18, 1822, 13:1730.
[43] Ibid., March 21, 1822, 15:2444.

the board mutually attacked each other's arguments, and the collector was granted the privilege of consulting the company's law officers, although not their actual help in fighting the case. Subsequently, the company's law officers were permitted to defend the collector in court, but the question of whether the government would pay the collector's court costs was left open.[44] Meanwhile, the collector did not confine himself to the marshalling of support for his legal defense but continued to engage in direct confrontation with the churchwarden by competing with his agents in the collection of revenue from temple lands and shops on temple property.[45] The board disapproved of these techniques. It suggested that the collector consult the company's law officers before taking any such measures. The advocate general advised the government that the collector's actions could not be legally justified, that he had exceeded his orders, and that he should simply plead "not guilty."[46] In transmitting this opinion to the chief secretary to government, the board rightly noted that the advocate general's opinion had evaded the central issue of the respective rights of the collector and the churchwarden.[47] The chief secretary approved the proposed mode of defense and simply shelved the more fundamental questions raised by the case.

By March 1823 the case appeared to be going in favor of the collector, the court having issued a writ of sequestration against the churchwarden. The board, accordingly, began to support the winning side. The collector, by a variety of techniques, began to reestablish his control of the temple. A petition was sent to the board by the pro-churchwarden faction in the temple, outlining the history of the issues in their favor and tacitly threatening confusion, disorder, and breakdown if the churchwarden was not fully reinstated to his original position. As late as April 1823, direct conflict between the collector's agents and the servants of the churchwarden continued over the collection of temple revenues. The collector continued to request permission to use heavy sanctions against his opponent. The board continued to advocate caution and increasingly referred all questions to the advocate general. From the board records of February 1825 it can be inferred that the court continued to favor the collector.[48] By this time the advocate general had drawn up a quasi-

[44] Ibid., March 11, 1822, 14:2237.
[45] Ibid., April 15, 1822, 17:3293–6; April 17, 1822, 17:3311–12.
[46] Ibid., April 18, 1822, 17:3409–18.
[47] Ibid., p. 3420.
[48] Ibid., February 24, 1825, 22:1762.

legal instrument containing a set of proposals for temple control predicated on the clear subordination of the churchwarden to the collector. The churchwarden had consented to these proposals.[49] The collector made some additions to this document, which clarified and elaborated his control over the churchwarden in economic affairs.[50] The collector's suggestions, however, were not accepted by the board and were excluded from the final document agreed to by the churchwarden in 1828.

These extraordinary proposals, which effectively made the churchwarden a servant of the collector of Madras, established the following propositions: (1) The *dharmakarta,* or churchwarden, "being appointed under the authority of government [was] to be subject to the immediate control of the Collector of Madras."[51] (2) Proposed temple budgets, actual accounts of incomes and expenditures (both past and present), and new gifts to the temple were to be regularly reported to the collector. (3) The company's bond, representing the investment of temple surplus income, was to be endorsed in such a manner that the churchwarden would not be able to transfer or sell it without prior governmental permission. (4) As for control of temple servants, the churchwarden was permitted to dismiss "ordinary" servants without the prior permission of the board (although subject to investigation by it). But in the case of *mirāsi* servants, he required the prior permission of the board. This distinction, between "ordinary" and "mirasi" servants, raised problems in the period after 1826, which are treated in the next chapter.

The suit, meanwhile, had been settled "amicably," and the churchwarden agreed to bear its costs. Thus, his challenge to the collector, and indirectly to the English administration, had failed. It was a costly failure, but the churchwarden had not lost everything. The collector's proposals for the contract had been rejected as follows: (a) "The Dharmakarta shall not be at liberty to rent any land or buildings belonging to the Pagoda without the knowledge and concurrence of the Collector and all Muchelkas [agreements] and securities taken on the occasion shall be executed in the joint names of the Collector and the Dharmakarta and be deposited in the Collector's treasury." (b) "An Ammeenah shall be appointed by the Collector to be always stationed at the Pagoda whose duty it shall be to bring to the notice of the Collector all abuses and irregularities if there exist

[49] Ibid., p. 1679.
[50] Ibid., July 13, 1826, 74:6843.
[51] Ibid., February 24, 1825, 22:1674–9.

any at the Pagoda." (c) "To prevent complaints on the part of the establishment, the Dharmakarta shall send on the fifth day of every month all the servants of the Pagoda to the Cutcherry of the Collector accompanied by a list of the wages due to them for the preceding month, and payment shall be accordingly made to them from the Collector's treasury out of the Church funds, after taking their receipts for the same."[52]

The rejection of these proposals left the churchwarden with considerable day-to-day control of the temple, but his authority had been formally and considerably diminished. To analyze the events that led to this outcome, two perspectives are useful: (1) the different ways in which the various protagonists viewed the conflict, and (2) the actual objects and issues around which the confrontation coalesced. These are considered serially in the following section.

Perceiving the situation

The collector's view

When the superintendent of police dismissed the case between the collector's agents and the servants of the *dharmakarta*, it was on the grounds that the actions of the collector with respect to the property of the temple were subordinate to another issue, namely, that the *dharmakarta* had not been suspended. Hence, the collector should have acted through him. The collector in a letter to the board considered this a trivial issue. But he argued that, in any case, "it is quite a new doctrine according to my apprehension the allowing of such irregularities because the superior is not suspended – the superior had my orders."[53] There was, thus, no doubt in the collector's mind of the clear-cut subordination of the churchwarden to his orders. As for any autonomous claims to authority on the part of the churchwarden, the collector was convinced that "the situation was not a hereditary one in the present family, for it has been given by government to such persons as were considered most likely to conduct the duties of that office to the satisfaction of the inhabitants of Madras."[54]

The board claimed that the collector had misinterpreted their original letter as an order to withdraw from all control of the temple

[52] Ibid., July 13, 1826, 74:6840–6.
[53] Ibid., February 18, 1822, 13:1726.
[54] Ibid., p. 1738.

in May 1821. The collector cited the relevant letter, saying that he was no longer to "appropriate or detain the funds of the Pagoda."[55] In addition to this restraint, argued the collector, if he was also deprived of control over the servants of the Pagoda, he felt he could "have no control in any shape whatever."[56] The board, early in 1822, asked the collector to conduct an inquiry into the dismissal of temple servants by the churchwarden during the previous year, when the collector had withdrawn all governmental control. The collector replied that he would comply but that "the Board must see the inutility of such inquiry on my part if I have not the authority of suspending and eventually removing the Churchservants."[57]

Furthermore, the collector argued, his lack of credible authority would exacerbate the situation. He noted that "accounts will be brought to me false or otherwise, and it will be impossible for me to ascertain their value, for the Brahmins, finding that I have not the power of redress (even should they be correct), will refuse their attendance, and such an enquiry will only add to that hostile feeling which now exists and is so much to be deprecated."[58] Because the churchwarden had refused to reappoint the dismissed servants and because his action was tacitly supported by the board, the collector complained that he could "only anticipate such will ever be the case when they [the orders] may not please him – which is in fact placing him in the entire command and excluding me from all control – whatever may be his conduct."[59]

When Annaswamy Pillay, the churchwarden, filed a suit against the collector on grounds of trespass, the collector defended his actions to the board in legal terms. He argued that the property of the temple was public, not private.[60] It is interesting to note, as well, that the rhetoric of "embezzlement" was not only employed by the native population to encode more complex concerns. It was also used by the collector, who hinted to the board that "this suit has been brought against me in the hope that it will deter inquiry into malversations said to have been committed on the public property of the Pagoda of Triplicane."[61]

The collector's attitude toward being brought before the court was ambiguous. On the one hand, he assured the board that their right to

[55] Ibid.
[56] Ibid., p. 1739.
[57] Ibid., February 28, 1822, 14:1961.
[58] Ibid., p. 1963.
[59] Ibid., March 11, 1822, 14:2236.
[60] Ibid., March 14, 1822, 15:2308.
[61] Ibid.

control the temple would be vindicated by the Supreme Court.[62] On the other hand, the collector did not think that the court had any business in this conflict. He adduced an example from 1807 to argue that "even at a time when the Supreme Court [was] most inimical to the measures of Government it never entered into its contemplation that the Pagodas could be interfered with by the Court, nor has that management I believe ever been questioned."[63] As for Regulation VII of 1817, the first explicit English legislation on temple management,[64] it was interpreted differently by the collector and by the board. The collector did not feel that it compromised his prior control of the Madras temples in any way.[65]

In essence, the collector blamed his being charged as a defendant in a legal action entirely on the board:

> This case has entirely and exclusively arisen from an act directed by the Board and that all the law suits that may arise out of the case originated from orders which I was obliged to obey as I was told that any hesitation or deviation must be at my own personal responsibility, for had the control of the Pagodas not been relinquished there would not have been an opportunity for the Churchwarden to have doubted an authority under which he had so long acted and up to the 22nd of May he had paid implicit obedience: it is therefore I argue that whatever may be the final result on this question the case has been brought forward by the doubts of the Board and the voluntary relinquishment of their own powers.[66]

The Board of Revenue's view

Although the available records do not permit a real understanding of how the board interpreted Regulation VII of 1817 regarding the Madras temples, it is clear that it was interpreted as being enforceable only "in the provisions."[67] That is to say, it warranted only a "watchdog" role for the state. This was the basis for the board's orders in May of 1821 to the collector to withdraw from all interference with the Madras temples. In the aftermath of the 1821 "with-

[62] Ibid.
[63] Ibid., March 21, 1822, 15:2438.
[64] The essential purpose of this regulation was to give a formal legislative basis to the powers of jurisdiction and supervision of the Board of Revenue and its agents over the native religious endowments. For a discussion of the inherent ambiguities in this regulation, particularly in the matter of the relative jurisdiction of the board and the courts, see P. R. Ganapathy Iyer, *The Law Relating to Hindu and Mohameddan Endowments*, 2nd ed. (Madras, 1918), pp. 35–6.
[65] BOR Cons. (IOL), February 18, 1822, 13:1739.
[66] Ibid., March 21, 1822, 15:2441.
[67] Ibid., February 28, 1822, 14:1974.

drawal," the board received petitions from both factions at the Triplicane temple requesting its return to temple affairs. In analyzing these petitions, the board reported to its superiors that "there is little doubt that these counter statements are attributable to the spirit of animosity and party which has usually existed among the Brahmins of the Pagoda."[68] Nevertheless, the board felt that "great room [was] left open for abuse where no controlling authority [was] exercised."[69] The board therefore recommended that "the general protection and patronage of the Government through its officers"[70] should be exercised as previously.

In recommending that the collector should resume charge of the Madras temples, the board laid great emphasis on the *auditing* function of the collector. He was to "superintend the receipts and disbursements of the Pagodas in order to ascertain that the revenues [were] properly administered and the contributions of government [were] correctly and faithfully appropriated."[71] Also, it was proposed that the "concurrence" of the collector was a prerequisite for the dismissal of servants by the *dharmakarta*.[72] In matters of dispute, the board enjoined the collector to bring about an "amicable adjustment."[73] Where recourse to law was found absolutely necessary, the board stated that the advice and assistance of the company's law officers "should be lent to the persons in authority as has heretofore been customary without compromising the government."[74]

The vague and conservative nature of the board's attitude toward temples is clearly seen in its summation of the preceding guidelines:

> Such has been the general course pursued by former Collectors. The Board are indeed aware that much of the advantage resulting from this species of superintendence and control must depend on the intelligence and discretion with which it may be exercised – but it is obvious that if all protection and superintendence are withdrawn, not only will the affairs of the Pagodas be liable to be improperly administered but the revenues thereof to become the prey of persons interested in promoting litigation.[75]

In a subsequent letter to the chief secretary to government, the board revealed that it had no clear understanding of the process by

[68] Ibid.
[69] Ibid.
[70] Ibid., para. 6.
[71] Ibid., para. 7.
[72] Ibid., para. 8.
[73] Ibid., para. 9.
[74] Ibid.
[75] Ibid., para. 10.

which the previous churchwardens had been nominated. The board's bias[76] toward a model of self-sufficiency for the temple, however, was obvious: The board also saw that its concern with "embezzled" property and its larger notion of itself as "protecting" the temple could be effected, in the last analysis, only "by application to the Supreme Court."[77]

When the collector reported to the board the churchwarden's refusal to reinstate the servants he had previously dismissed, the board bluntly replied that it had no information on the basis of which to decide "the propriety or otherwise of the proposed measure."[78] The board reiterated its earlier emphasis on the inspection of the temple accounts in order to decide whether "embezzlement" had in fact taken place and at the same time hinted that such charges had in the past been found to have been baseless. As for the reinstatement of the dismissed servants, the board restated its laissez-faire attitude by suggesting that the churchwarden had "a great responsibility attaching to him" and that the reversal of his decisions and judgments might involve "very injurious consequences."[79] The board concluded this letter to the collector by repeating its analysis of factionalism in Triplicane and making explicit its conception of the collector as an *arbitrator* rather than a *controller* by enjoining him to make a "full, temperate and impartial investigation" of both parties.[80]

In February 1822 the board quoted an opinion of the advocate general of Madras in response to the criminal proceedings involving the collector's agents. The board informed the collector that the property in question was the property of the "Triplicany Pagoda."[81] The board did not apparently perceive the contradiction between this laissez-faire view and its ideology of "protection" or clarify the concrete agent of this ownership. It simply informed the collector that "the superintendence you are authorized to exercise is an amicable, not a hostile, one."[82]

On March 11, 1822, in response to the news that the collector had been named as a defendant in a suit of trespass, the board expressed its regrets that an officer of the government should be forced into

76 Ibid., January 7, 1822, 10:218–19.
77 Ibid.
78 Ibid., February 25, 1822, 14:1906.
79 Ibid., pp. 1906–7.
80 Ibid., p. 1907.
81 Ibid., February 28, 1822, 14:1974.
82 Ibid.

court as a defendant. The board revealed its radical ambivalence toward the judiciary by chastising the collector thus: "It was in anticipation of such a consequence that we have so frequently pressed upon you the necessity of a cautious and very considerate line of conduct, and of ascertaining in every instance your competence to do acts of compulsion before you resorted to them and . . . to call in the aid of Court to protect the funds, rather than by hasty measures to involve the government in law suits as defendants."[83]

When the collector indicted the board for having precipitated the conflict by its dilatory policy, the board responded with a detailed apologia for its actions and a direct indictment of the collector, which was presented to the chief secretary to government.[84] In this document the board completely disassociated itself from the collector's actions. It argued that "it is not only difficult to determine to what extent the Collector's conduct has been inconsiderate and needlessly violent, but also doubtful whether he [would] be able to bring sufficient judicial proof of his general right of control, to justify before the Court the sealing up of the Pagoda property."[85] The board frankly admitted its ignorance of past policy but correctly recalled that the interference of the officers of the government had, in the past, "never been regularly defined, nor uninterruptedly exercised."[86] The board noted as well that "much has been frequently left to the Dharmacurta, whose proceedings appear to have been too often for a length of time together not at all enquired into."[87]

In response to the churchwarden's legal initiative, the board itself assumed a quasi-legal posture and defined the *dharmakarta*'s right of possession of temple property as that of a "trustee." Consequently, they argued, the collector's only defense could be that he was a "superior trustee."[88] The board expressed its doubts, however, as to the credibility of this claim. It further recommended that the government should bear the collector's legal costs only after he had been successful in the court. In short, the board accused the collector of having been hasty and imprudent, in contrast to its own posture of judiciousness and caution.

[83] Ibid., March 11, 1822, 15:2239–40.
[84] Ibid., March 21, 1822, 15:2437–46.
[85] Ibid., p. 2438.
[86] Ibid., p. 2443.
[87] Ibid.
[88] Ibid., pp. 2443–4.

For the remaining period of the conflict, the board and its bureaucratic superiors increased their dependence for guidance on the company's law officers and eventually relied wholly on the advocate general of Madras to bring about an equitable and authoritative settlement. Even when the board had come to recognize that all particular questions concerning the collector's actions were subordinate to the fundamental question of "the right of government to exercise authority over the Dharmacurta,"[89] its own perception of the priorities remained unchanged. In the board's view, the security of the property of the temple took precedence over "the control of the persons who may be temporarily vested with its custody."[90]

The churchwarden's view

The churchwarden's perception of the situation emerges in the records more through his actions (which are described in the following section on "The Currency of Conflict") than in written statements. But there are two situations in which he places his views on the record. The first is his written plaint to the Supreme Court initiating his action of trespass against the collector.[91] In the plaint he repeatedly described himself as being "in possession of" the property of the temple. Indeed, he described the temple itself as being his property and claimed that he was entitled, in legal terms, to its "possession, use, occupation and enjoyment." The collector's actions, he argued, had deprived him "of the use and benefit of the Pagoda."[92] It is important to note that unlike the board, which was inclined to grant him the right of possession of the temple's property by virtue of his "trusteeship" (in keeping with its conception of the temple as a charity in the contemporary English legal sense), the churchwarden did not even mention the concept of trusteeship in his plaint.

The second document in which the preoccupations of the churchwarden can be seen is in a set of proposals, in the form of a contract, that he submitted to the collector when it had become clear that the case was going against him.[93] This was a last-ditch attempt to bolster his position while appearing to make major concessions to govern-

89 Ibid., April 18, 1822, 17:3420.
90 Ibid.
91 Ibid., March 14, 1822, 15:2309–13.
92 Ibid., p. 2311.
93 Ibid., February 24, 1825, 22:1671–4.

mental authority. In this proposed agreement, Pillay conceded that he was "appointed by the Collector under the sanction of government." But in the very first article of the agreement he subtly suggested his concern for control over temple servants: "All servants attached thereto are to obey Annaswamy who should report their appointment and dismissal to the Collector." This was clearly no compromise at all.

In the matter of payments from the government to the temple, Pillay proposed that they should be continued as before. As far as the scrutiny of temple accounts was concerned, he proposed that in future the accounts he presented to the collector were to be open to scrutiny only for a period of three months subsequent to their submission, after which they were to be considered conclusive and unopenable. Similarly, past accounts during his tenure and that of his ancestors were to be considered final and conclusive. He concluded by proposing that each party in the suit was to pay its own costs and that the case was to be withdrawn from court. Although the conclusion of the case and the final agreement were considerably less favorable to him, these two documents reveal Pillay's aspirations. His conception of his role, fostered by his previous tenure and that of his predecessors, was clearly one of considerable local autonomy and minimal supervision by government.

The advocate general's view

In the period of his mediatorship between the collector and the churchwarden and his advisory role regarding the government, the advocate general's position underwent some interesting changes. In a letter to the company's solicitor dated April 14, 1822, the advocate general, in a narrowly legal vein, opined that the actions of the collector were not justifiable or defensible and that, therefore, he must simply plead "not guilty."[94] The basis of this analysis was that the collector, in sealing the property of the temple, had not a clear mandate from the board. The advocate general agreed with the board that only a "limited and defined authority" had been given to the collector. The collector, in the advocate general's opinion, had exceeded his authority. Therefore, "it was impossible to justify the acts complained of under the authority of government." In short, the advocate general, at this stage, was more concerned with the

[94] Ibid., April 18, 1822, 17:3413–18.

subordination of the collector to the board than with the subordination of the churchwarden to the collector. As the board subsequently complained, the advocate general had evaded the question of the right of government to control the churchwarden.[95]

However, in February 1825, after the collector had tacitly won the case and Pillay had submitted his proposals for a contractual agreement, the advocate general's critique of these proposals and his own suggestions for the legal instrument to be signed by the churchwarden were considerably more pointed. He made it clear that no settlement of the disputes satisfactory to the government could take place "unless there be an unqualified admission on the part of Annaswamy that he has been appointed Dharmakarta of the Pagoda under the authority of the government."[96] Having stated this clearly, the rest of the advocate general's proposals explicitly presumed "that the remedy adopted in England to protect the charities should be pursued here."[97] Accordingly, the majority of the advocate general's proposals were geared to rigorously auditing the temple.

His aim was to "provide for the security of the property and funds of the Pagoda; determine when, where, by whom and how the jewels, paraphernalia and funds of the pagoda shall be preserved or protected and examined – what reports shall be made of donations or gifts to the institution and how, when, to whom and in what manner the periodical accounts of the Dharmakarta shall be rendered, examined and adjusted."[98] The advocate general clearly pointed up the delicate balance between "protection" and "subordination" in the government's handling of the temple. He recognized the possibility that these regulations might become a legal issue at some future date. He therefore laid great emphasis on clarifying the duties and responsibilities of the *dharmakarta*, "at the same time affording to him due support and protection while he shall perform the functions of his office in conformity with regulations."[99]

The police superintendent's view

In February 1822 one of the temple servants who had been dismissed by the churchwarden in the previous year, the *māṉiyakkāraṉ*,

[95] Ibid.
[96] Ibid., February 24, 1825, 22:1674–5.
[97] Ibid., April 18, 1822, 17:3411.
[98] Ibid., February 24, 1825, 22:1678.
[99] Ibid., p. 1679.

attempted to regain his powerful position with the support of the collector and failed.[100] He, therefore, prosecuted several temple servants in the Police Office, where the police superintendent decided criminal cases in his capacity of justice of the peace. The *māṉiyakkāraṉ*'s case was based on the flouting of his orders (given by the collector) by the churchwarden and the temple servants under his control.[101] The churchwarden and his henchmen, by contrast, argued that they had "nothing to do with the Collector."[102]

The police superintendent judged that since the *māṉiyakkāraṉ*'s authority was subordinate to that of the churchwarden, his own previous behavior had followed this axiom, and, consequently, he had no case. Specifically, the police superintendent argued that the case had to be dismissed because the churchwarden had not been suspended and "the present order was not given through his means."[103] In insisting on this chain of command, the police superintendent tacitly recognized the board model of local autonomy for the churchwarden in the control of the temple.

In a letter to the collector of Madras dated February 12, 1822, however, the superintendent gave an even more interesting argument for his decision.[104] He perceived, first, that the conflict was not merely one concerning the relative subordination of various individuals to one another but was also a subtler distributive question: Thus he reported that "the question for decision has appeared to resolve itself into one of respective rights in a Pagoda."[105] He underscored, moreover, that whereas the conflict was brought into his court as a criminal proceeding, it was in fact a civil matter; thus, it did not fall under his purview.[106] It is intriguing to observe that in laying primary emphasis on the questions of "subordination" and "respective rights," the police superintendent touched the most important issues at stake throughout the conflict.

The view of the Triplicane residents

The views of the Triplicane community are expressed in petitions to the government during this period, which fall into two groups

[100] See report from *māniyakkāraṉ* to collector, in BOR Cons. (IOL), February 18, 1822, 13: 1729.
[101] Ibid., p. 1731.
[102] Ibid.
[103] Ibid.
[104] Ibid., p. 1730.
[105] Ibid.
[106] Ibid.

divided along factional lines. These factions were contrasted according to their wishes for or against the continuation of Annaswamy Pillay as churchwarden of the temple. The views of the anti-Pillay faction are considered first.

In January 1822 the anti-Pillay petitions forced the board to reconsider its earlier decision to restrict the collector's control over the temple. These early petitions complained of "maladministration," "abuse," and "frauds" perpetrated by Pillay and explicitly invited the government to resume control[107] and to remove Pillay from his position. A later petition, written in February 1822 during the first direct skirmishes between the collector and the churchwarden, was more elaborate.[108] The petitioners thanked the government for responding to their pleas "for the better preservation of [their] pagoda," and they decried Annaswamy's contempt for the collector's orders in reference to temple property. This outrageous behavior, they claimed, was responsible for the stoppage of certain calendrical festivals and for disturbances in the routine religious ceremonies in the temple. They also reported a rumor that Pillay was planning to take the matter to the Supreme Court. Similarly, they also speculated that it was in order to establish the economic viability of this plan that he had recently asked the government to give him possession of a company bond in the name of the temple.

The last document on the anti-Pillay side was a deposition made principally by the Chetti merchants of Triplicane.[109] This document is especially important because it is the first recorded case of a specific *jāti* establishing its role in the temple in relation to an external authority (such statements become common currency after 1878). The Chetti merchants established first that in the early days of British rule their *jāti* fellows (many of whom were "middlemen" in the early colonial economy in Madras) controlled the temple as churchwardens under British patronage and performed charities "from their own money and from the pagoda revenues."[110] They went on to assert that the Chettis voluntarily resigned their monopoly of the churchwardenship "from an unwillingness to give the government continual trouble by frequent complaints on account of the disputes in the pagoda of the Brahmins of this village."[111] The

[107] See Petition No. 594 of 1821, in BOR Cons. (IOL), August 2, 1821, 88:6964–5; and similar petition in ibid., January 7, 1822, 10:217–18.

[108] Ibid., February 18, 1822, 13:1735–7.

[109] Ibid., April 25, 1822, 13:3677–80.

[110] Ibid., p. 3677.

[111] Ibid., pp. 3677–8.

petition concluded with a suggestion of embezzlement by Pillay and a claim that the annual and other festivals of the temple were subsidized by their money and not by the funds of the churchwarden.

Although the evidence is scanty, the anti-Pillay faction appears to have included: dismissed temple servants wishing to reclaim their positions, members of the Brahmin community who might have been dissatisfied with their shares in the distributed leavings of the deity, and a section of the commercial castes at Triplicane who appear to have preferred direct government interference to the control of the churchwarden, possibly because this permitted greater display of their subsidy of temple ritual than the churchwarden was likely to allow.

On the pro-Pillay side, a contrastive, but complementary, rhetoric obtained. On January 3, 1822, a petition was presented to the government by the "ghosty Brahmins" who were entitled to recite the Tamil Prabandams in the temple and thus, also, to a fixed and sizable share of the divine leavings.[112] The petitioners first extolled the virtues of the churchwarden in much the same terms as in an 1809 petition, when Pillay was proposed for the churchwardenship.[113] His appropriateness was indicated by stressing (a) tacitly, his descent from previous temple controllers; (b) his endowment of the temple both by new physical extensions and by the gift of jewels to the deity; (c) his performance of all the festivals; (d) his "protection" of the petitioners; and (e) his increasing of the wealth of the temple.

The petitioners described the opposite faction:

> Some wicked Brahmins who have no manner of concern in the Pagoda and who had already preferred false complaints against the Churchwarden to the several successive authorities and were punished by them for the same, have now presented a petition to the government . . . with an evil design to injure the institution, to disgrace the persons who wish to make gifts, and to deprive the Church of her property by obtaining some authority from the government.[114]

This analysis was followed by a reminder to the government that it, the government, was "naturally disposed to protect the churches as well as the Brahmins" and by a request that "the institution be continued on its present and usual footing under the immediate management of the present Churchwarden."[115]

112 Ibid., January 3, 1822, 10:27–9; see Chapter 4.
113 Ibid., December 4, 1809, 46:9406.
114 Ibid., January 3, 1822, 10:27–8.
115 Ibid., p. 29.

The second pro-Pillay petition was recorded on April 3, 1823, when things were already going badly for the churchwarden.[116] This lengthy document began with a more detailed historiography of the factional conflict at the temple from 1800 onward. The language of "embezzlement" was used but in two curiously opposed ways. On the one hand, all complaints of "embezzlement" against the churchwardens since 1800 were held to be a product of malice, disgruntlement resulting from dismissal, and the like. On the other hand, the petitioners argued that the anti-Pillay faction was composed of persons who were creating disturbances because the temple was being managed in such a way that "they could not embezzle the pagoda's property."[117] The attempts of the collector to reestablish control were described as being "contrary to *mamool* [custom]." The petitioners also suggested that the hidden motivation of the anti-Pillay faction was to reestablish governmental control of the temple. Finally, the petition concluded with a series of predictions (which sound much more like veiled threats) as to what would happen if the government decided to disturb the previous autonomy of the churchwarden: Those who had endowed the temple would cease to do so, "confusion" would reign, there would be "disturbances" at the temple; in short, disorder would be rampant.[118]

The preceding analysis of variation in the "perception of the siutation" by various groups and individuals was meant to suggest not only the complexity of the concerns that were expressed in this period but also that the radically disparate categories that different persons brought to bear on their concerns with the temple were themselves a partial explanation of the conflict. What follows is an analysis of the concrete objects and issues around which the confrontation between the collector and the churchwarden actually coalesced.

The currency of conflict

The following analysis of the concrete concern of the major protagonists in the 1821–6 conflict is perforce an analysis of the substantive and empirical meaning of temple control insofar as temple control is an issue that confuses the boundary between temple and state. The subject can be considered from the following three distinct, but

[116] Ibid., April 3, 1823, 48:3390–6.
[117] Ibid., p. 3391.
[118] Ibid., pp. 3395–6.

interrelated, points of view: material inputs, control of people, and temple property.

Material inputs

It has already been noted that the conflict between the collector and the churchwarden was partly expressed by competition over, and manipulation of, a series of economic inputs into the temple. The most important of these were: (1) two routine compensatory payments from the government to the temple (analyzed in the following chapter), which were withheld by the government throughout the period of the conflict;[119] (2) the urban land tax on land granted to the temple; the ground rent on bazaars and shops on temple property, which was previously collected by the *dharmakarta* but during the conflict was competed for by him as well as by agents of the collector, each claiming it as their right;[120] (3) "voluntary" contributions from some local shopkeepers to subsidize temple festivities whose closure was threatened in a pro-Pillay petition;[121] and (4) the company bond representing the temple's invested capital, which had originally been in the name of the churchwarden but in the contract eventually signed by him was to be jointly in his and the collector's names so that he would not be able to alienate or misuse it. By the end of the conflict, the churchwarden's relatively autonomous control over these inputs had been greatly attenuated, and the government, in the person of the collector, had considerably greater control over their allocation.

Control of people

Even more important than the control of material flows into the temple, in the eyes of the collector and the churchwarden, was the control of people. Under the larger ideological penumbra of the churchwarden's subordination to the collector, the specific issue was their relative control over two sets of people: temple servants and shopkeepers.

The patron–client relationship of temple servants to the churchwarden in the temple polity obliged them to defy the collector's

[119] See letter from collector at Madras to Board of Revenue, April 2, 1923, in BOR Cons. (IOL), April 3, 1823, 48:3389.
[120] Ibid., April 25, 1822, 18:3674–5.
[121] Ibid., April 3, 1823, 48:3395.

orders blatantly. Thus, the collector's inordinate concern with the question of the dismissal of temple servants does not reflect an obsession with correct procedure but rather a recognition that controlling temple servants was a large part of the key to the credibility of his control over the temple. It has already been noted that the collector attempted to incorporate into the final contract signed by Pillay a stipulation whereby the monthly wage payments to temple servants were to be made at his office rather than by and through the churchwarden. Although phrased in the rhetoric of avoiding "abuse," this provision really constitutes an attempt to shift the client role in reference to temple servants from the churchwarden to himself. Simlarly, the collector's proposal for the permanent appointment of an *amīnā* at the temple, also phrased in the rhetoric of abuse prevention, represents a bid for direct and constant control over temple servants.

The constant (and violent)[122] battle between the collector's agents and the churchwarden's agents for the loyalty of the *shopkeepers*, in their capacity as temple endowers, is another symptom of their mutual concern for the control of people.

Temple property

The final set of objects competed for by the collector and the churchwarden was the movable property of the temple, specifically, the temple jewels and temple accounts.[123] For several reasons, both items are enduring tokens in temple conflict throughout the nineteenth and twentieth centuries. Of all the items that incarnate the temple and whose possession connotes temple control, these share the following characteristics: (1) Their substance is necessarily subject to periodic fluctuation (resulting from fresh endowments in the case of jewels and rapid obsolescence in the case of accounts); (2) they are easily subject to "misappropriation," both because of their disaggregated nature, which makes auditing difficult, and their high ratio of value-to-weight, which makes them eminently mobile and portable; (3) unlike cash, they are both items that are, in principle, meant to be preserved and not spent or destroyed. Thus, they are the

[122] See a petition to the board complaining of oppressive conduct by collector's agents in enforcing certain "voluntary" payments: BOR Cons. (IOL), April 17, 1822, 17:3311; and a report from the Amildar to the collector in ibid., April 25, 1822, 18:3674–5.

[123] See, for example, a report from the *māniyakkāran* to the collector in BOR Cons. (IOL), February 11, 1822, 12:1276–7.

only two items that occupy a strategic position between the fixed (physical) property of the temple and its liquid capital.

The three sets of items that have been analyzed in the preceding discussion cannot be controlled in isolation from one another. The control of "things" and the control of "people" not only support each other (by controlling wages, you control servants; by controlling shopkeepers, you partially control endowments) but are in an important sense two sides of the same object. This object is that diachronic relationship between "things" and "people" that, over time, organizes the redistributive *process,* which is the core of the temple. To control this relationship, therefore, is in part to control the temple. (The other aspect of temple control, discussed elsewhere in this study, involves that relationship between "things" and "people" that defines the *output* of the temple, the distribution of "honor.")

What had changed and why? 1800–1826

Between 1800 and 1818 the temple had been a largely self-regulating institution. Its incapacity to arbitrate its own conflicts, however, had invited the state to involve itself in temple affairs, albeit in a sporadic, uneven, and ad hoc manner. By 1826 the temple had lost much of its autonomy and the state, in turn, had considerably expanded its control over the temple. This control was defined in systematic, rule-governed, and self-conscious terms. What accounts for this change?

The preceding analysis of the conflict between the churchwarden and the collector suggests the following explanation. The change in the nature of temple control can be attributed to the dialectical interaction between three sets of forces: (1) the structural (and traditional) incapacity of the temple to resolve its conflicts internally; (2) the clear articulation of a tension in English rule, which was already incipient before 1818, between its executive/administrative arm and its legal/judicial arm; and (3) the elaboration of a previously tacit contradiction in English administrative ideology between the ideas of temple "protection" and temple "subordination." How did these three factors interact to produce change?

The specific precipitant of conflict was bureaucratic confusion concerning Regulation VII of 1817. The board apparently interpreted it as placing the temple under the purview of the Supreme Court of Madras. It therefore directed the collector to attenuate his control of the temple and to retain merely a "protective" function. The collector, whose concern with temple control was much less abstract, interpreted this as an order to withdraw from any involvement in temple affairs. Given the temple's lack of self-sufficiency in resolving its conflicts, withdrawal generated a series of complaints and accusations to the state, compelling it to resume control.

Meanwhile, however, the churchwarden had enjoyed complete autonomy for almost a year and was not willing to graciously accept the resumption of governmental control. In opposing the collector he ran up against the collector's conception of temple control, with "subordination" (particularly of the churchwarden himself) as its cornerstone. Also, the collector, because of his emphasis on "subordination," lost the sympathy of his superiors, the board, whose members saw the collector's ideas and actions as a gross travesty of their ideology of "protection."

But the conflict was not merely precipitated by the question of the relative jurisdiction of the board and the Supreme Court over the temple and exacerbated by the contradiction between the board's emphasis on "protection" and the collector's concern with "subordination." The churchwarden's capacity to resist the collector would have been negligible if the Supreme Court of Madras had not been available to him as an independent guarantor of his rights, which could be deployed against the collector. Nor was it simply the functional division of authority from power in English rule that made this tactic possible. In the "protective" ideology of the board itself lay the seeds for recourse to the court. As has already been noted, this was apparent even before 1818. But after 1818, it became more explicit.

In the board's ideology of "protection" a curious synthesis had taken place. Building on the indigenous idea that rulers are obliged to protect temples, the English had grafted on to it (as is clear in the advocate general's arguments) the contemporary English view of public trusts and charities, which could ultimately be "protected" not by the executive but only by the judiciary. Thus, access to the courts was not opened to natives simply by the recent and increasing separation of the executive from the judiciary. Access was also built into the ideology of the English bureaucracy regarding temples. These considerations account for the structure of the conflict between 1821 and 1826. But why this outcome? Why was the temple not restored to some state of self-sufficiency rather than radically subordinated to the English bureaucracy?

For an empirical answer to this question, more information is required than is available on the actual course of the litigation between the collector and the churchwarden. It is known that in issuing a writ of sequestration against the churchwarden,[124] the court favored the collector sufficiently so that the churchwarden was persuaded to tacitly concede his failure and propose compromise. A description of the structural constraints that made this outcome highly likely is possible if a further fact about the board is recalled. The board expressed the tension between executive and judiciary by holding views that seem paradoxical. On the one hand, they recognized their dependence on the judicial system for the fulfillment of their "protective" mandate. On the other hand, they wished to restrict their involvement and the involvement of persons and institutions under them in litigation. This anti-litigious attitude is understandable on the part of administrators who often saw the courts as a waste of time, a drain on revenues, and occasionally, a threat to the efficiency and effectiveness of bureaucratic control.

But the board and its superiors were convinced that the institution in question was a constant prey to "abuse." This perspective was in large part a consequence of native petitions using the language of "embezzlement" to express more complex issues in the redistributive politics of the temple. In this situation, if recourse to the court was viewed with distaste, how could the ideal of "protection" be realized without an elaboration of control or, in other words, "subordination"?

It is this syllogism that was recognized and enacted in the advocate general's formulations for a contract of subordination to be signed by the churchwarden. The quasi-legal and rule-oriented nature of this document reveals that two elements of the previous style of bureaucratic interaction with the temple were now obsolete: executive fiat and ad hoc decision making. The British had come to control this temple by 1826 not by a vertical policy decision but by a complex three-way interaction between the "explosive" nature of temple conflict, the functional separation (and consequent tension) between the executive and the judiciary branches of the colonial state, and the contradiction between the ideas of "protection" and "subordination" in English bureaucratic policy with regard to the temple.

[124] BOR Cons. (IOL), March 24, 1823, 47:3233.

4

FROM BUREAUCRACY TO JUDICIARY, 1826–1878

British bureaucratic involvement with the temple reached its zenith and then was gradually withdrawn in the half century from 1826 to 1878. As a consequence of these two phases of the relationship, a new meaning began to apply to the term *Teṉkalai*. Increasingly, it lost its pan-regional, sectarian, and ritual connotations and began to acquire the status of a local sociopolitical category that designated the political constituency of the temple. This chapter examines the logic of this development: First the period from 1826 to 1840 will be discussed, then the period from 1841 to 1878.

British involvement: 1826-1840

In the period from 1826 to 1840, three processes are of primary importance: (1) the alteration and exacerbation of temple conflict resulting from the directness of British bureaucratic control; (2) the transformation of the preexisting tensions in British ideology (between the ideas of "protection" and "subordination") into new idioms; and (3) the beginnings of a new sectarian politics.

Temple conflict and British control

By 1832 the temple had lost most of its economic autonomy. It was dependent for all its regular income on the British revenue administration in the form of the collector's office.[1] This income was of four sorts: (1) a *mērai* payment, in compensation for lands belonging to the temple that had been "resumed," or appropriated, by the British in the first years of the nineteenth century; (2) a *makamai* payment, in compensation for certain taxes on sea and land customs, which had been assigned to the temple in the eighteenth century through the influence of native *dubashis* who were also temple mangers (this payment had also been abrogated); (3) an allowance in lieu of the quitrent originally collected by the temple (referred to in the preced-

[1] BOR Cons. (IOL), October 30, 1834, 53:11630–1.

ing chapter); and (4) taxes on shops, carts, and so on in the temple's vicinity, previously collected by the temple but interrupted in 1832.

This last set of "taxes," the last vestige of the local economic autonomy of the temple, had apparently been stopped by the superintendent of police "as liable to prove vexatious to the public and lead to abuse and litigation."[2] When this happened, petitioners from the temple presented the collector with the following subtle analysis of the indispensability of these payments: "There are four poojas daily performed at the Pagoda, for which purpose rice, ghee and various other articles have been purchased from the tax levied on carts etc; that the discontinuance of those poojas would, in consequence of its bringing the pagoda into less repute, hinder the performances of the grand festivals usually celebrated there, and that the poojas in question are therefore considered by those interested in the Pagoda indispensable."[3]

The collector accepted this argument. The board of revenue agreed to his proposal that payment should be made to the temple to compensate for this loss from the annual residue from the quitrent to the temple after the fixed allowance had been made.[4] Thus, even this local capacity of the temple was converted into a dependency on cash flowing from the collectorate. The only economic resources left in temple hands were private endowments, whether of cash or kind, to the temple by local citizens. These were subject by the agreement of 1826 to the strictest audit by the collector.

In considering these four cash flows from the collectorate to the temple, it is striking that all these payments are forms of cash *compensation* for abrogated or expropriated local economic privileges. Although the British saw their payments to the temple as an extension of the indigenous model of royal patronage, these payments, in fact, consisted of a series of compensations for appropriation of local revenue sources. Thus, although previous royal endowments to temples were, functionally speaking, attempts to redistribute resources using the local economic autonomy of temples,[5] British patronage precisely attemped to compensate for the appropriative acts of a centralized revenue apparatus that had already radically reduced the economic autonomy of temples.

[2] Ibid., p. 11631.
[3] Ibid., p. 11630.
[4] Ibid., p. 11631.
[5] Burton Stein, "The Economic Function of a Medieval South Indian Temple," *Journal of Asian Studies* 19, No. 2 (1960):163–76; see also, T.V. Mahalingam, *South Indian Polity* (Madras, 1967), Chap. 8, Sect. 5.

The result is an irony. The collector's office, the par excellence instrument of revenue exaction, is turned into a source for subsidizing temple activity. This irony is part of a larger tension in the economic relations of early British domination between the urge to maximize the upward flow of revenue (at whatever cost to local economic relations and privileges) and the urge to maximize stability and order in economic relations (i.e., to preserve local economic relations and rights). This contradiction (i.e., necessary conflict between two objectives of a system) is expressed in numerous major policy conflicts in the eighteenth and nineteenth centuries.[6]

This tension between the "extractive" functions of British rule, with its emphasis on direct control, vertical accountability, and formal bureaucratic categories, and the "subsidizing" function of British rule, with its emphasis on indirect control, local autonomy, and tacit indigenous categories, can be seen best in the conflict over *mirāsi* rights in the temple during the 1826–30 period. The term *mirās*, which is of Persian origin, refers to a "right by inheritance" over a share of the agricultural produce, as well as over other privileges, either in virtue of a service or in virtue of a putative royal grant.[7] The question of who had *mirāsi* rights in the pre-British period, what these rights consisted of, and how to deal with them in assessing land revenue was one of the thorniest problems of the British revenue administration in Madras in the eighteenth and nineteenth centuries. It generated a vast and confused bureaucratic literature, and insofar as it represented real privileges in the apportionment of agricultural products, it was abolished by the British by the 1860s.

Without going into the details of *mirāsi* rights in early British revenue systems, it is important to realize that the complex of local revenue privileges connoted by the term *mirās* was poorly understood by the British and its meaning was radically transformed. An English administrator, writing in 1879, analyzed the British impact on this set of privileges in Chingleput district:

[6] In the nineteenth century, this tension between revenue maximization and stability took many forms: in land policy, in the choice between the *zamindari* and *ryotwari* systems of tenure; in law, between the tendency to collapse executive and judiciary functions in the collector's office to maximize efficient extraction and the tendency to separate these two functions, to make the revenue officialdom judicially accountable, and thus to "protect" the rights of the individual; in bureaucratic organization, it took the form of tension between the urge to maximize vertical accountability and the fantasy of *pancāyat* models of local self-sufficiency.

[7] This definition of the term *mirās* extends most standard definitions, which treat it exclusively as a form of favorable and hereditary tenure.

In going over the bulky reports, proceedings, minutes of consultation, and "orders thereon", not to mention the dispatches of the East India Company, nothing strikes the reader more strongly than the change which has come over the nature of the right itself, ever since the district was first handed over to the Company. During that period many portions of the right at one time inherent in it have disappeared, owing to the changes produced by flux of time and the altered conditions of the country, while others have been expressly abrogated by government itself. Yet this seems generally to have been overlooked and additional perplexity has thus imported into the discussion of a subject already sufficiently intricate and obscure.[8]

Given the relatively high urbanization of temple lands by 1800, the usage of the term *mirās* to describe various rights in the temple had lost all connection with the rural model of privileged shares of agricultural resources. Instead, it had come to encode the arguments of individuals and families both to hereditary claims on temple jobs and to the perquisites and shares in the divine leavings attached to these jobs.

Until 1826, board records are silent on any conflict in the temple concerning *mirāsi* rights. The background for the 1826 issue was the conflict between the collector and the *dharmakarta* in 1822 and the resultant contractual agreement, proposed by the advocate general, to be signed by the *dharmakarta*. In this document the advocate general proposed that for "ordinary" servants the *dharmakarta* should have the power of dismissal subject to investigation by the board. But in the case of *mirāsi* servants, he could not dismiss them without prior permission from the board.[9] This gratuitously introduced distinction immediately provoked a scramble among temple servants to have their jobs defined as *mirāsi*. Similarly, it renewed the conflict between the collector and the churchwarden as to the relative propriety of several such conflicting claims.

On May 29, 1826, the collector sent the board a list of *mirāsidār*s proposed by the *dharmakarta*, Annswamy Pillay.[10] This list was clearly contested by several petitioners. In a letter to the board on July 13, 1826, the collector cited a series of counterclaims. He cited the churchwarden's defense of the status quo (i.e., of the list of present holders), which he, the churchwarden, had already formalized in several different ways.[11] First, in the case of rival claims to the *mirāsi* role of reciting the Vēdas (*Vēdapārāyaṇam*), Pillay

[8] C. S. Crole, *Manual of the Chingleput District* (Madras, 1879), pp. 214–15.
[9] BOR Cons. (IOL), February 24, 1825, 22:1678.
[10] Ibid., May 29, 1826, 69:4849.
[11] Ibid., July 13, 1826, 74:6834–40.

discredited the contestant to the present incumbent by citing improper descent and, therefore, a null hereditary basis for his claim. Second, in some cases, he attacked the counterclaimants as unworthy or dishonest. In the case of the temple cook, for example, he cited a previous collector's order of dismissal. Third, in another case, he said the claimant had not claimed his right for more than twenty-four years, and, therefore, the right could not be recognized. Fourth, he identified some claimants in minor slots as "common coolies and not mirasidars, their ancestors not having been servants of the pagoda." And fifth, he denied, in one case, that the claim was a *mirāsi* situation at all.

In response, the board asserted that they were only interested in immediately settling all *mirāsi* situations among present pagoda servants and "not in counter-claims."[12] As for those roles considered *mirāsi* by the collector but not by the *dharmakarta*, the board suggested the formation of a native *pancāyat* (committee) to "ascertain what has been the custom of the pagoda with respect to the offices in question, whether the succession to them has been hereditary or whether they have been filled by the appointment of the dharmakarta."[13] When the *pancāyat* was formed, the *dharmakarta* complained to the board of the embarrassment of "being placed in competition with individuals who had been doing duty under his immediate direction in the capacity of common coolies."[14] The board chastised the collector for his indiscretion in permitting the *dharmakarta* and his servants to come into conflict at the same meeting, but they insisted that the discreet selection of a *pancāyat* must go on.[15]

Meanwhile, the board received a petition that had been sent directly to the chief secretary to government by the dismissed claimant to the *mirās* and superintendence of the temple kitchen.[16] The principal complaint of the petitioner was that Pillay owed him a large sum of money for the provision of "kitchen services." He then went on to argue his *mirāsi* claim on three grounds: (1) the *sannad* given in 1805 by the collector to the then *dharmakarta* confirming his position; (2) the *mucilika* (contract) signed by the claimant promising the government to perform according to certain rules; and (3) the *mahazarnamā* (petition) signed by the other *mirāsi* servants of the

[12] Ibid., August 10, 1826, 77:8036–7.
[13] Ibid., p. 8036.
[14] Ibid., August 24, 1826, 78:8397–8.
[15] Ibid., pp. 8400–1.
[16] Ibid., December 21, 1826, 90:13587–93.

temple upholding his claim. The petitioner concluded his argument by suggesting that Pillay's denial of his *mirāsi* right was in order to evade the account owed to the petitioner.

Subsequently, the board accepted the collector's verification of the petitioner's later dismissal by a collector for misconduct. It decided that "the claim of the petitioner to be readmitted into the service in the Pagoda cannot be recognized."[17] In September 1828 the board essentially vindicated all of the churchwarden's arguments concerning *mirāsi* positions. In so doing, it recognized his formalization of the *status quo* with respect to temple service of a privileged or hereditary sort.[18]

Noteworthy, in the context of this *mirāsi* "crisis," is the code of "accusations" of embezzlement employed in petitions against the churchwarden from the *māṉiyakkāraṉ* (reappointed by the collector) and some of the *mirāsi* servants of the temple.[19] In the accusations, importance was given to the fabrication of false accounts by the *dharmakarta;* to his sale of jewels presented to the deity for personal profit; and, most significant, to his fabrication of *mirāsi* service holders so that he could pad his claims for wage expenses to the collectorate. The petition concluded with the following prayer for further extension of governmental control over the temple: "Under the foregoing circumstances we humbly pray you will at your earliest convenience be pleased to recommend to the Board and the right honourable the Governor-in-Council that the magamah may not be paid into the hands of Annaswamy Pillay the Churchwarden, but that the charities of the pagoḍa may be conducted under the orders of the circar according to mamool whereby the Honourable Government will acquire fame, virtue and success."[20]

The extension of governmental control did not only exacerbate conflict over rights in the temple in the idiom of *mirāsi* positions. Conflict also took the form of a relatively more arcane dispute in 1835, which was a direct product of the extended role of the collectorate in temple affairs. The context for the conflict was that the temple had not had a churchwarden since the last one resigned in 1832. Until the appointment of another churchwarden in 1836, the power of the collectorate was even greater than the power that had been already technically granted to it. An elaborate analysis of the conflict

[17] Ibid., April 12, 1830, 44:4241.
[18] Ibid., September 11, 1828, 64:8711–15.
[19] Ibid., January 3, 1828, 47:430–34.
[20] Ibid., p. 343.

is contained in a letter from the acting collector to the board dated August 11, 1835, in which the acting collector condenses and responds to a petition addressed to the government by certain *mirāsidārs* who "call themselves the Tengala Brahmins of Triplicane."[21]

In reporting the claims of the petitioners, the acting collector said that they "assert their sole right to the Pagoda there to the exclusion of the *Vadagalas*."[22] The collector, however, disregarded this first systematic claim for Teṉkalai control over the temple, arguing that "this is a question on which it is not perhaps necessary that any inquiry should be instituted for the present."[23] The petitioners charged, first, that the head sheristadar (a revenue official immediately subordinate to the collector), who was of the Vaṭakalai persuasion, was causing disturbances at the temple. Second, that at the sheristadar's instigation, the affairs of the temple were being run without consulting the *mirāsidars*, in contradiction to their previous consultative role. Third, the petitioners charged that "during the celebration of any grand festival, the Sheristadar prevents the Mirasidars etc. of the Pagoda from approaching the image, whilst this privilege is freely allowed to persons of his own sect." Fourth, that the sheristadar ordered them "to convey to him what is termed 'holy rice' which should be distributed among the mirasidars." Fifth, that he was alleged to have disregarded the protests of the petitioners and on "a certain respect being paid, on a particular occasion, to the person celebrating an annual festival, the Sheristadar caused it to be paid at first to himself."

Having listed these charges, the collector proceeded to exonerate his subordinate on the basis of an inquiry he claims to have conducted at the temple.[24] The collector then argued with respect to the final charge that "due respect was paid to the party entitled to it, and that ultimately a small garland of flowers was given to the Sheristadar in common with other respectable natives who were present."[25] In regard to the other charges, the collector claimed that the petitioners were not cooperative in the conduct of an investigation into them. The collector went on to document that the petitioners were troublemakers. They had been involved in a police case in 1831 provoked by "a regular riot over the distribution of 'cakes'."[26] A peti-

[21] Ibid., August 20, 1835, 1:9229–30.
[22] Ibid., p. 9229.
[23] Ibid.
[24] Ibid., p. 9231.
[25] Ibid., p. 9233.
[26] Ibid., pp. 9237–40.

tion from the "Tengala Gosty Brahmins and others" confirmed this view of the petitioners.[27]

It was argued further that this troublemaking propensity explained the fact that no applicants had applied for the position of *dharmakarta*, although a vacancy had existed since 1832.

The collector concluded his argument by describing the charges as "frivolous, vexatious and incapable of proof" and summed up his exoneration of the sheristadar by the following description of the limits of his mandate:

> It is only on the occasion of any grand festival that the Sheristadar is directed to attend at the Pagoda to ascertain that the funds allotted for the purpose are not misappropriated, but he is by no means authorized to interfere in deciding upon the rights and privileges of any particular sect, or in any other matter concerned with the religious ceremonies of the Pagoda.[28]

The board agreed with the collector to dismiss the above charges. But it is clear that they were not empty charges. They demonstrate that, in part, the bureaucratic ideology of preventing "misappropriation" was an ideological wedge for some native employees of the bureaucracy to directly manipulate key elements of the redistributive process, which was the essence of the temple. Such manipulated elements included: proximity to the deity, shares in the *prasātam* leavings of the deity, and "respects" in such forms as garlands worn by the deity, which carried the significance of status. The battle over the distribution of "cakes" (a form of *prasātam*) in 1831, for which no data are available other than the preceding allusion, also suggests a general atmosphere of conflict over the redistributive process in this period. The second "honors" case is better documented over the period under discussion.

The second honors dispute apparently involved the subsidy of a certain ritual event as part of the ten-day annual festival of the main deity of the temple, Śrī Pārtasārati Svāmi, by a caste of Mudaliyārs from Poonamalėe, a section of Madras adjoining Triplicane.[29] This caste-subsidized event, it appears, had not been celebrated as part of the ritual calendar since 1818. Consequently, the customary regulations concerning which members of the caste were qualified to receive the honors associated with the event had become obsolete. In 1829 an attempt was made to revive this caste's participation in the ceremony. An agreement was signed by some members of the caste to the effect that "the presentation of a garland of flowers to

[27] Ibid., p. 9234.
[28] Ibid., p. 9236.
[29] BOR Cons. (IOL), April 30, 1840, 32:5709–13.

Nagamooney Narainsamy Moodelly was to be continued only as long as he conducted himself to the satisfaction of all parties and was to be discontinued if he acted in any respect against their wishes."[30] These same signers appear to have objected to its continuance in 1838 (the ceremony had not, in fact, been performed in the intervening years). They subsequently changed their minds. But one faction, led by Appasamy Moodelly, the headman of the caste, refused to give its consent.

The conflict between the two proposed incumbents for the honor in question was analyzed to have begun over another question of temple rights. Appasamy Moodelly had selected one dancing girl to be *manicantall* (apparently a specially privileged role among the fifteen *mirāsi* positions after 1826). The conflict's result, however, was to provoke disagreement in a more visible honor arena, expressed by the garland of flowers.

The *dharmakarta*, Narasimloo Naick (appointed in 1836), reported to the collector that in this complex situation he did "not feel authorized to permit the ceremony to be performed on his personal responsibility, but that, if peremptory orders be sent to him for the ceremony being observed, he would be prepared to carry these out as he is apprehensive that he may render himself liable to a prosecution in the Supreme Court if he was to act on his own responsibility."[31] In reporting this situation to the board, the then acting collector recalled that Mr. Smalley, who had been the collector in 1830, had given an order supporting the 1829 agreement. In reviewing the collector's analysis of bureaucratic precedents and in his request for guidance from the board, it becomes clear that the sustained opposition to the 1829 agreement was made possible, in part, by both the authoritative presence of the government in temple affairs and by the possibility of continued resistance to adverse decisions through appeal to successively higher echelons of the British bureaucracy. The records do not, unfortunately, reveal the final outcome of this episode except to report the recommendation of the collector to appoint a native *pancāyat* to resolve the conflict.

The evidence on three types of dispute over rights and privileges in the redistributive process of the temple between 1826 and 1840 has been considered. The argument concerning the causal relationship between the extension of British control and the exacerbation of temple conflict can be disaggregated as follows. First, as was argued

[30] Ibid., p. 5710.
[31] Ibid., p. 5711.

in the discussion of the *mirāsi* question, the fundamental problem was the contradiction between the "extractive" function of British rule (with its abrogation of local economic rights and relationships) and the "investive" functions of British rule (with its wish to preserve local economic rights and privileges in the interests of stability and productivity). This led to a process of "codification" of local rights and privileges, which was necessarily both *arbitrary* (because the original economic nexus of the relationships in question had been severely disturbed) and *stimulative of conflict* (because individuals and groups used those fractured categories in order to achieve, consolidate, or legitimize claims in the present). This is the explanation of the turmoil around *mirāsi* positions.

Second, this loosening of questions of rights and privileges from an original and specific economic nexus made them a relatively "free" calculus for establishing claims credible to the contemporary bureaucratic and political authority. Thus, a "ripple" effect was created whereby disputes over honors of other types, involving more condensed and discrete symbols of shares in the temple process, became more common. Third, the extension of governmental control presented a new basis for native members of the bureaucracy (who were also "interested" in the temple) to siphon honors in this already conflicted domain.

And finally, the capacity of the *dharmakarta* to arbitrate redistributive conflicts (always finite, as has been argued, owing to the poor distinction between temple and society and the peculiar autonomy of discrete "shares") was further diminished by his willingness (and obligation) to consult a multitiered hierarchy of superiors and by his fear of being dragged into a competing domain of legitimate authority, the court. These four interrelated factors explain the necessary exacerbation of temple conflict by the extension of British control.

British ideology: interference versus self-sufficiency

As previously argued, in the period from 1800 to 1826 British interest in the temple changed from an ad hoc and largely laissez-faire policy to a direct, self-conscious, and rule-governed control of temple administration. This outcome was explained in terms of the three-way interaction between the "explosive" nature of temple conflict, the tension between the executive and judicial branches of the colonial government, and the contradiction between protection and subordination in British administrative policy vis-à-vis Hindu temples. In the preceding section I argued that in the period from 1826 to 1840 the first factor (i.e., the "explosive" nature of temple conflict) was systematically exacerbated by the extension of British control over the temple. What form did the second two factors take in the period 1826–40?

The conflict between executive and judicial authority, so prominent up to 1826, is less visible in the subsequent period, but there is evidence that it continued, although latently, to be a powerful structural factor. It has already been noted that in the *dharmakarta*'s unwillingness to arbitrate a serious temple conflict, a large role was played by his fear of being taken to court. Also, in 1838, evidence exists that the then *dharmakarta* did in fact get involved simultaneously in two suits in the Supreme Court of Madras.[32] Although details of these suits were not available for this study, it is clear that one suit was "an action of Trespass" and the other was for breaking a temple wall. Nevertheless, it seems highly likely that these suits against the *dharmakarta* were additional expressions of the general ferment over temple rights in this period. The board reported to the chief secretary to government that "these actions are apparently brought by a party hostile to the administration of Narasimloo Naick in order to harass him with vexatious suits."[33] It is also interesting to note that one of these suits was on the same grounds as the case against the collector in 1822, except that the reduction of the *dharmakarta* to a subordinate public servant is neatly reflected in his shift from plaintiff to defendant. Significant also is the reaction of the governor-in-council who responded to Narasimloo Naick's appeal for legal and monetary support in exactly the same unsupportive way that he had reacted to the collector's predicament in 1822–6. The chief secretary to government rejected Naick's plea on the grounds that he acted "without proper instructions and in any case the acts complained of were not done in his official capacity as a public officer."[34]

The board, still sympathetic to the plight of the *dharmakarta*, in line with their earlier views, recommended the government's support, "providing he can be shown to have acted within the strict line of his duty."[35] Eventually, the government paid the *dharmakarta*'s costs in one suit out of accumulated temple funds, which he won, but withheld their support in the other suit, pending its result. The

[32] BOR Cons. (IOL), March 1, 1838, 23:2719–20; March 22, 1838, 24:3589–95.
[33] Ibid., March 22, 1838, 24:3594.
[34] Ibid., March 1, 1838, 23:2720.
[35] Ibid., March 22, 1838, 24:3593.

records do not appear to contain this latter outcome. The evidence is sufficient, however, to warrant the assertion that the availability of the court as an alternative arena within which temple rights could be contested continued to exacerbate temple conflict, even though the extension of government control had shifted the structural slots of the contestants.

As for the tension between the protective and subordinative ends of British policy with respect to the temple, it was no longer strictly represented in the tension between the board and the collectors, although elements of that structural conflict remained. This was due to the extension of governmental control and the reduction of the *dharmakarta* to "a public servant." The ideological tension, however, remained powerful, although its mode of expression was somewhat altered. In order to appreciate the transformation of the shape of this problem, it is important to note that in the period 1826-40 there were three *dharmakarta*s, as well as a succession of collectors and acting collectors in Madras to whom these *dharmakarta*s were subordinate. In part, therefore, the tensions in administrative policy reflected, and were caused by, the discontinuities in the incumbency of crucial offices. But it is also clear that a definite and continuous variant of the earlier tension between protection and subordination continued, indeed, in a sharper form than before.

On the one hand, throughout this period it is clear that the radical extension of British control over the temple after 1826 was not merely nominal but real. In 1828, when the contractual agreement was finally signed by the *dharmakarta*, the collector's suggestion for specific control over temple wages, rents, and endowments was rejected.[36] In practice, however, the collectorate did continue for the next twelve years to exercise substantial control over these and other areas. The subjection of the jewels and accounts of the Temple to systematic governmental scrutiny was begun. The *dharmakarta*, already reduced virtually to a public servant, was made to sign a bond worth Rs. 40,000 as a guarantee against peculation. On the death of Annaswamy Pillay in December 1830 and pending the appointment of a successor, the collector proposed that a sizable number of his native subordinates (one *amīnā*, two accountants, and six peons) should be put in joint custody of the temple "with those already there" in order to "prevent the illicit removal of any property from it."[37] This bureaucratic phalanx was to be paid out of the funds of

[36] BOR Cons (IOL), January 3, 1828, 47:448–55.
[37] Ibid., December 30, 1830, 71:1570–1.

the temple. The proposal was approved. At the same time, a proposal by Annaswamy Pillay's widow for certain nominations to the vacancy was flatly rejected. Furthermore, the government reiterated both its now formalized prerogative to appoint *dharmakartas* and also Pillay's quasi-legal admission that the office was held "at the pleasure" of the government and "subject to the immediate control of the governor of Madras."[38]

In 1831 C. Streenivasa Pillay was appointed *dharmakarta* of the temple on the recommendation of the collector. In July 1832, however, Streenivasa Pillay tendered his resignation to the board on grounds of excessive interference from the collectorate.[39] He wrote that he had applied for the job "from the honourable distinction which follows it." But the collector, he argued, treated him like a "mere Ameen in his service," issued orders on matters not worthy of his notice, and because he was "not inclined to dispute the authority of the Collector of Madras for the sake of my honour," he begged to resign.

In explaining his position to the board, the collector alluded to complaints against the *dharmakarta* regarding the performance of festivals and the nonpayment of servants. He said that in this situation there was no choice but to replace him.[40] The collector went on to propose that pending the appointment of a successor, an *amīnā* be appointed for "a few days." The few days of temporary control by the collectorate, however, turned into four years. It was only in 1836 that a new *dharmakarta* was appointed. It was during this period of de facto governmental administration of day-to-day temple affairs, as has already been noted, that the *sheristadar* from the collector's office used his official position to manipulate the redistributive process of the temple.

These government incursions did not go without protest. In 1835 certain *mirāsidārs* of the temple protested against the reappointment of an *amīnā*, previously dismissed, they claimed, for embezzlement.[41] The collector defended the retention of the *amīnā* on the subtle technical ground that the *amīnā*'s name was no longer on the roster of his revenue subordinates. In short, that he was not a temple servant.[42] Even before this, when Annaswamy Pillay had been the

[38] Ibid., January 3, 1831, 2:641–3.
[39] Ibid., July 12, 1832, 46:6408–9.
[40] Ibid., January 3, 1831, 2:641–3.
[41] Ibid., December 10, 1835, 11:14151–2. As was noted in Chapter 1, in 1973 the *amīnā* was very much a temple servant, and no one now recalls the origin of the office, although it is conceded that the term smacks of revenue officialdom.
[42] Ibid., December 14, 1835, 11:14234.

dharmakarta, there were complaints in 1822 that he did not permit the *māṉiyakkāraṉ* (the collector's agent) to examine his accounts or the *sheristadar* to properly audit the temple jewels.[43]

Throughout this period, at the same time that bureaucratic control of the temple was being radically increased, there was a growing and paradoxical affirmation of the ideology of "noninterference" at all levels of government. The board variant of this ideology, generally accepted by the highest echelons of government, continued to express itself in a tendency (seen most clearly in the 1822–6 period) to support the *dharmakarta* in most of his specific complaints against the collector. Specifically, this is seen in their vindication of the *dharmakarta*'s list of *mirāsi* positions in 1828 and in their concomitant rejection of the then collector's additional proposals for the contract to be signed by the *dharmakarta*.

There was, however, a change in the board's conception of how "protection" must be given to the temple. Prior to 1826, "protection" was conceived in terms of the extension of governmental control and the ultimate recourse to the courts. After 1826 there was an increased emphasis on self-regulation for the temple, especially in matters of conflict. During the *mirāsi* controversy in 1826–8, the board suggested the appointment of a native *pancāyat* to make a determination on the rights in question. Eventually, however, the idea seems to have petered out.

The *dharmakarta*'s definition of the situation was accepted. Even at the levels of the collectorate, the fantasy of self-government for the temple was strong. When Annaswamy Pillay died, the then collector proposed a successor for him. At the same time, he suggested to the board that in order to avoid "misappropriation" a permanent body of three native "trustees and auditors" should be formed, who would ease the auditing burden on the collectorate.[44] He suggested several native government employees to fill the positions. His proposal was concluded with the following opinion:

> Upon the whole, I am inclined to think that the Superintendence of the Pagoda should be left as much as possible to the control of the heads of the Hindoo society, and that the Collector should no further interfere than to prevent any abuse, and to receive the annual accounts.[45]

It should be remembered that this was the very same collector who, by the humiliating nature of his interference, had caused the resigna-

[43] Ibid.
[44] Ibid., February 14, 1831, 5:1960–2.
[45] Ibid., p. 1962.

tion of the new *dharmakarta* in 1832. The board rejected this proposal but endorsed the principle on which it was based.

The collector's proposal was not entirely hypocritical. It reflects a real contradiction between the systematic extension of his control in order to "protect" the temple and the necessity of interpreting and arbitrating an increasingly complex series of temple conflicts. For this type of increasingly delicate arbitration, neither the collector nor the board had the capacity or patience. Similarly, in the 1840 honors case involving the Poonamallee Mudaliars, the board accepted with alacrity the collector's proposal that a native *pancāyat* should investigate and resolve the matter.

This micro problem, of turning to *pancāyat* models of self-government in response to increasing conflict exacerbated by executive control of the temple, has a macro context. From 1816 onward, but especially after 1828, under the administration of Governor Munro, there had been an increasing shift to *pancāyat*s for the arbitration of local conflicts.[46] Munro had supported and systematized this tendency on the basis of three arguments: (1) the increasing expenditure on judicial establishments because of the multiplication of courts, (2) the "traditional" efficacy of *pancāyat*s for local disputes, and (3) the resulting hope that the revival of this institution would render the government more acceptable to the people. It has been noted often that this was only one policy expression of a larger myth concerning the traditional self-sufficiency of the Indian village that was shared by a large and significant body of English administrators throughout the late eighteenth and nineteenth centuries.

Louis Dumont has pointed out the peculiar construction of this myth, which conceded the economic dependency on the state of the village but at the same time insisted on the political self-sufficiency of the village.[47] Whereas Dumont is interested in this contradiction for other reasons, it seems to be the most direct expression of the contradiction in British rule, noted previously, between the motives of extraction and investment. Specifically, it reflects a desire to avoid the responsibility of dealing with conflicts generated by British disturbance of agrarian relations through a stubbornly high revenue assessment, with a relatively low regard for local rights and privileges *and* encouraged by the availability of the courts to deal with such local conflicts.

[46] M. P. Jain, *Outlines of Indian Legal History* (Bombay, 1972), pp. 275–80.

[47] Louis Dumont, "The 'Village Community' from Munro to Maine," in *Contributions to Indian Sociology* 9 (Paris, 1966):66–89.

Here the investment aspect of British ideology is seen in a wish to maximize stability, to minimize lengthy and expensive litigation, and to increase the popularity of government. The *pancāyat* ideology of Munro was also a response to the basic division of authority between the judiciary and the executive. The *pancāyat* was seen explicitly as an attempt to reunite judicial and executive powers in the same body at the local level, and in so doing, effectively to contain local conflict before it entered the courts and thus avoid lengthy and expensive litigation.

By 1840, therefore, the British bureaucracy found itself in a rather strange dilemma. The wish to protect the temple had resulted in a radical extension of its control of the temple. In thus extending their control, the British escalated temple conflict, leading to disputes that they found impossible and distasteful to arbitrate. This regenerated at all bureaucratic levels the older emphasis on noninterference in the new form of *pancāyat* rule for the temple. The increased subordination of the temple to the control of the revenue bureaucracy had neither eliminated the accusations of misappropriation nor preempted the shift of conflicts to the court. Thus, just at the time when the idea of protection seems to have become subsumed by the idea of subordination, the laissez-faire element in the board's protection policy resurfaced in a repeated desire for *pancāyat* rule. Until 1840 this wish was a fantasy. The complete dependence of the temple on British subsidy and control made internal resolutions of conflict more unrealistic than they intrinsically were. Thus the tension between protection and subordination had not disappeared, although its expression had. Subordination was systematized, and the idea of protection had changed into the fantasy of temple self-government, by implication a fantasy of "withdrawal."

A new sectarian politics

The preceding chapters have discussed the Vaṭakalai-Teṉkalai schism in medieval South Indian Vaisnavism and its transformation from a scholastic controversy to a full-fledged battle for temple control in the late sixteenth, seventeenth, and eighteenth centuries. An analysis was also made of conflicts between the Teṉkalais and Vaṭakalais in Triplicane in the eighteenth century and of the tacit control of the temple at the end of the eighteenth century by the Teṉkalais. Between 1800 and 1831 there is little evidence that the idea of Teṉkalai affiliation was a crucial element of the political identity of the native community interested in the temple. During this period, the Teṉkalai community apparently did have de facto control over both temple ritual and temple management. But in their descriptions of the issues underlying temple conflicts, their *mahazarnamā*s in support of candidates for the churchwardenship, and in their self-description in any of the petitions to government, there is no mention of their Teṉkalai affiliations. In these petitions to the government, where individuals and groups were anxious to describe themselves as possessing a legitimate and credible interest in the temple, they preferred to rely on specific roles, rights, ranks, or caste affiliations. Thus, the petitioners described themselves variously as: *mirāsi* servants, Śrī Vaisnava Brahmins (Ghosty Brahmins), Nattars, Desayees, "all the inhabitants of Triplicane," and so on. In no case did a petitioner justify his interest on the basis of being a "Teṉkalai" or of representing Teṉkalais.

But in 1831 the idea of being Teṉkalai begins to become an important referent in temple politics. When C. Streenivasa Pillay applied for the churchwardenship of the temple in 1831, his application was based, in part, on being of the "same sect and caste" as his predecessor.[48] This tacit reference to his Teṉkalai affiliations is the first explicit and self-conscious invitation to the British to formalize the sectarian idea as a principle for local temple control. In 1833 the acting collector of Madras reported to the board an attempt by a Vaṭakalai to take over the churchwardenship in the confused 1832–6 hiatus.[49] The collector reported that he was then desired to "obtain the usual *mahazarnamā* from the respective Brahmins of Triplicane and the inhabitants in general, but he has failed in doing so, and the Ghosty Brahmins of the Pagoda and the Nattars and Desayees of the village have objected to Nullah Rimga Pillay being appointed because he is of the Vadagala sect – the Former Dharmakarthas were all of the Tengala sect and it is their wish that a person of that description should be selected."[50]

In 1835, in reporting complaints against manipulation of the redistributive process by the *sheristadar* from the collector's office, the collector noted some significant facts. He reported to the board that "the petitioners who call themselves the Tangala Brahmins of Triplicane assert their sole right to the Pagoda there to the exclusion of the Vatakalas, but this is a question on which it is not perhaps

48 BOR Cons. (IOL), February 1, 1831, 5:1959.
49 Ibid., January 24, 1833, 68:961–2.
50 Ibid., p. 962.

necessary that any inquiry should be instituted for the present."[51] On the other hand, the collector also reported that a *mahazarnamā* from "Tengala Gosty Brahmins and others"[52] testified that the petitioners were troublemakers, the ultimate cause of the confused condition of the pagoda.

Finally, in 1836, when Narasimloo Naick was proposed for the churchwardenship, the temple community became divided along lines of "right and left hand castes,"[53] and the government received petitions claiming that Naick was a member of the right-hand caste and that his nomination would create riots and disorder. The collector had already reported to the board that Naick is "of the Beljee caste and the same sect with former Dharmakartas – persons of this description appear to have held the office prior to the appointment of the late Annaswamy Pillay's ancestors."[54] In response, the board, concerned about threats of conflict between the right- and left-hand castes, asked to "know to what sect the former Dharmakarta therein alluded to belonged."[55]

In reply, the collector gave formal, if unconscious, recognition to Teṉkalai temple control by reporting that "the former Dhurmacurtahs of the Triplicane Pagoda were all Tengalahs, the sect to which S. Narasimloo Naick belongs."[56] The right/left conflict, as is its nature, was soon resolved and Naick took control. But the idea of Teṉkalai monopoly of temple control had taken root in the interaction between changing native self-descriptions and British bureaucratic formalization. The interaction itself had a broader context, which has been analyzed in the previous two arguments concerning renewed temple conflict and the tensions in British ideology regarding the temple.

The general flux over temple rights and the hiatus in temple control between 1832 and 1836 provoked Vaṭakalai attempts to control or manipulate the distributive process of the temple. In response, the temple community began to define its rights explicitly in terms of Teṉkalai affiliations. With the general British urge to fix temple rights and their specific tendency to render the temple "self-

[51] BOR Cons. (IOL), August 20, 1835, 1:9229.
[52] Ibid., p. 9234.
[53] For a general discussion of this phenomenon, see Arjun Appadurai, "Right and Left Hand Castes in South India," *Indian Economic and Social History Review* 11, Nos. 2–3 (June–September 1974):216–59.
[54] BOR Cons. (TA), August 25, 1836, 1518:11601–2.
[55] Ibid., August 4, 1836, 1514:10567.
[56] Ibid., p. 10570.

governing," it was natural that they gravitated toward formalizing Teṉkalai affiliation as the dominant criterion for temple control. Nevertheless, until 1840, the semantic function of the term *Teṉkalai*, in its use by all parties, remained essentially contrastive with external (i.e., Vaṭakalai) claims and pretensions.

The shift to court: 1841–1878

Starting in 1841, and in response to pan-Indian as well as domestic pressures, the court of directors of the East India Company decided to withdraw from "all interference with native religious establishments,"[57] a move that was viewed with alarm by at least some natives in Madras. In response to a petition requesting the reconsideration of this decision, the chief secretary to the Madras government reiterated its orders to the board: "The Board will further carefully explain to the Petitioners that the object of the recent orders is to give them the sole control of their own religious institutions, that they will still be protected by the Courts of Justice, and that the Magistrates will take care that the peace shall be maintained on all occasions."[58]

The collector of Madras was given the responsibility of making appropriate arrangements for withdrawal from "interference" with the temples in Madras city. On January 16, 1843, the collector recommended that two men, Narasimloo Naick (the current *dharmakarta*) and Vencatanarayana Pillay, be appointed trustees of the Triplicane temple. As for the selection of successors, the collector made the following statement, which for the subsequent century of temple politics was a major referent: "The selection of a trustee on the occurrence of a vacancy may be left to the suffrage of the community of the Tengala sect as has heretofore been customary on the occasion of the appointment of a Dharmakarta."[59] Later that month the collector added another trustee, V. Sadagopachariar (the first Brahmin trustee since 1795), and enclosed *mahazarnamās* in favor of all three members by groups identifying themselves as Teṉkalais interested in the temple.[60] The board ratified these appointments.

[57] BOR Cons. (TA), August 8, 1836, 1515:10711–12.

[58] On the process and context of British "withdrawal" from temples, see Chandra Y. Mudaliar, *The Secular State and Religious Institutions in India: A Study of the Administration of Hindu Public Religious Trusts in Madras* (Wiesbaden, 1974), pp. 16–23.

[59] BOR Cons. (IOL), January 17, 1842, 741:37.

[60] Ibid., January 16, 1843, 25:1420.

Regarding the principles for filling vacancies, the board tacitly rejected the collector's suggestions and said that the government was considering legislation that would provide a standard for judging various claims to the vacancy.[61] This tacit rejection was never mentioned again in any subsequent discussion. The collector's suggestion, by its very decisiveness, became, as we shall see, a monumental political charter. In 1847 C. Narasimloo Naick died. The surviving trustees proposed that his son, T. Ramanjulu Naidu, should be appointed trustee. They sought the ratification of the collector for the appointment. The then collector refused involvement but reiterated the 1843 collector's statement about the "suffrage of the community of the Tengala sect."[62] In so doing, he elevated this mere suggestion to an accepted principle. In any case, this was apparently taken as adequate ratification, and the appointment does not appear to have been contested.

Act XX of 1863 was the first major legislation pertaining to South Indian temples since Regulation VII of 1817. Its major contribution was the creation of Native District Committees to oversee temples within their jurisdictions.[63] In 1865 there was apparently a move toward creating such a committee to oversee the Triplicane temple, consisting of Teṉkalais, Vaṭakalais, and Smārta Brahmins. In September 1865 a petition from "the Thengalai inhabitants of Triplicane" to the collector of Madras protested this proposition in elaborate and instructive terms.[64] The petitioners referred to the already classic 1843 dictum and its 1847 reiteration as a charter for Teṉkalai control over the temple. They attributed the long-standing "peace and tranquility" of the temple to "the non-holding of any mirassi right or privilege whatever in it by any other sectarians but Thengalais, and to the non-interference of any other sectarians but of Thengalais in the conduct of the duties and worship and in the management of the affairs thereof."

The petitioners predicted that the Vaṭakalai and Smārta members of the committee would "try to introduce such innovations in the temple as might create some right" or other to the persons of their respective sects. Whether or not the trustee acceded to such attempts, there would be "continual disturbances, quarrels and dis-

[61] Collector to BOR secretary, January 25, 1843, in list of documents attached to Writ Appeal 17 of 1953 against Writ Petition 4840 of 1951 (Madras High Court).

[62] BOR Cons. (IOL), February 13, 1843, 27:2457–8.

[63] On Act XX of 1863, see Mudaliar, *Secular State*, pp. 23–31.

[64] Collector at Madras in reply to petition, February 17, 1847, documents cited in Writ Appeal 17 of 1953.

putes" in the temple. When the collector transmitted this petition to the government, the officials decreed that because the government had severed its connection with the temple in 1843, it would not fall under the jurisdiction of a committee appointed under Act XX of 1863.[65] This important decision rendered the temple allegedly self-governing. Similarly, it altered the substance of its future politics, if not its structure.

In one crucial respect, that is, economically, the government found itself incapable of severing its connections to the temple. Of the four payments to the temple that the government was making by 1832, two were dropped. The *makamai* allowance was canceled on the grounds that "it was a pure act of indulgence by the government for which they received no equivalent, and which they are in no way bound to continue."[66] The compensation for the resumed taxes on such items as shops and carts allotted in 1832 was simply forgotten. The allowance paid out of the quitrent of the temple to subsidize its ritual was seen as a firm commitment in 1804 that could not be reneged upon. Thus, it was to be continued at the rate of Rs. 1,050 per annum.[67] A wish, expressed by the government in 1853, that the trustees themselves might resume making these quitrent collections, rather than continuing to burden the government with this task, came to nought. The payment continued to be made to the temple by the collector of Madras until 1870 and by the accountant general at Fort St. George thereafter.

Finally, the *mērai* payment (also referred to as a *tastīk* payment), in lieu of resumed lands, also continued to be paid to the temple, through the collector of Chingleput (because the resumed lands were in that district). Attempts in 1857 to force the trustees to choose lands in lieu of the cash *tastīk* (so as to aid bureaucratic disengagement) had apparently failed. Instead, the payment continued to be made. This last payment was worth Rs. 1,793 per annum.[68] These two payments, reminders of the government's prior financial involvement in the temple, provided the instruments for factional conflict in the 1870s, conflict that ended up in the High Court of Judicature at Madras.

In March 1872 V. Sadagopachariar, the Brahmin trustee, died. The accountant general of Madras received a petition from a group

[65] See documents cited in ibid.
[66] Ibid., Government Order, October 13, 1865.
[67] BOR Cons. (TA), August 8, 1853, 25:2382, 9472.
[68] BOR Cons. (IOL), February 6, 1854, 25:2076–8.

in Triplicane to withhold the customary payments to the surviving *dharmakartas* until a third trustee had been properly elected.[69] The accountant general also received a counterpetition from another group "who claimed the right of selection."[70] They requested that the payments should continue to be made to them, pending the appointment of a third trustee. This request was granted, and until December 1874 the two surviving trustees continued to receive the payments in question. Early in 1875 conflict erupted again, in response to the attempts of the two surviving trustees to involve the dead trustee's son in temple affairs.[71] They tried to make him the third trustee by having him cosign the receipt for the government payments. This was protested by an opposed faction at Triplicane, and later attempts to legitimize his appointment by petitions were decried as improper and unpopular. Between 1875 and 1876, the accountant general received a total of nine petitions from both sides, arguing their positions.[72] This placed the accountant general in a quandary. Payments to the temple were frozen.

The arguments of the faction led by the surviving trustees began, as usual, with both an invocation of the 1843 bureaucratic charter and a claim that their action in electing the dead trustee's son "was by the suffrage of the Tengala Community, as has heretofore been customary."[73] In a subsequent petition, this position was given a more specific and self-interested meaning. It was argued that the previous practice had been for the surviving trustees to appoint a successor from among the heirs or the nearest male relations of the dead man.[74] The Teṉkalai community, it was argued, had only the right to acquiesce in the choice by their silence or to oppose it by presenting counterpetitions to the relevant authority. This was followed by an argument in favor of restricting the positive rights of the community in electing a successor. "In the event of leaving the selection itself to the community of such a large populous place it was to be apprehended that the selection would not be likely to fall upon a proper person considering the transition state of the Hindu society as well as the anxiety prevailing generally among all ranks of the Hindu community especially among those in opulent and influential

[69] Ibid., February 6, 1858, 1:2528–30.
[70] Petition of March 9, 1872, in documents cited in Writ Appeal 17 of 1953.
[71] Petition of March 19, 1872 in ibid.
[72] Written statement of first defendant in C.S. 486 of 1878 (High Court of Judicature at Madras), Record Room, Original Side, High Court of Madras.
[73] See documents in C.S. 486 of 1878, High Court of Judicature at Madras.
[74] See plaint in ibid., December 11, 1878, para. 13.

circumstances to get into the management of such a rich and reputed Pagoda and the consequent facility for the latter to canvas votes."[75] The surviving trustees based their case, for the right to appoint a successor, on the government's refusal to interfere in the 1846 succession issue, which they read as a proof that they were competent to fill the vacancy.[76] As for their opponents, the view of the surviving trustees was to deny their credibility on prima facie grounds. They claimed that the persons objecting to their procedure were not competent to do so, for "the party or parties making such objection ought properly to establish his or their right before a competent authority."[77]

On the side opposed to the surviving trustees and their proposed candidate for the vacancy, a different set of arguments was made. The counterpetitioners argued that in attempting to nominate the dead trustee's son, the surviving trustees were trying "to make their place hereditary and to create a mirassi right."[78] In reviewing the previous history of the temple, the counterpetitions argued that the selection and nomination of new trustees had always been made by the "Tengalai goshti" (community) and that in no sense had there ever existed any hereditary rights to the trusteeship.[79] It was further argued that those who had signed petitions in favor of the trustees were not "competent" to vote: Some were alleged not to be natives of Triplicane, some were not concerned with the temple, some were the relatives of the proposed candidate, and some were menial servants in the temple.[80]

These petitioners prayed that the government payments should be made only to the two surviving trustees until "the question of Civil Right involved in the appointment of Churchwardens by a Civil Tribunal"[81] was determined. If the new candidate insisted on being acknowledged, they prayed that "he might be ordered to go to a Civil Court to establish his right if any."[82] In later counterpetitions the lack of credibility of the trustees' supporters was reiterated and

[75] Written statement of first defendant, January 20, 1879, in C.S. 486 of 1878, para. 7.

[76] Ibid., para. 12: letter to accountant general, Fort St. George, October 22, 1875.

[77] Ibid., para. 13: letter to deputy accountant general from two trustees, October 26, 1875.

[78] Ibid., para. 5: petition to accountant general, February 1, 1875.

[79] Ibid., para. 6: petition to solicitor general, government of Madras, from certain "Tengalai Goshti Brahmans," February 8, 1975.

[80] Ibid.

[81] Ibid.

[82] Ibid.

insinuations of corrupt patronage were leveled. It was argued that instead of making an open claim to hereditary trusteeship, the surviving trustees "made the false petitioners acknowledge that the right to nominate belongs to the surviving Churchwardens at the sacrifice of public interest."[83]

By late 1875 there was a deadlock. All parties were threatening, or demanding, legal action. In October the accountant general refused to resume the payments to the temple unless an order was obtained from the High Court of Judicature at Madras.[84] In December 1878 a plaint was filed by the two surviving trustees and the proposed candidate, citing the secretary of state for India in Council as the first defendant and eight members of the Triplicane community as codefendants. Titled *Vencatanarayana Pillay* v. *Secretary of State for India in Council*, this suit is discussed in Chapter 5 as representing the first phase in a new epoch of the political history of the temple. At this point it is sufficient to note that in the petitions of this period both sides described themselves as appropriate representatives of the "Teṉkalai Community of Triplicane." Similarly, both sides took as their charter the collector's dictum of 1843 whereby the filling of vacancies in the trusteeship was to "be left to the suffrage of the community of the Tengala sect as has heretofore been customary."

The problem, of course, was to define the appropriate constructtion to be placed on this 1843 dictum. This, the government was neither willing nor capable of doing.

The shift of scenario to the court was inexorable. It is important to note, as well, that the term *Teṉkalai*, in its political usage, had already lost its strictly *contrastive* meaning. That is to say, it was no longer a matter of keeping Vaṭakalais out of shares in temple control. Rather, it was a matter of deciding the concrete, operational, and substantive definition of Teṉkalai control over the temple.

This chapter began with certain observations regarding the fundamental differences between Hindu sovereigns and the British rulers of South India in their relations with temples. Summarily, these differences were in: (1) the basic abolition of *king-deity honors transactions* that were the cultural and moral basis of temple-state relations and the concomitant shift from sectarian groups and leaders as the operational machinery of this relationship to centralized bureau-

83 Ibid., para. 11: petition, September 14, 1875, from "Thengalai Goshty Brahmans and Sthallatars."

84 Ibid., para. 14.

cratic structures as the mediators of this relationship; (2) the replacement of the pre-British emphasis on *minimal* day-to-day "bureaucratic" involvement by sovereigns in temple affairs and highly valued, direct arbitration in temple conflict by a reversed emphasis on maximal rule-governed, day-to-day state control, accompanied by an avoidance of the arbitration of most temple disputes; and (3) the shift from the unitary model of the Hindu king as judge-cum-administrator to an institutional structure in which the supervision of temples was divided between bureaucracy and judiciary.

Changes between 1800 and 1878 in the relationship between the colonial state and Hindu temples can be accounted for partly in terms of the macro interaction of these factors all over India.

The decision of the directors of the East India Company to accede to the demands of missionary lobbies in India, as well as in the English press and Parliament, to withdraw from the "patronage" of native religious institutions in 1842 reflected a readiness to end the illusions of continuity between pre-British and British sovereign attitudes to temples. Given that the core of this indigenous relationship, predicated on honors transactions between kings and deities, had never engaged British policy or ideology,[85] it is not surprising that the husk was willingly discarded, especially as such illusions were increasingly unnecessary for the security of the colonial regime after 1830.

Certainly after the passage of Regulation VII of 1817, the legislative basis for state interference in temples became paramount. Built into Regulation VII and Regulation XX of 1863 was the notion that, in the last analysis, only the courts could decisively arbitrate temple conflict. The withdrawal of the British bureaucracy from direct involvement in temple affairs after 1842 and the shift of temple conflicts to the court were the inevitable consequences of the separation of executive and judiciary under British rule and the reluctance of British bureaucrats to arbitrate temple disputes.

However, the active interaction of the British bureaucracy with Hindu temples up to 1842 had serious consequences. In the case of

[85] The outcry of missionaries and publicists against British governmental involvement in native temples (accusing it, for example, of being the "dry nurse of Vishnu"), notwithstanding, the only serious aspect of all these criticisms was that the English government ought not to be economically subsidizing native temples. This "subsidy," I have tried to show, is radically different, in its bureaucratic and compensatory character, from the style of Hindu sovereigns. Certainly, the other forms of British "patronage" of native temples, such as having government troops at festivals to maintain "order," are *sui generis* and have no real counterpart in the style of their Hindu predecessors.

the Śrī Pārtasārati Svāmi Temple, the bureaucratic tendency toward codification combined with an arbitrary bureaucratic definition in 1843 to generate a new, constitutive meaning for the term *Teṉkalai*. With the dissolution, under British rule, of the king-sect-temple connection, the term *Teṉkalai* ceased to connote sectarian rivalry in the pan-regional medieval sense.

In the course of the nineteenth century, the term *Teṉkalai* acquired a primarily local and constitutional connotation. The decipherment of this new, local, and constitutive meaning of the term *Teṉkalai* kept the temple in court continuously from 1878 to 1924. The interaction between temple and court in this period is the subject of the following chapter.

5

LITIGATION AND THE POLITICS OF SECTARIAN CONTROL, 1878–1925

The continuous interaction between the temple and the Anglo-Indian judicial system between 1878 and 1925 has features of both local and comparative interest. In the first place, it reveals the process by which native litigants appropriate an alien legal language (both literally and metaphorically) to their own purposes. More important, it reveals the transformation of previously social categories into actual social organizations, of previously ritually constructed privileges into bureaucratically defined ones, and of a relatively fluid system of alliances into a relatively rigid and antagonistic set of interest groups. These three processes, which are here discussed in a highly specific cultural and historical milieu, might constitute the key processual features of a more generally applicable model of how modern colonial regimes (especially those based on Anglo-Saxon legal traditions) affect indigenous political and cultural systems.

For organizational and stylistic reasons, this chapter is divided into two parts. The first section places the argument of this chapter in the context of the preceding chapters, as well as in the general theoretical context of the impact of English law and legal institutions on Indian society in general and South Indian temples in particular. This provides a general theoretical and historical backdrop for the specific ethnohistorical analysis of data from the Śrī Pārtasārati Svāmi Temple during this period. The second section, therefore, locates the general issues raised in the first in a specific micro context.

English law and temple legislation

In the first chapter of this study, it was argued that the sovereign personality of the deity in the South Indian temple was, potentially, a structural source of conflict in the temple, as well as a potential hindrance to the smooth resolution of such conflict. Chapter 2 argued that in pre-British South India the transactions between kings and temples, through sectarian intermediaries, provided a framework within which the sovereignty of human rulers was maintained and extended and the arbitration of temple disputes was authoritatively performed. With the arrival of the British in South India and the consolidation of their rule in the eighteenth and nineteenth centuries, key features of the relationship between the temple and the state were altered. In Chapters 3 and 4, it was argued that the separation of the executive and the judiciary, along with British administrative vacillation between ideas of protection and subordination in respect to the temple, resulted in the exacerbation of temple conflict and the incipient reification of a new sociopolitical category, "the Teṉkalai community of Triplicane." After 1842, and the withdrawal of British bureaucratic "interference" (unthinkable under the indigenous model of shared sovereignty), it became increasingly clear that the dominant external factor in temple politics would be the English judicial system in South India.

Before going on to analyze the impact of the English judiciary on Śrī Pārtasārati Svāmi Temple, the analysis of royal arbitration of temple conflict in the pre-British period (following Lingat, in Chapter 2) must be briefly recapitulated. The actions of the Hindu king, in authoritatively solving temple disputes, resembled those of an *administrator,* not a legislator. Thus, decisions were made to suit contexts and did not either strictly follow or generate a body of general rules. Thus, although the "Hindu Law" (*dharmasāstra*) was subject, in fact, to historical change, it was not considered to be either the direct source or the logical outcome of decisions in particular cases. English courts, on the other hand, followed a mixture of legislation (contained in a series of acts, codes, and regulations) and "precedent" generated by previous judicial decisions.[1] In both respects, the "context-sensitive" model of previous royal arbitration of temple disputes was altered. The general rules, as well as the "judge-made" law of the English courts, had unanticipated effects on temple politics, effects that this chapter will describe and analyze.

British law in the Indian colonial context

As in other areas of British policy in India, so in the realm of law, the pragmatic and ideological needs of British rule largely overcame any intentions of "preserving" the indigenous cultures and institutions of the subject population. Just as British revenue policies oscillated

[1] For an excellent general discussion of this aspect of English law, see R. Cross, *Precedent in English Law* (Oxford, 1961). For cross-cultural discussions that place the ideal of "precedent" in context, see Lloyd A. Fallers, *Law Without Precedent: Legal Ideas in Action in the Courts of Colonial Basoga* (Chicago, 1969), passim, but especially pp. 17–19; also, Max Rheinstein, ed., *Max Weber on Law in Economy and Society* (New York, 1967), Chap. 5, passim.

between laissez-faire and utilitarian/reformist goals, so British policies in respect of law and the judicial system in India oscillated between the wish to leave Indian "custom and usage" intact and the wish to create rationality and uniformity in indigenous law. The cumulative effect of these ambivalent motives was the massive, though often covert, importation of English ideas and mechanisms into the legal system in India and the serious, though unintended, alteration of key features of Indian society and culture.

Until 1862 the British-Indian courts were organized in a two-tiered system of bifurcated type: Supreme Courts in the presidency towns (Madras, Bombay, Calcutta), which were wholly modeled on the Court of the King's Bench in England, and *mofussil* (provincial) courts, which were under the authority of the East India Company. In 1862, four years after the English crown had assumed direct rule over India, these two systems were fused. High Courts were created in Bombay, Madras, and Calcutta, which were the original and appellate courts of the presidency towns, and in their respective provinces appellate courts comprised the lower judical apparatus. Thus a single system of courts was established in 1862 in which there was only one major departure from the English model: The English distinction between law and equity, which had never been important in British India, was ignored, and English common law and English equitable doctrines were fused, both in Indian legislation as well as in case law, partly through the powerful influence of the judges of the High Courts and the percolation of their synthetic use of English principles of law and equity into the lower courts.[2]

As early as 1781, judges in Indian courts were enjoined to operate on the English maxim of "justice, equity and good conscience,"[3] thus creating a major channel for the entry of English legal concepts into Indian courts. This tendency was encouraged by the growing impulse of British administrators in India in the nineteenth century to codify the diverse laws of Indians in the interests of uniformity, regularity, and certainty, a plan that was Roman in its aspirations and Benthamite in its inspiration.[4] The result of this process of codification was the importation, on a considerable scale, of portions of English law,[5] now in a more explicit form than in the covert guise of "justice, equity and good conscience," although even the latter

[2] M. C. Setalvad, *The Common Law in India* (Bombay, 1970), pp. 32–3 and 57–62.

[3] Lloyd I. Rudolph and Suzanne H. Rudolph, *The Modernity of Tradition: Political Development in India* (Chicago, 1967), pp. 282–3.

[4] Ibid., pp. 284–5.

[5] Sir Benjamin Lindsay, "Law," in L. S. S. O'Malley, ed., *Modern India and the West* (London, 1941), p. 112.

concept was a fruitful channel for importation.[6] English law, thus imported in both overt and covert forms, had the most serious effects on Indian society. This was so at many levels. According to one analyst of the British law in India:

> The jural postulates that underlie the British introduced courts – equality in the eyes of law, judicial ignorance of the complainants, the idea that economic relations are based on contract not status, the goal of settling the case at hand and only that case, and the necessity of a clear-cut decision rather than a compromise – were at odds with a wide range of adjudication procedures followed in the villages of India.[7]

More specifically, the doctrine of *stare decisis*, embodying the fundamental importance of precedent in English common law, began, after the 1820s, to take increasing hold in the Anglo-Indian legal system, creating its own powerful tendency toward the rigidification and stabilization of a law that had previously been remarkably adapted to various and changing conditions.[8] Although the results of this Anglicization of the law were generally a source of pride to the British in the realm of criminal law and much of the civil law, they were a constant embarrassment in the realm of "personal" law (i.e., the law that applied to Hindus and Muslims in matters relating to marriage and divorce, adoption, joint family guardianship, minority, legitimacy, inheritance, succession, and religious endowments).[9]

From the beginnings of British rule until at least the end of the nineteenth century, a pious fiction was propounded and frequently reaffirmed that in these matters Hindus were to be ruled according to "Hindu Law." What this so-called Hindu Law was remained unclear, and for the first century of British rule an astonishing process of search, translation, compilation, and distribution was unleashed for "Hindu" texts that would provide the basis for a "Hindu Law" to be applied by the courts in all "personal" matters to Hindu natives.[10] The goal that underlay this massive production of "Hindu" texts was to assure "clarity, certainty and finality in terms foreign to Hindu tradition."[11] Its results, predictably, were to

[6] J. D. M. Derrett, *Religion, Law and the State in India* (London, 1968), pp. 311–12.

[7] Bernard S. Cohn, "Anthropological Notes on Disputes and Law in India," *American Anthropologist* 67, No. 6 (December 1965):105, Pt. 2.

[8] Lindsay, "Law," p. 130; Setalvad, *Common Law in India*, pp. 48–52; Bernard S. Cohn, "From Indian Status to British Contract," *Journal of Economic History* 21 (December 1961):614–15.

[9] Cohn, "Anthropological Notes," p. 111.

[10] Derrett, *Religion, Law and the State*, Chap. 8, passim.

[11] Ibid., p. 269.

further confuse matters and, to some extent, to ossify and standardize a law that had previously been highly various and adaptable.[12] In addition, codification and case law made their inroads into "Hindu Law," which by the end of the nineteenth century was "mainly based on published cases and was to be to a lesser extent based on Indian legislation."[13] The drastic effects of this massive new Anglo-Indian law on social relations in the realms of caste,[14] land,[15] and family[16] in India are well established. But in the matter of religious endowments, the complex consequences of this Anglo-Indian system of law are less clearly understood. It is to this gap in our knowledge that this chapter is partially addressed.

Unlike other areas of the "personal" law of Hindus, where it was possible to discover "Hindu" law texts (however dubious their origin and unclear their scope), in the area of religious endowments, the texts are uniformly meager. This has been the consensus of English codifiers,[17] Anglo-Indian judges,[18] and twentieth-century compilers of the "law of endowments."[19] Although there have been numerous explanations of this strange paucity of indigenous law on so transparently important a subject, the most plausible theory follows from the analysis of the kingly role in respect to temples, extending Lingat's general model, which is presented in Chapter 2.

Because the activities of Hindu kings in respect to temples were "administrative" and not "legislative," and because their resolutions were context specific and not absorbed into a general body of evolving case law, it is no surprise that a "law of endowments" had not

[12] For a trenchant critique of this "Hindu Law" by a nineteenth-century English administrator, see the following three works by J. H. Nelson: *A View of the Hindu Law as Administered by the High Court of Judicature at Madras* (Madras, 1877); *A Prospectus of the Scientific Study of the Hindu Law* (London, 1881); and *Indian Usage and Judge-Made Law in Madras* (London, 1887).

[13] Cohn, "Anthropological Notes," p. 113.

[14] An important series of articles by Marc Galanter has discussed the relationship between caste and law; see particularly, "Law and Caste in Modern India," *Asian Survey* 3, No. 11 (1963):544–59, and "The Abolition of Disabilities – Untouchability and the Law," in J. Michael Mahar, ed., *The Untouchables in Contemporary India* (Tucson, 1972), pp. 227–314.

[15] For example, Cohn, "From Indian Status," pp. 618–22.

[16] J. D. M. Derrett, *Hindu Law Past and Present* (Calcutta, 1957).

[17] T. Strange, *Hindu Law*, 2 vols. (London, 1830), 1:32.

[18] Judgment in *Girijan and Datta Jha* v. *Sailajanund Datta Jha*, in *Indian Law Reports*, 23:653, cited in P. V. Kane, *History of Dharmasāstra*, 2nd ed., 5 vols. (Poona, 1974), 1:32.

[19] Kane, *History of Dharmasāstra*, 2:910 ff., Pt. 2; A. Ghosh, *The Law of Endowments (Hindu and Mohameddan)*, 2nd ed. (Calcutta, 1938), pp. 3–4; P. R. Ganapathy Iyer, *The Law Relating to Hindu and Mohameddan Endowments*, 2nd ed. (Madras, 1918), pp. 20–23.

developed; instead, only an inscriptional record of specific instances of royal intervention and arbitration existed. But this seeming gap was rapidly filled by the British impulse to legislate and codify, especially where such an obvious vacuum was seen to exist. What was the specific content of British legislation and codification that had a bearing on the legal resolution of temple conflict? What was the scope and source of these newly created provisions?

The specific portions of British-Indian law to affect the legal resolution of temple conflict between 1878 and 1925 were portions of the Religious Endowment Act XX of 1863 (briefly discussed in Chapter 4) and portions of the Civil Procedure Code of 1877, 1882, and 1908. The relevant portions of the 1863 act were Sections 14 and 15:

Section 14. Any person or persons interested in any mosque, temple or religious establishment, or in the performance of the worship or of the service thereof, may, without joining as plaintiff any of the other persons interested therein, sue before the Civil Court the trustee, manager or superintendent of such mosque, temple or religious establishment or the member of any committee appointed under this Act, for any misfeasance, breach of trust or neglect of duty, committed by such trustee, manager, superintendent or member of such committees in respect of the trust vested in, or confided to them respectively; and the Civil Court may direct the specific performance of any act by such trustee, manager, superintendent or member of committee, and may decree damages and costs against such trustee, manager, superintendent or member of a committee, and may also direct the removal of such trustee, manager, superintendent or member of a committee.

Section 15. The interest required in order to entitle a person to sue under the last preceding section need not be a pecuniary, or a direct or immediate interest or such an interest as would entitle the person suing to take any part in the management or superintendence of the trusts. Any person having the right of attendance, or having been in the habit of attending, at the performance of the worship or service of any mosque, temple or religious establishment, or of partaking in the benefit of any distribution of alms, shall be deemed to be a person interested within the meaning of the last preceding section.[20]

The second specific statutory provision that had important effects on temple conflict was Section 539 of the Civil Procedure Code of 1877, which was slightly altered in Section 539 of the Civil Procedure Codes of 1882 and 1908. The three consecutive texts that represented this provision in the three codes were:

[20] Ghosh, *Law of Endowments*, p. 1016.

Section 539 of the Civil Procedure Code of 1877:
In case of any alleged breach of any express or constructive trust created for public charitable purposes, or whenever the direction of the Court is deemed necessary for the administration of any such trust, the Advocate General acting *ex officio,* or two or more persons having a direct interest in the trust and having obtained the consent in writing of the Advocate General, may institute a suit in the High Court or the District Court within the local limits of whose jurisdiction the whole or any part of the subject matter of the trust is situate, to obtain a decree

(a) appointing new trustees of the charity
(b) vesting any property in the trustees of the charity
(c) declaring the proportion in which its objects are entitled
(d) authorizing the whole or any part of its property to be let, sold, mortgaged or exchanged
(3) settling a scheme for its management or granting such further or other relief as the nature of the case may require. The powers conferred by this section on the Advocate General may (where there is no Advocate General) be exercised by the Government Advocate or (where there is no Government Advocate) by such officer as the local Government may appoint in this behalf.

Section 539 of the Civil Procedure Code of 1882:
In case of any alleged breach of any express or constructive trusts created for public charitable or religious purposes, or whenever the direction of the court is deemed necessary for the administration of such trust, the Advocate-General acting *ex-officio,* or two or more persons having an interest in the trust and having obtained the consent in writing of the Advocate-General, may institute a suit in the High Court or the District Court within the local limits of whose civil jurisdiction the whole or any part of the subject-matter of the trust is situate, to obtain a decree –

(a) appointing new trustees under the trust;
(b) vesting any property in the trustees under the trust;
(c) declaring the proportions in which its objects are entitled;
(d) authorizing the whole or any part of its property to be let, sold, mortgaged or exchanged;
(e) settling a scheme for its management;

or granting such further or other relief as the nature of the case may require. The powers conferred by this section on the Advocate-General may, outside the presidency-towns, be, with the previous section of the Local Government, exercised also by the Collector, or by such officer as the Local government may appoint in this behalf . . .

Section 92 of the Civil Procedure Code of 1908:
In the case of any alleged breach of any express or constructive trust created for public purposes of a charitable or religious nature, or where the direction of the Court is deemed necessary for the administration of any such trust, the Advocate-General or two or more persons having an interest in the trust and having obtained the consent in writing of the Advocate-General, may institute a suit, whether contentious or not, in the Principal Civil Court of original jurisdiction or in any other court empowered in that behalf by the

Local Government within the local limits of whose jurisdiction the whole or any part of the subject-matter of the trust is situate to obtain a decree –

(a) removing any trustee;

(b) appointing a new trustee;

(c) vesting any property in a trustee;

(d) directing accounts and enquiries;

(e) declaring what proportion of the trust-property or of the interest therein shall be allocated to any particular object of the trust;

(f) authorizing the whole or any part of the trust-property to be let, sold, mortgaged or exchanged;

(g) granting such further or other relief as the nature of the case may require.

(2) Save as provided by S. 14 of the Religious Endowments Act (XX of 1863), no suit claiming any of the reliefs specified in subsection (1) shall be instituted in respect of any such trust as is therein referred to except in conformity with the provisions of that subsection.[21]

The third provision, also contained in the Civil Procedure Code, which had unforeseen effects on temple conflict in South India, was Section 30 of the Civil Procedure Code of 1877 and 1882, revised as Order 1, Rule 8 of the Civil Procedure Code of 1908. Because the wording of this section is precisely identical in the code of 1877 and 1882 but was somewhat altered in Order 1, Rule 8 of the code of 1908, only these two versions are presented:

Section 30 of the Civil Procedure Code of 1877:
Where there are numerous parties having the same interest in one suit, one or more of such parties may, with the permission of the Court, sue or be sued, or may defend in such suit, on behalf of all parties so interested. But the Court shall in such case give, at the plaintiff's expense, notice of the institution of the suit to all such parties either by personal service or (if from the number of parties or any other cause such service is not reasonably practicable), then by public advertisement, as the Court in each case may direct.

Order 1, Rule 8 of the Civil Procedure Code of 1908:
Where there are numerous persons having the same interest in one suit, one or more of such persons may, with the permission of the Court, sue or be sued, or may defend, in such suit, on behalf of or for the benefit of all persons so interested. But the Court shall in such case give, at the plaintiff's expense, notice of the institution of the suit to all such persons either by

[21] Section 539 of the C.P.C. of 1877 is taken from J. H. Nelson, *Commentaries on the Code of Civil Procedure, Act No. X of 1877* (Madras, 1878), pp. 514–15; Section 539 of the C.P.C. of 1882 is taken from J. O'Kinealy, *The Code of Civil Procedure Being Act XIV of 1882, As Amended by Acts VI, VII and X of 1888, with Notes and an Appendix* (Calcutta, 1889), p. 454; Section 92 of the C.P.C. of 1908 is taken from Nand Lal, *The Code of Civil Procedure (Act V of 1908), With the Case-Law Thereon*, 3 vols. (Lahore, 1926), 1:661–2.

personal service, or, where from the number of any such persons or any other cause such service is not reasonably practicable by public advertisement, as the Court in each case may direct.

(2) Any person on whose behalf or for whose benefit a suit is instituted or defended under subrule (1) may apply to the court to be made a party to such suit.[22]

Before considering the cumulative scope of these various provisions, it is important to note their sources in contemporary English law. The sole model that nineteenth-century British officials, both administrative and judicial, brought to bear on their dealings with the South Indian temple was the English model of the "charitable trust." In the contemporary English law, which had roots going back to A.D. 1600, the protection of charitable trusts was vested in the king, as *parens patriae*.[23] It was concretely exercised under the general equitable jurisidiction of the Court of Chancery, which acted upon information provided by the attorney general in his capacity as forensic representative of the crown.[24] During the nineteenth century, the relationship of the British-Indian courts to religious and charitable endowments was considerably influenced by the doctrines of the English Courts of Equity.[25] In 1846 an important decision of the High Court of Madras explicitly extended the prerogatives of the Court of Chancery in England to the Supreme Courts in India, and this became applicable to the integrated judicial system, under the High Courts, after 1861.[26]

The English model of the trust, whereby endowed property was transferred to, and vested in, a trustee for the benefit of others, called "beneficiaries," was clearly not applicable to the Hindu temple, where property clearly was vested in the idol[27] and was only "managed," on its behalf, by the trustee.[28] Although this fundamental difference between the English and Hindu conceptions was repeatedly noticed by Anglo-Indian judges in the nineteenth century,[29] an alternative model for the Hindu temple was never generated,

[22] Section 30 of the C.P.C. of 1877 (unaltered in the Code of 1882) is taken from L. P. Delves Broughton, *The Code of Civil Procedure Being Act X of 1877 With Notes and An Appendix* (Calcutta, 1878), p. 133; Order 1, Rule 8 of the C.P.C. of 1908 is taken from Lal, *The Code*, p. 1134.

[23] Ghosh, *Law of Endowments*, pp. 725–6.

[24] Ibid.

[25] Ibid., pp. 46–7.

[26] Iyer, *The Law*, p. 36.

[27] This was argued at the beginning of Chapter 1.

[28] Ghosh, *Law of Endowments*, pp. 42–3.

[29] Ibid., pp. 267–9; it was noted in Chapter 3 that British administrators in the nineteenth century also adhered to this model.

and the English idea of the "trust" continued to provide the cognitive framework within which judges treated Hindu temples throughout the nineteenth century.[30] It was in view of this persistent ambiguity that religious endowments were explicitly exempted from the scope[31] of the Indian Trusts Act, which was passed in 1882. Nevertheless, for lack of a systematic alternative, the English model of the trust continued, by analogy, to inform the judgments of the Anglo-Indian courts, as will be seen in the cases discussed in the body of this chapter.

Sections 14 and 15 of the Religious Endowments Act of 1863 clearly and powerfully reflected the contemporary English view that the "protection" of trusts was the business of the courts. Although the bulk of Act XX of 1863 was no doubt tailored to the context of British bureaucratic withdrawal from the affairs of Hindu temples, its overall orientation was considerably influenced by contemporary legislation concerning charitable trusts in England. From the very beginnings of the nineteenth century, moves to refine the supervision of charities in England had continued to gain strength.[32] Between 1853 and 1860, three acts concerning charitable trusts were passed in England, in which the powers of a new supervisory body, the Charity Commission, were defined and clarified.[33] Nevertheless, the new English legislation continued, to the dismay of many, to vest a great deal of power in relation to charities in the Courts of Equity.[34]

It is thus hardly surprising that in framing an act for the benefit of Hindu temples, which had been deprived of the "protection" of English administrators and were hence subject to wholesale "mismanagement," immense reliance should have been placed on the role of the courts in solving future temple disputes. Similary, Section 539 of the Civil Procedures Code of 1877 and 1882 (later Section 92 in the Civil Procedure Code of 1908) was directly modeled on a particular portion of the English Charities Procedure Act of 1812, popularly known as Sir Romilly's Act, which was meant to provide a "summary" remedy for the mismanagement of English trusts.[35] Lastly, Section 30 of the Civil Procedure Code of 1877 and 1882 (refined in Order 1, Rule 8 of the Civil Procedure Code of 1908),

30 Ghosh, *Law of Endowments*, pp. 271–2.
31 Ibid., p. 42.
32 David Owen, *English Philanthropy 1660–1960* (Cambridge, Mass., 1964), p. 181.
33 Ibid., pp. 202–8.
34 Ibid.
35 Ibid., p. 183; *Indian Law Reports* (Madras Series) 17 (January–December 1894):462–9; Lal, *The Code*, 2:662.

which was meant to enable "representative" suits in matters involving persons sharing the same interest, was based on a practical solution of the English courts to the inconvenience created by their general rule, "not to dispose of any matter, not to bind any man's interest, or to make any declaration of any man's rights, in his absence."[36]

The decisions of the Anglo-Indian judicial system in respect to Hindu temples after 1877 were guided by the previously cited sections of Act XX of 1863 and of the Civil Procedure Code of 1877, 1882, and 1908. In the period from 1878 to 1925 an immense body of case law was generated all over India, which defined the scope of every clause of these sections, refined their applicability, explicated their interrelationship, removed their ambiguities and overlaps, and influenced the changes in the wording of some of these sections.[37] Severally and jointly, these specific products of British legislation in India provided the framework as well as the impetus for a vast body of pan-Indian litigation in the period from 1878 to 1925, which provoked judicial codification of a large variety of rights, wrongs, and rules concerning "public" aspects of conflict in Hindu temples, as all these pieces of legislation applied only to "public" rights and interests.

It was clear from the start, however, that these enactments did not preclude or prevent the legal pursuit of "private" rights and interests in temples, which fell under ordinary common law as it applied to civil rights in British India.[38] In practice, this distinction between "private" and "public" interests was hard to make in the conflicts that brought Hindu temples to English courts, and frequently "private" rights were codified under these sections having to do with "public" interests. In any event, the cases from the Śrī Pārtasārati Svāmi Temple, which provide the "legal dramas" of this chapter, all fell under one or another aspect of these provisions of Anglo-Indian law. The outcome of this legislatively stimulated interaction between the temple and the court was a complex process, in which structures were defined, rights codified, and authority consolidated or fragmented in a way that was unintended by judges and

[36] Broughton, *The Code*, p. 134; Lal, *The Code*, 2:1134.

[37] Lal, *The Code*, 1:661–98 and 2:1134–46; Ghosh, *Law of Endowments*, passim, particularly Chaps. 2 and 3 and pp. 1016–22; Iyer, *The Law*, passim, but especially Chaps. 2, 24, and 28; T. V. Sanjiva Row, *The Code of Civil Procedure, 1908 (Act V of 1908) With the Case-Law Thereon*, 2 vols. (Madras, 1909), 1:832–58 and 2:76–82.

[38] O'Kinealy, *The Code*, p. 454; Lal, *The Code*, pp. 687–8.

litigants alike. It is this process that is documented in the narrative of the cases from this temple in the period from 1878 to 1925.

In *The Concept of Law,* H. L. A. Hart has lucidly argued that the differences between the alleged uncertainties of communication by authoritative example (precedent) and the certainties of communication by authoritative general language (legislation) are often exaggerated.[39] In the case of English law, he argues that both these sources of judicial activity are "open-textured," and thus the courts, although they might pretend otherwise, perform a creative and generative function:

> Here at the margin of rules and in the fields left open by the theory of precedents, the courts perform a rule-producing function which administrative bodies perform centrally in the elaboration of variable standards. In a system where *stare decisis* is firmly acknowledged, this function of the courts is very like the exercise of delegated rule-making powers by an administrative body. In England this fact is often obscured by forms: for the courts often disclaim any such creative function and insist that the proper task of statutory interpretation and the use of precedent is, respectively, to search for the "intention of the legislature" and the law that already exists.[40]

This feature of the English judicial system had even more radical generative consequences in British India, given the peculiarities of the context discussed earlier in this chapter. Put briefly, and in anticipation of the detailed narrative to follow, the judicial activity of the English courts in Madras between 1878 and 1925 had two far-reaching effects on the Śrī Pārtasārati Svāmi Temple: First, the notion of a Teṉkalai community in Triplicane, which had the exclusive right to control the temple, was elaborated, refined, and codified; at the same time, and paradoxically, various subgroups and individuals within this Teṉkalai community were encouraged to emphasize the heterogeneity of their interests and to formulate their *special* rights in a mutually antagonistic way, thus making authority in the temple even more fragile than it previously had been.

Litigation and the Śrī Pārtasārati Svāmi Temple, 1878–1925

The Śrī Pārtasārati Svāmi Temple was involved in seventeen legal suits in the High Court of Madras between 1878 and 1925.[41]

39 H. L. A. Hart, *The Concept of Law* (Oxford, 1961), pp. 121 ff.

40 Ibid., p. 132.

41 The primary sources for this analysis are the legal documents generated in seventeen civil suits between 1878 and 1925 involving the Śrī Pārtasārati Svāmi Temple, fought on the original side of the High Court of Judicature at Madras. These

The data available on these cases is sufficiently rich to permit numerous kinds of analysis of a microsociological sort. For example, the data from these cases could be used to make a careful analysis of changing patterns of alliance and factionalization, in terms of kinship, patron-client relationships, and so forth. Alternatively, the analysis could focus on caste as an attribute of the litigants and as a substantive theme in these cases. Or these cases could be used as a lens through which to observe, from the ground up, the sociological formation of the Anglo-Indian legal profession. Other possibilities exist. But the approach taken here, which accords best with the general thrust of this study, involves an emphasis on the *relationship* between the Anglo-Indian judicial system and the litigants interested in the Śrī Pārtasārati Svāmi Temple.

This relationship has two aspects. The first is a systematic aspect under which the interaction of temple and court exhibits certain consistent patterns and tendencies, which constitute an ongoing political cycle (discussed later) uniting these two institutions. The second aspect of this relationship is a matter of consequence and is therefore a substantive and diachronic feature of the interaction. Of these diachronic consequences, two are fundamental: (a) the gradual evolution and legal codification of the idea that the Teṉkalai community of Triplicane had control over the management of the Śrī Pārtasārati Svāmi Temple and (b) the concurrent, and paradoxical, encouragement by the court of fissiparous tendencies within this community and the resulting fragmentation of authority in the temple.

The diachronic and substantive elements in this process can only be discussed in the unfolding context of the cases themselves. But the synchronic/systemic element, the political cycle uniting temple and court, can be briefly summarized (Figure 9). Put in the simplest terms, the temple and the High Court became inextricably linked because the actions of the court consistently had effects opposed to those that were intended. The broad intention of the judges of the court was to define the boundaries of the Teṉkalai community of Triplicane, conceived as an electorate, and to create a machinery, on

voluminous records are now preserved in the Record Room of the original side of the High Court, where they are filed by number, viz., C.S. 161 of 1891 (i.e., Civil Suit No. 161 of the year 1891). As I refer to these cases in the text by their names (viz., *Vencatanarayana Pillay* v. *Secretary of State for India in Council*), following the format of the law digests, for reasons of economy and also to reflect the system according to which I had access to them, I have used the number system in the footnotes.

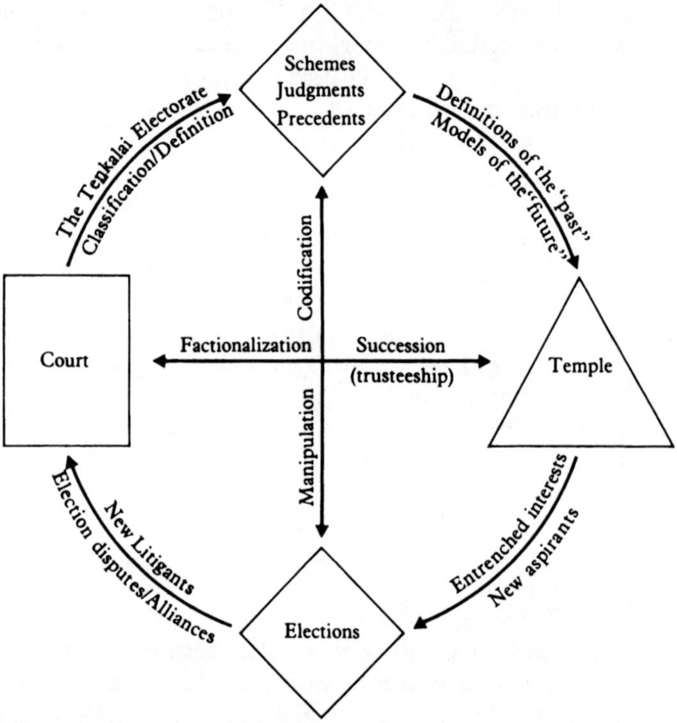

Figure 9. The dialectic of temple and court

the contemporary Western model, that would enable this constituency to elect trustees who would manage the temple on their behalf. This task was not, as it turned out, a simple one.

The court's efforts to classify, define, and demarcate the concrete meaning of the concept of the "Teṉkalai community of Triplicane" generated more tensions than it resolved. The "schemes" for the governance of the temple and the judgments and the precedents created by the court provided opportunities for litigants to reflexively refine their self-conceptions and their political aspirations. The legal "texts" encouraged the multiplication of ideas of the "past" as well as models of the "future" in respect to the temple. The elections held on the basis of these "texts" became, in fact, arenas for the enactment of factional struggles, for the manipulation of the redistributive process of the temple, and for the naked exercise of physical power and patronage connections. In turn, these elections, transformed from "contexts" into "texts," provided fresh fuel for accusation and counteraccusation, for new grievances and for fresh factional alliances on the parts of various groups. The resolution of these renewed disturbances placed the temple once again in the hands of the judges of the court, who had no choice but to refine their schemes, review old precedents, and revise prior judgments. The final result was that the cycle of interaction between temple and court was reenacted in yet another case.

It would be misleading, however, to view these cycles of interaction as indicating a static relationship between temple and court. With the occurrence of new cases, the cycles take on a helical quality, as more participants enter the litigation, new issues eclipse old ones, and conflict grows more intensified and disaggregated. The evolution of this dialectical and helical interaction had direct and substantive consequences on the idea and the reality of the "Teṉkalai community of Triplicane" in relationship to the Śrī Pārtasārati Svāmi Temple. Each of these cases constitutes a "legal drama" and, in another sense, an act in an extended drama.

In the analysis of these cases, therefore, I have borrowed from Victor Turner the concept of the social drama, which he develops in *Schism and Continuity in an African Society.*[42] In the course of this extended analysis of conflict and equilibrium in an African micro-context, Turner develops the concept of the "social drama," that is, a dramatic episode of conflict and redress, which provides "a limited area of transparency on the otherwise opaque surface of regular, uneventful social life."[43] Turner persuasively argues that these episodes of conflict reveal a common processual form and that the detailed analysis of these dramatic episodes can be highly revealing of the rules of, and tensions in, a given social structure:

> But it is necessary to remember that after disturbance has occurred and readjustments have been made, there may have taken place profound modifications in the internal relations of the group. The new equilibrium is seldom a replica of the old. The interests of certain persons and groups may have gained at the expense of those of others. Certain relations between persons and groups may have increased in intensity while others may have diminished. Others again may have been completely ruptured while new relationships have come into being . . . In one aspect, the social drama is a process which reveals realignment of social relations at critical points of structural maturation or decay; in another, it may be regarded as a trial of strength between conflicting interests in which persons or groups try to

[42] Victor W. Turner, *Schism and Continuity in an African Society: A Study of Ndembu Village Life* (Manchester, Eng., 1957).
[43] Ibid., p. 93.

manipulate to their own advantage the actually existing network of social relations, both structural and contingent, within the system. Thus the social drama may represent either the natural, inherent development of a given social system through spacetime at a distinct phase, at a critical point of maturation, or the deliberate attempts by some of its members to accelerate or retard that development. It may be either an index or a vehicle of change. In most cases both aspects are present.[44]

This chapter is concerned, by analogy, with a similar approach to an extended and interconnected series of "legal dramas" in a particular period in the history of a single South Indian temple.

The dramatistic metaphor here is somewhat different from Turner's original application. Because of the archival, and necessarily partial, nature of the sources in this context, the processual regularities discovered by Turner in the structure of the social dramas he discussed are difficult to establish in these "legal dramas," although they might well exist. In treating these cases as "legal dramas," my intentions are somewhat more idiosyncratic.

The main concern is to treat the temple and the court themselves as the primary "characters" in the series of dramatic/legal episodes to be discussed. What is intended here is not a puerile personification of these institutions but rather a device for making stylistically coherent the fact that the encounter of these two institutions is tense, unpredictable, and often jagged. Nevertheless, an underlying coherence is gradually revealed, which is partly structural and in juxtaposition, that makes the description of them as "legal dramas" worthwhile. In this particular analysis, the relationships between various individuals provide the background, the material, and the fabric of the drama. But the genuinely dramatic fact is the encounter between the two institutions themselves. As in Turner's analysis of the African case, the potential reward for the detailed reproduction of episodes is the discovery of key principles of tension within a changing social structure.

The interaction between the temple and the court in the period from 1878 to 1925 can be divided into two phases, which are dealt with sequentially but separately in what follows. The first phase, which is concerned with nine court cases fought between 1878 and 1916, involves the legal process of demarcating the sectarian basis for temple control and the machinery of elections for the trusteeship. The second phase, which runs from 1916 to 1925, is dominated by

[44] Ibid., pp. 161–2.

the structural fragmentation of the community into legally defined interest groups.

In the first phase of the interaction between temple and court a number of interlinked processes are observed. The judges of the High Court of Madras seek to legally define a sectarian electorate for the temple and in the process encourage a variety of groups to refine their political self-conceptions and to use legal language and legal categories to pursue their interests. The role of the trusteeship grows increasingly central to temple control, with a concomitant increase in conflicts between trustees, which in turn affect the redistributive process of the temple as well as its day-to-day management. Elections turn into arenas for the often gross manipulation of their followers by aspirants to temple control and for the actualization of shifting alliances. Models of the managerial past and future of the temple proposed by litigants interact in an increasingly sophisticated fashion with the judicially formulated schemes (or constitutions) for temple management. Such managerial documents constantly become interpreted as charters for new forms of political alliance and action, as well as for cultural redefinition.

These processes evolve through the helical intensification of litigation and politics, in which legal judgments addressed to the solution of one problem generate the context for another problem. Thus, the early conflicts over a vacancy in the trusteeship, resolved in a substantive fashion by Justice Muttusami Iyer, open up the issue of criteria for the future election of trustees. The idea of election rapidly becomes an assumption (though it is a political and cultural innovation in temple control), but the actual machinery for elections and the concrete identity and limits of the electorate come to be contested. As a result, in a decision of 1889, all non-Teṉkalais were excluded from the electoral process. But this negative definition of the electorate was inadequate, and one response to the ambiguity was for groups to redefine the relevance of their varna and caste affiliations as charters for their share in the slots for the trusteeship. A court scheme of 1894 eliminated the idea of Teṉkalai persuasion as a basis for membership in the electorate and substituted for it the even vaguer notion of membership in the "Teṉkalai sect," a definition whose application was to be determined by the incumbent trustees. As a consequence of such inflation of the role of the trustee, elections became increasingly naked arenas for competition between various alliances and for direct conflicts between incumbent and aspirant trustees. As such battles grew more intense, trustees increasingly expanded their prerogatives in the economy of the temple. Further, legal procedures were often manipulated by one or another party in an effort to gain information (and thus control) over the activities of its opponents in temple management. Conflict between trustees (and the alliances and followings they represented) increasingly affected the redistributive process of the temple and the delicate relations between donors and the new managerial center of the temple. By the end of this period, "contested elections" ceased to be the dominant motif of temple politics, and substantive issues, both cultural and political, affecting the management of the temple dominated litigation after 1916. But this brief narration of the events of the period from 1878 to 1916 captures little of the rich detail that constitutes the political drama of these cases. We turn therefore to a more detailed description of some of the materials in these cases in order to make their import more graphic and contextual.

The first major case to embroil the Srī Pārtasārati Svāmi Temple and the High Court of Madras was *Vencatanarayana Pillay* v. *Secretary of State for India in Council.*[45] Because this case constitutes an important transition in the political life of the temple, it is considered here in some detail. In the course of attempts to fill the vacancy in the trusteeship caused by the death of V. Sadagopachariar in 1872, two factions arose in the Teṉkalai community of Triplicane.[46] Not only did these factions represent opposed candidates for the vacancy, but in the course of their appearance before the High Court of Madras, it became clear that neither side had any coherent understanding concerning the procedure for filling vacancies in the trusteeship. This procedural vacuum was part of a larger uncertainty about the concrete definition of temple control, which was stimulated, though not resolved, by the bureaucratic charter of 1843, whereby the filling of vacancies in the trusteeship was "to be left to the suffrage of the community of the Tengala sect, as has heretofore been customary." The two factions had divergent interpretations of this powerful, though excessively formalistic, charter, and it became the business of the High Court of Madras to assign some concrete meaning to this proposition and resolve the immediate conflict in light of such a concrete interpretation. Thus the statements of litigants on both sides of the case, as well as the final judgment of the presiding judge, represent an extremely important transition in the

[45] C:S. 486 of 1878. The background and stimulus for the filing of this suit were disccused in Chapter 4.

[46] See pp. 159–62.

cultural definition of political life in the temple. Litigants began the process of defining their concerns in English legal language, and the judgment rendered the court responsible for the resolution of temple disputes as well as for the creation of the categories and rules that were henceforth to define temple control.

Because the immediate stimulus for the conflict over the vacant trusteeship was the freezing of payments owed to the trustees from the government, the secretary of state for India was named as the first defendant in the suit. The plaintiffs were the two surviving trustees, T. Vencatanarayana Pillay and P. T. Ramanjulu Naidu, and V. Raghavachariar, the son of V. Sadagopachariar, whom they had made the new Brahmin trustee. Their opponents, in addition to the secretary of state for India, were eight other members (both Brahmin and non-Brahmin) of the Teṉkalai community of Triplicane, who had supported other candidates for the vacant trustee slot.

The arguments of the plaintiffs and the defendants have been discussed in some detail in Chapter 4 and need not detain us here. What is of considerably more importance is the judgment and the decision of the presiding judge in this suit.

Justice Muttusami Iyer, the first native judge of the High Court of Madras, passed judgment on this case on February 24, 1880. His judgment was a major referent for later judges who had to deal with conflict at the Śrī Pārtasārati Svāmi Temple.[47] In the first place, this judgment gave the 1843 bureaucratic charter a fresh legal lease on life by simply confirming the notion that the customary practice had been to leave the election of trustees to the "suffrages" of the Teṉkalai community of Triplicane and that the "contest in this suit is whether the 3rd Plaintiff's appointment is in accordance with the custom indicated by government."[48]

In reviewing the evidence pertaining to the appointment of trustees from the time the British took possession of Triplicane until 1843, Justice Muttusami Iyer asserted that it "throws however no light on the mode in which the Tengalai sect expressed its opinion and it is clear that the right now claimed for the surviving trustees to nominate to a vacancy could have no existence during this period."[49] Using evidence from the cases of succession in 1831 and 1836,[50] the

[47] Judgment, February 24, 1880 in C.S. 486 of 1878, High Court of Judicature at Madras.
[48] Ibid.
[49] Ibid.
[50] Chapter 4.

judge asserted that the custom was "to leave to the Tengalai community in deference to usage to name a qualified person, to the Collector to express an opinion whether the person named was duly qualified, and if several persons were named, which of them was most eligible, and to the Board finally to confirm the nomination."[51]

In his shrewd analysis of the government's arrangements in 1843 when it withdrew from temple affairs, Muttusami Iyer noted that although they left future nominations to the "suffrages" of the Teṉkalai community, implying that future nominations should be elective, it was also clear that "whether the elections should take place under express enactment or by usage sanctioned by prescription should form a subject of future consideration."[52] In any case, the judge was clear that the argument of the plaintiffs that the surviving trustees could nominate a new trustee and that the Teṉkalai community had only *veto* power was a distortion of "usage" as sanctioned by the 1843 charter. Thus, he decreed that V. Raghavachariar's appointment was illegal, primarily on the grounds that petitions in support of his candidacy were obtained only *after* his selection by the surviving trustees.

Justice Muttusami Iyer succinctly summarized this view by asserting that "the appointment is bad because it was made in contravention of the usage of the institution and in improper assertion of a right which has no legal basis."[53] The judge confessed that there was considerable room for doubt, given the paucity of clear-cut rules for "election," but in this situation he felt that it was not a problem of rival candidates but of conflict "between the trustees and the Tengalai sect as to the extent of the right possessed by the trustees."[54] He then decreed that a judge "in chambers" would "elect a Dharmakarta with reference to the opinion and usage of the Tengalai community, and that if the 3rd Plaintiff should be indicated as most eligible by the voice of the community, there is no objection to his appointment by the court."[55]

Subsequently, Justice Muttusami Iyer himself, "in chambers," elected V. Raghavachariar (whose previous election he had judged to be illegal) as the third trustee "with reference to the opinion of the Tengalai community and the usage of the institution."[56] He reported

51 Judgment in C.S. 486 of 1878.
52 Ibid.
53 Ibid.
54 Ibid.
55 Ibid.
56 Judge's Certificate of November 12, 1880, in C.S. 486 of 1878.

that he had made this decision after receiving proposals and petitions on behalf of three candidates and "after reading such statements of fact and proposals, affidavits and Mahazarnamahs and taking such oral evidence as necessary."[57] The style and context of this decision by Justice Muttusami Iyer represent an interesting transitional form, from the particularistic, administrative, and authoritative style of Hindu kings in relation to temple disputes to the generalizing, legislative, and reluctant style of later judges in the Anglo-Indian judicial system. In the course of the proceedings in this case, however, too many questions had been raised in "legislative" terms, and the judge's actions solved the immediate problem but did not answer the general questions. Some of this unfinished business erupted in the next case to be discussed.

In a subsequent suit,[58] the judges of the High Court of Madras found themselves obliged to explicitly formulate a scheme for the management of the temple. In the course of this case, members of the Triplicane community were explicitly invited to participate in the case through a proclamation in Tamil and Telugu, which was displayed in and around the temple. An English translation of this proclamation follows:

> Whereas under Section 30 of the Civil Procedure Code it was ordered by an order of this Honourable Court made herein and bearing date the 30th day of April 1884 (amongst other things) that a Proclamation be made through Triplicane inviting all persons interested in the Shree Parthasardhy Pagoda at Triplicane in Madras to come in and be made parties themselves or see that some other or others by whom they are content to be made parties defendant to this suit and that copies thereof be stuck up in at least four conspicuous places on the gates or walls of the said Pagoda. It is hereby proclaimed and notified that all parties desirous of coming in and applying to be made parties to this suit or of nominating some person or persons for the purpose of representing them in this suit – and of protecting their interests herein are to come in and apply accordingly to this Honourable Court before the Honourable Mr. Justice Hutchins the Judge before whom this case is pending within one month from this date.[59]

On April 3, 1884, Justice Hutchins also ordered that this suit be referred to chambers in order to settle a scheme "for the election of future trustees, to determine the qualification and registration of the electoral body and to settle and approve the general form and mode

[57] Ibid.

[58] C.S. 36 of 1884, High Court of Judicature at Madras.

[59] Proclamation, September 9, 1884, in C.S. 36 of 1884. This English translation, along with the Tamil and Telugu originals and other documents in this case, is preserved in the High Court at Madras.

of publication of the accounts statement."[60] Accordingly, both the plaintiffs and the defendants presented the judge with model schemes, through their lawyers, whose common elements and contrasts provide a fascinating set of texts for the political aspirations of various segments of the community.

The lengthy model scheme presented by the defendants[61] proposed an electoral structure for the trusteeship in the Śrī Pārtasārati Svāmi Temple. The suggested qualifications for voters were that they should be Teṉkalai males over eighteen years of age who resided in Triplicane (defined in precise geographical terms by reference to five bounding streets). It was also proposed that the Brahmin, Pillay, and Naidu castes should fill the three trustee positions and that vacancies should be filled in accordance with this caste quota. Emphasis was placed on the fact that no pecuniary restrictions should be placed on either trustees or voters and that in the case of trustees their residence should not be an issue either.

As for the actual machinery of the election (publication of notices, preparation of lists of voters, and so forth), the most important suggestion of this model scheme was that the surviving trustees should call upon the headmen of the subcastes to provide *mahazarnamās* (petitions) demonstrating the preferences of their constituents. The defendants also proposed that provision be made for recourse to the High Court in case of electoral fraud. Finally, and most naturally, this proposed scheme contained the suggestion that the mere fact of the existence of a vacancy or of a disputed election would not affect the right of the surviving trustees to act in behalf of the temple and to collect and disburse the sums payable to it. Interestingly enough, this scheme (representing the faction of the surviving trustees) proposed that "the Tengalay community of Triplicane, shall not as such have any right of control, direct or indirect, over the Dharmakartas of the Temple."[62]

The whole tenor of this document, with its emphasis on a wide electoral base, with no pecuniary restrictions on the electorate or the candidates for trusteeship, and with its wide mandate for the powers of the trustees in respect to this electorate, suggests that the defendants represented an alliance focused on the surviving trustees, who were supported by a large, though impoverished, section of the

60 Judge's order, April 3, 1884, in C.S. 36 of 1884.
61 Defendants' scheme, in C.S. 36 of 1884.
62 Ibid., para. (k).

Teṉkalai community of Triplicane and were anxious to reduce their potential accountability to rival elites and their followings.

By contrast, the vastly more elaborate model scheme proposed by the plaintiffs[63] suggests a relatively wealthy segment of the Triplicane Teṉkalai community, seeking to make inroads into temple control. It proposed considerably more selective economic criteria both for voters and for candidates for the trusteeship, especially in property terms.[64] In addition, this scheme made numerous concrete proposals for the actual electoral machinery, the publication of notices concerning the election, the preparation of voter lists, the terms of trustee appointment, and so on. In all these matters, this scheme laid great emphasis on the directive and supervisory role of the court. It proposed as well the creation of a Board of Control to supervise the trustees, which would be composed of six persons elected in the same way as the trustees.

On the basis of the two model schemes presented to him, Justice Hutchins published his own authoritative scheme.[65] This document, which represents the first authoritative constitutional text for temple control and which was a primary referent in much litigation up to 1924, is reproduced in full in Appendix B.

This scheme, and the elections based on it, led to a flurry of efforts on the part of various groups to carve out a niche for themselves in the three trusteeships and in the electoral process that governed access to them. In 1889 a local headmen of a Vellala subcaste protested to the court that the surviving trustees had deliberately excluded him from the electoral process and had instead called upon his assistant headman (who was a Teṉkalai) to furnish the list of voters from this subcaste in Triplicane. The response of the Brahmin trustee graphically illustrates the delicacies of transforming a locally understood ritual identity into a managerial category and at the same time displays the hold that the idea of Teṉkalai management of the temple had already taken:

> That throughout the scheme and the decree, care is particularly taken to avoid all discord in the proceedings for election which might, by any possibility, result from the introduction of any element other than the Tengalai element in the said proceedings. That from the fact that the headmen entitled to be present at the meeting of voters for finally determining the voter's list and at the meeting of voters for voting, at which meeting

63 Plaintiffs' scheme, in C.S. 36 of 1884.
64 Ibid., paras. 2 and 3.
65 Justice Hutchins's scheme of November 7, 1885, in C.S. 36 of 1884.

no other than Tengalai voters or Tengalai Dharmakarthas are entitled to be present and from the fact that the Headmen who are entitled to be present are to aid the surviving or continuing Dharmakarthas if required in their deliberations as to the competency of persons who claim to be entitled to vote, and also in the proceedings at the meeting of the voters assembled for voting, it is clear that such important privileges could not have been contemplated to be conferred upon others than Tengalais, as it is sure that in such an event grave complications both as to the interests of the temple and the preservation of order and purity of vote would result.

That the hostility between the Saiva and the Vaishnava and the Vadagalai and the Tengalai is well known and is the recognized basis of the scheme and the decree themselves in the suit. And it is not difficult to see that the introduction of any Headman other than Tengalai will give rise to frequent false personation and disorder in the assemblies of voters above mentioned.

That the determination (even without the disturbing influence of the presence of sectarian opponents) of what people among the Sudras are Tengalai is difficult, and the presence of a non-Tengalai Headman would surely aggravate the difficulty in many ways.

That, besides, the mere fact that a man wears a Tengalai mark (and among the Sudras many wear one mark at one time and another at another time) does not make him a Tengalai unless he is really of the Tengalai persuasion. And this a non-Tengalai Headman cannot determine as he cannot be expected to know the essentials of the Tengalai creed.

Many people who wear the Siva mark on many days wear the Tengalai mark on other days as, among others, for instance, in the Parattasi month and Amavasia days, and others wear these marks indiscriminately. And in such cases the question is one of the man's persuasion, and the presence of a Siva caste headman at the meeting of the voters for determining the voter's list will be of no help to the Dharmakartha who is to decide whether a candidate is Tengalai or not.[66]

After a judicial decision that upheld the position of the Saivite headman, there was a further appeal on the above grounds by V. Raghavachariar, and the Chief Justice of the High Court of Madras finally upheld the position of the Brahmin trustee.[67] This landmark judgment, which excluded non-Teṉkalais from any role in the electoral process, was the first major legal demarcation of the boundaries of the Teṉkalai community of Triplicane. This far-reaching decision, and the legal proceedings that led up to it, laid the basic foundation for the enduring relationship between the temple and the High Court of Madras.

But sectarian credentials were not the only mode in which legitimate claims to temple control were discussed. In a subsequent

66 Counteraffidavit of V. Raghavachariar, September 2, 1889, in O.S.A. 24 of 1889 (C.S. 36 of 1884), paras. 12 and 13.

67 Judgment, August 21, 1890, in O.S.A. 24 of 1889.

case,[68] we observe caste-based groups attempting to document, in legally credible terms, the link of their traditional prerogatives to the newly evolving legal framework for temple control. This case deserves close scrutiny because it shows in graphic terms the growing mastery of Western legal usages and concepts by native litigants. The factional structure underlying this case was complicated: On the one hand, there was a collusive alliance between a wealthy merchant triumvirate (of Kōmaṭṭi Seṭṭis), who were the first three plaintiffs, and V. Raghavachariar, the surviving Brahmin trustee (the first defendant); on the other hand, there was an ad hoc alliance between dismissed and disgruntled temple servants, individuals denied honors by the Brahmin trustee, opponents of his from previous litigation, and members of the Yātava sub-caste threatened by the Kōmaṭṭi bid for a share in temple control.

After several years of delay, the sole surviving trustee, V. Raghavachariar, around June 26, 1890, published a list of voters and notified the community of his intention to hold an election to fill the two existing vacant trustee positions. He had no sooner done this when a new suit was instituted against him in the High Court of Madras.[69] This suit, which carried on for four years, involved twenty plaintiffs and fourteen defendants from various sections of the Teṉkalai community of Madras, a host of lawyers representing them, a series of decisions, appeals, and reversals by both the original and appellate sides of the court, a modification of Justice Hutchins's scheme of 1885, and one successfully held election, which was subsequently held to be invalid.

In the course of the litigation it was clearly established and confirmed by several judges that the suit was the outcome of collusion between the surviving trustee and the plaintiffs, with a view to postponing elections and perpetuating the sole control of V. Raghavachariar.[70] The plaintiffs, who belonged to different castes, appeared to be led and financed by a wealthy triumvirate of merchants of the Kōmaṭṭi Seṭṭi caste, none of whom actually resided in Triplicane. Although these plaintiffs vociferously denied the charges of collusion with the Brahmin trustee, and though their plaint took great care not to impugn his character, there is no doubt that this suit was partly motivated by a genuine wish on the part of these merchants to carve

[68] *A. Condiah Chetty* v. *V. Raghavachariar*, C.S. 161 of 1891, High Court of Judicature at Madras.

[69] Plaint, July 11, 1891, in C.S. 161 of 1891, High Court of Judicature at Madras.

[70] Affidavit of T. Raghunatha Pillay, January 15, 1894, in O.S.A. 9 of 1893 and Judgment, January 28, 1895, in O.S.A. 22 of 1894 (both under C.S. 161 of 1891).

out a place for the Kōmaṭṭi caste in temple control. In one of their many affidavits, they argued that the members of this community "are staunch Thengalay Vaishnavites and have long been and still are large benefactors to the said temple, larger benefactors indeed than any other class of people in Madras: Their exclusion is highly prejudicial to the best interests of the said temple."[71] In the atmosphere of collusion in this case it is hard to judge whether these threats to the interests of the Kōmaṭṭi caste were real or imagined, but their claims did elicit a fascinating response from the Brahmin trustee, V. Raghavachariar.

In his written statement to the court, V. Raghavachariar argued, first, that the claims of the Vaisya caste (which these Kōmaṭṭis claimed to represent) "were neither urged, considered nor recognized in the discussions which preceded and led to the decree in C.S. 36 of 1884."[72] He further claimed that the court would have to make some decisions on the question of Vaisya monopolies over a trustee position, because "the question of the several castes and subcastes which should be represented on the management of the temple of Sri Parthasarathi Swami in Triplicane is not capable of discussion on the strength of any well-established or binding usages in the past."[73] He reported, further, that when the details of Justice Hutchins's scheme of 1885 became known, it excited class jealousies, and the list of voters, owing to the want of any property qualifications and other like limitations, grew so enormous and so unsatisfactory as to give general dissatisfaction.[74] In a later affidavit, V. Raghavachariar impugned the motives of several of his opponents and alleged that in several instances this suit was the outcome of malice on the part of individuals from whom he had legitimately withheld certain crucial honors. This accusation indicates that honors issues were often behind the legal dramas in this period, even if they were rarely the direct subjects of litigation.

One of the outcomes of this attempt by the Seṭṭi caste, representing themselves as Vaisyas, to gain additional shares in temple control was the impetus this gave to local members of the Piḷḷai (or Yātava) caste to make their own claims. In the course of making these claims

[71] Affidavit, July 11, 1891, of M. Gooroomoorthy Chetty and P. V. Nayudoo in C.S. 161 of 1891.

[72] Written statement of the first defendant, September 1, 1891, para. 4.

[73] Ibid., para. 7.

[74] Counteraffidavit of first defendant, September 9, 1891, in C.S. 161 of 1891, para. 24.

it was revealed that leadership within the Yātava community in the urban context of Madras was fragmented and incoherent: In one case a certain I. T. P. Pillay decried another caste fellow who wished to "represent" the Yātavas by saying that "the said Karikristna Pillay is not the head of the Yadava caste, nor is there any particular person who is recognized as such head to the said caste which is broken up into various sub-castes."[75] Eventually, with the support of affidavits from several other members of this community, I. T. P. Pillay was made a party to the suit, "representing" the interests of the Yātava community.

It is interesting to note how sensitive native litigants already were to the court's power to sanction certain cultural categories as appropriate markers for certain roles, as we see in the following claims by I. T. P. Pillay:

> That if the Court should hold that the Komity or Vysia contention in this suit shall prevail, I state that I belong to the Vysia community. I am informed that the original Vysia caste is on very good authorities divided into: (1) "Go Vysia," or those who make their living by rearing cows (2) "Bhoo Vysias," or those who till the land and earn their bread (3) "Thana Vysias," or those who live by trade or dealings in money. That I aver that I belong to the first class of Vysia sub-sect and I have better and preferential claim to the other sub-sects aforesaid.[76]

On the part of the plaintiffs and the first defendant, V. Raghavachariar, the court was besieged with arguments for the modification of Justice Hutchins's scheme of 1885. In addition to a number of minor technical changes that were requested, the most telling argument was the continuing difficulty of delineating the Teṉkalai electorate according to the 1885 scheme in a practical and efficient manner. It was alleged by various litigants that the mandate for "all Tengalais" to vote led to confusion,[77] that the use of the expression "of the Tengalai persuasion" in the 1885 scheme led to false personation,[78] and that the partisan spirit of many caste headmen exacerbated these problems.[79] These arguments found favor with the

[75] Further affidavit of I. T. P. Pillay, November 30, 1891, in C.S. 161 of 1891, para. 2.
[76] Ibid., para. 10.
[77] Written statement of supplemental plaintiffs, November 18, 1891, in C.S. 161 of 1891, para. 3.
[78] Affidavit of M. K. Lutchmanachariar and three others, November 2, 1891, in C.S. 161 of 1891, para. 6.
[79] Ibid., para. 8.

court, and accordingly new model schemes were proposed by several sets of litigants.

In his decree in September 1892 Justice Best of the High Court of Madras largely upheld the terms of the 1885 scheme, with a few minor alterations, and ordered that a new election should take place immediately.[80] Accordingly, an election was held on February 19, 1893, and L. Vencatarangam Naidu and T. Raghunatha Pillay were named to the two vacant trustee positions. Both the decree of September 21, 1892, and the results of the election of February 1893 immediately stimulated a renewed spate of litigation, which lasted until 1897. As a result, this suit was remanded for retrial, a fresh scheme was passed by Justice Best on August 31, 1894, and it was decided that the effect of this new scheme was not retroactive: The election was held valid and contestable not by an appeal but only by a fresh suit.[81] Such a suit was instituted and it will be discussed shortly.

Justice Best's final scheme of 1894, which remained substantially unaltered for the next twenty-five years, made a few key alterations in the previous scheme, but adhered to it in much of its detail. It did not alter the previous scheme in the matter of the caste of trustees. As for the other qualifications for the trusteeship, a property qualification was introduced. The age of voters was raised from eighteen to twenty-one years, and in the crucial matter of clarifying the boundaries of the Teṉkalai electorate, the judge left it to the trustees "to decide who are the members of the Tengalai sect, the phrase 'Tengalai persuasion' in the 1885 scheme being altered to 'Tengalai sect.' "[82] Lastly, the obligation of the surviving trustees to consult caste headmen was completely expunged, and it was also reiterated that only Teṉkalai headmen were entitled to be present at the receipt and counting of votes.

In the course of this case, the elements that formed the cultural framework for the interaction between temple and court continued to evolve. Judges, operating on both the procedural as well as the substantive ideas of Anglo-Indian law, were forced to make precedents commensurate with new conflicts. Litigants continued to use the structure and language of the court to pursue their political ends. The schemes generated by this interaction provided the "texts" around which both litigants and judges refined their expression of

[80] Decree of September 21, 1892, in C.S. 161 of 1891.
[81] Judgment on remand in C.S. 161 of 1891, August 31, 1894.
[82] Ibid.

the basic categories that underlay the politics of temple control. Legal codification and the self-understanding of contestants for temple control continued to stimulate each other.

Elections steadily became the opposite of what the courts intended them to be. Instead of being instruments of order, regularity, and participatory democracy, they were, more often than not, unruly and violent affairs. An excellent example of this was an election held on February 19, 1893, whose outcome was contested in *Rajaruthnum Naidu* v. *Venkatarangam Naidu*.[83] For legal purposes, this suit was brought by three members of the Teṉkalai community of Triplicane against the three trustees of the temple: V. Raghavachariar and the two newly elected trustees, L. Vencatarangam Naidu and T. Raghunatha Pillay.[84] But the wishes of the plaintiffs as well as other documents in this case make it quite clear that the plaintiffs were sympathetic to the Brahmin trustee, V. Raghavachariar, and their primary object was to nullify the election of the two newly elected trustees and to oust them from office. Depositions made by representatives of both factions involved in this case left little doubt that a state of cold war existed between V. Raghavachariar and his newly elected colleagues and that the utter lack of cooperation between the trustees had seriously interrupted the performance of several important festivals.[85]

The major issue in this case, however, was the validity of the election of L. Vencatarangam Naidu and T. Raghunatha Pillay as trustees on February 19, 1893. Justice Boddam's notes, based on his examination of oral evidence from several witnesses of the election, give a fascinating glimpse of the chaotic nature of this event.[86] In keeping with the factional alliances in the community, led by the newly elected trustees and V. Raghavachariar, respectively, the depositions of the witnesses fell into two categories: One consisted of witnesses claiming that the election was a fraudulent, noisy, corrupt, mob-ruled travesty of the scheme, whereas the other claimed that, in spite of seeming "confusion" at the temple on election day, the election itself was fair and valid. Each side attacked the motives of the other.

[83] C.S. 137 of 1895, High Court of Judicature at Madras.

[84] Plaint, June 1, 1895, in C.S. 137 of 1895.

[85] Plaint, June 1, 1895, in C.S. 137 of 1895, para. 6; affidavit of plaintiffs two and three, June 5, 1895; counteraffidavit of third defendant, June 5, 1895; affidavit of defendants one and two, March 4, 1896.

[86] Judge's notes on examination of witnesses in C.S. 137 of 1895.

On the (tacit) side of the Brahmin trustee, witnesses painted a gory picture of mass manipulation, mob frenzy, and corruption. A certain Y. Partasarady Iyengar, a Teṉkalai lawyer, claimed that voters were being "coached" about how to vote by their headmen, that people who knew nothing of the election cast votes, that people squeezed improperly onto the dais, and that it was impossible to keep order in spite of the presence of the police. He also accused a certain Saivite, Sholliappa Mudaliar, an agent of the newly elected trustees, of causing confusion and manipulating voters. Of the voters, this witness claimed that "some wore Shiva marks, others wore other marks." M. Tirumalachary, a Teṉkalai landed proprietor, also reported a mob and said that he "could not vote because I did not want to push my way in." P. Parthasarathy Iyengar, a Teṉkalai merchant of Triplicane, said that agents of the newly elected trustees distributed voting papers at the houses of voters ten days before the election and that "dependent on whose paper you were carrying you were or were not let in."

The reports of the witnesses questioned on the second day of depositions, August 11, 1896, grew more graphic and outraged. Venkatesa Pillay, a non-Teṉkalai, claimed that Sholliappa Mudaliar, the agent of the newly elected trustees, with the help of others "solicited votes and paid voters." He also reported that headmen of various castes collected voting papers and handed them to the Brahmin trustee. With surprising and charming candor, Venkatesa Pillay admitted that "I paid voters myself . . . only a few . . . I also gave money to headmen to pay voters . . . paying was done secretly . . . I followed because they paid one of our voters . . . he had promised to vote for us."

The mass manipulation of the poor and illiterate emerged in the deposition of a Teṉkalai fisherman named Murugappa Chetty. He reported that "my Headman took me to his house and asked me to sign a paper and take it to the temple." This was apparently paid for with half a rupee. When he reached the temple, "a Brahmin led me up and I handed up my paper to a man pointed [out] by the Brahmin." This fisherman's vote was for L. Vencatarangum Naidu, whom he had never seen before that day. He also reported that the agent, Sholliappa Mudaliar, whom he knew, was on the portico of his headman's house when he received the half rupee, as did three other caste headmen: "My master told me that the third defendant [i.e., the Brahmin trustee, V. Raghavachariar] favored our side."

Embarrassment on the part of the Brahmin trustee, who did not wish to seem pleased with this farce, and the fear of being unseated on the part of the two newly elected trustees led to denials from all three of all these charges of electoral irregularity. But in the face of the graphic evidence, such denials were weak, and Justice Boddam found the election to be invalid on numerous grounds, such as a poor ratio of actual voters to registered voters (697:2,857), bribery, false personation, and the alteration of voting papers.[87] But even while this case was being argued in court, the conflict between V. Raghavachariar and his new colleagues had generated a concurrent, though separate, suit at the High Court of Madras.

The previously discussed case, although embedded in the specific factional opposition between V. Raghavachariar, the Brahmin trustee, and his two non-Brahmin co-trustees, established a major motif – "disputed elections" – which lasted for the next twenty years. What it shows is the utter impracticality of imposing a Western, nineteenth-century democratic model of politics on an institution that had neither cultural nor historical acquaintance with such a model. This case is, therefore, not simply a paradigm of the "corrupt election." It is an example of how the rules and structures of an alien political model simply provide a scaffolding, which complicates and in some ways facilitates preexisting political ties and concepts. The debate on such "elections" in court, in this case as in future cases, demonstrates the difficulty of establishing the "facts" in such a partisan affair. That the real issues lay elsewhere than in such artificial procedural matters became clear in the following case, in which the newly elected trustees responded to the hostility of their Brahmin colleague, V. Raghavachariar.

In the increasingly ambiguous and polarized state of affairs, conflict between trustees began to take the form of heated accusations of mismanagement. In *Srinivasa Ayyangar* v. *V. Raghavachariar*,[88] for example, allies of two newly elected trustees accused the third trustee, V. Raghavachariar, of a large variety of improprieties. The major accusations were: The plaintiffs claimed that "the defendant has been guilty of numerous acts of misfeasance, breach of trust and neglect of duty." They claimed that V. Raghavachariar had used the income from a certain pillared hall in the temple called the

[87] Judgment, August 17, 1896, in C.S. 137 of 1895.
[88] Plaint, December 5, 1895, in C.S. 293 of 1895.

Gānkaikkoṇṭān Maṇṭapam for his own benefit; that he had failed to deposit into the temple accounts various sums of money entrusted to him by worshippers for making a jeweled crown for the deity; that the list of temple jewels furnished to the new trustees was incomplete; that, instead of lodging them in the Bank of Madras, he kept in his own house temple cash and government promissory notes to the value of Rs. 1,21,000 and some temple records; that "with the intention of benefiting his friends and dependents," he had been levying smaller rents than were appropriate for houses belonging to the temple and had allowed rental arrears to accumulate to the extent of Rs. 1,500. These, and a number of other complaints, were concluded with a prayer to the court that V. Raghavachariar be removed from office.

This period also sees litigants making clever use of legal provisions and courtroom strategies to aid their cases, such as the use of legal provisions of a technical and procedural sort to subvert their opponents, and attempting to use the subpoena powers of the court to gain access to temple documents that would benefit them and prejudice the claims of their opponents.

Further, the judges of the High Court, both Indian and English, found that in order to respond to the increasing legal sophistication of litigants, they had to clarify, expand, and delimit the precise meaning of legal statutes. Thus, in one case in the last years of the nineteenth century, Justice Shepherd had to contend with a subtle objection to a suit based on Section 30 of the Civil Procedure Code of 1882. This involved the clarification of a series of English precedents, the precise discrimination of a series of types of case, the classification of the case in question in its appropriate category, and a general clarification of the meaning and scope of the statutory provision. In this case, as in many others, the politics of the contested election were transformed, in part, into the politics of legal procedure.

Conflicts between trustees and their adherents, acted out in bitterly fought elections and extended court cases, also began to have an increasingly direct effect on the ritual and redistributive process of the Temple, with the issue of honors at its center. In 1905 the death of V. Raghavachariar, the Brahmin trustee, led to conflict between the surviving trustees, P. M. Appasawmy Pillay and P. Rajaruthnum Naidu, and the family of the deceased trustee. Two suits filed in 1905 reflect the attempts of the two sides to use the court to their advantage.

The case of *Appasawmy Pillay* v. *Ramanuja Chariar* was filed on July 14, 1905, by the two surviving trustees against V. Ramanujachariar and seven other surviving male members of the family of the late Brahmin trustee, V. Raghavachariar.[89] The main issue of the plaint concerned the control of the Gaṅkaikkoṇṭāṉ Maṇṭapam, whose importance already was clear in C.S. 293 of 1895. On much the same grounds as in that previous case, the plaintiffs asked the court to declare this property as belonging to the temple and that "the Defendants have no manner of right to the same."[90]

The response of the defendants provides rich evidence concerning a basic source of structural tension in the temple (previously discussed in Chapter 1), namely, the relative autonomy of donors in the redistributive process of the temple, often displayed in concern over honors.[91] In addition to citing their family's construction and continued subsidy of this structure and the commercial establishments in it, the defendants explicitly linked their claims to the ownership of this property with the honors they received in this structure on key ritual occasions:

> The Defendants submit that during the annual festivals in the said temple, on certain special occasions, the God, while processioning through the four streets around the temple, used to alight in the said Mantapam where certain offerings used to be made to the deity at the expense of the Defendants and the Defendants are honoured with garlands in token of the said family having constructed the said Mantapam for the use of the deity.[92]

This impassioned defense was concluded with a plea that the suit should be dismissed, because it was filed on the eve of the impending election "with the sole object of lowering the 1st Defendant in the estimation of the voting public."[93] The suit was dismissed by Justice Boddam on September 5, 1906,[94] and a subsequent appeal against this judgment was also dismissed.[95] But an election had been held on July 23, 1905, and shortly thereafter partisans of the late Brahmin

[89] Plaint, July 14, 1905, in C.S. 108 of 1905, High Court of Judicature at Madras.

[90] Ibid., para. 15.

[91] Written statement of defendants one and three, July 31, 1905, in C.S. 108 of 1905.

[92] Ibid., para. 6.

[93] Written statement of defendants one and three, July 31, 1905, in C.S. 108 of 1905, para. 16.

[94] Judgment, September 5, 1906, in C.S. 108 of 1905.

[95] Plaint, September 21, 1905, in C.S. 169 of 1905, High Court of Judicature at Madras.

trustee and his family filed a suit, *Krishnasawmy Moodeliar* v. *Rajaruthum Naidu,* contesting the validity of the election.

The main target of attack by the plaintiffs in this new suit was the newly elected trustee, M. Parthasarathy Iyengar, who had previously been the *amīnā* of the temple and had defeated the plaintiffs' favored candidate, V. Ramanujachariar (the brother of the late V. Raghavachariar). The plaintiffs made the usual charges of "undue influence, bribery, false personation, and other material irregularities,"[96] and the defendants issued the standard denials.

But some of the evidence in this case brought to light a variety of interesting ways in which features of the redistributive process of the temple were manipulated for factional ends. A letter written by some worshippers to the trustees, a week before the election, detailed four ways in which the *amīnā* might have used his key role in the redistributive process of the temple to influence his victory in the election.[97] First, they said, he had been lenient toward those temple servants who had supported his candidacy and had overlooked irregularities in their conduct. Second, it was claimed that the man who was contracted to sell the edible leavings of the deity *(prasātam)* to the public had the support of the *amīnā* in selling unwholesome articles to the public. The reason for this, according to the deponents, was that "this Amina is allowed to make free use of the articles of the hotel for bribing the voters who support his candidature."[98] Third, they claimed that the *amīnā* had been diverting some share of the sacred leavings of the deity meant for special visitors *(tecāntari prasātam)* away from this use to the canvassers of votes for his own election. Finally, they claimed that the *amīnā* had been excessively strict toward those temple servants who opposed his election, "for instance by curtailing their honors, etc."[99]

In the three major suits that occurred between 1910 and 1916, although vacancies in the trusteeship and contested elections continued to provide the backdrop for temple politics, conflicts between trustees more explicitly centered on the details of the day-to-day management of the temple as an economic and administrative entity. In C.S. 176 of 1915, the two non-Brahmin trustees were opposed to the Brahmin trustee, V. Parthasarathy Iyengar. The office of temple

96 Ibid., para. 9.

97 P. Kristnaswamy Aiyer and Raghavachari to the trustees, July 19, 1905, brought on record by the plaintiffs in C.S. 169 of 1905.

98 Ibid.

99 Ibid.

manager was a newly created one, and its incumbent was a partisan of the two non-Brahmin trustees. On the other hand, the *amīnā* was a cousin of the Brahmin trustee and his direct link to the day-to-day economics and ritual of the temple. The question here was: Whose man would have direct and routine control of temple affairs?

The judgment in this case established that the majority of the trustees could overrule the minority. This important administrative decision was made in the context of lively and detailed recourse to the legal past of the temple by all concerned, litigants as well as the judge. In addition to filing the judgments and records in the suits of 1911 and 1914 and the judgment and schemes in C.S. 486 of 1884 and C.S. 161 of 1891, the defendant asserted that "in 1843 when the government handed over charge of the temple to three trustees they were expressly directed to look after the management of the temple themselves personally and the same was affirmed in C.S. 161 of 1891." Similarly, one of the plaintiffs cited the judgments and proceedings in C.S. 108 of 1905, C.S. 233 of 1911, and C.S. 29 of 1914. The judge bolstered his own judgment in behalf of the majority with both English and South Indian precedents in order to show that this apparent innovation was not really contrary to "custom and usage."

This suit, in a way, encapsulated four decades of legal precedents in the history of the temple. Henceforth, the question of trusteeship, its incumbents, their mode of election and so forth became subordinate to the more fundamental questions with which the early cases in this period were concerned: the meaning and definition of the Teṉkalai community, the rights of various groups within it, and the issue of the accountability of the trustees to their electorate. But when these fundamental issues reappeared, it was in a more radical, organized, and serious fashion than in the last decades of the nineteenth century. Three and a half decades of acculturation to the language and ideology of Anglo-Indian law had not been wasted on the community interested in the politics of the temple.

In the years between 1916 and 1925 the propensity of the court to create new definitions of rights and roles in the temple, born of its twin orientation to legislation and precedent, helped to transform what had been a relatively fluid system of alliances, factions, and cleavages into a structurally fragmented community. In many respects this was the logical outcome of patterns established between 1878 and 1915. Because the seven major cases that occurred between

1916 and 1925 are so intimately interconnected, it is not worthwhile to isolate them analytically. The following analysis treats them as part of a single, though immensely complex, set of events.

The seven suits involving this temple, which were fought at the High Court of Madras between 1916 and 1925, present the following chronological profile: *Parthasarathy Iyengar* v. *Appasawmy Pillay,*[100] occupied the attention of the court from 1918 to 1925 and was filed by three Teṉkalai Brahmin voters against the temple trustees; *Vijayaraghava Mudaliar* v. *Ranganadham Chetty*[101] was filed by some non-Brahmin worshippers against the temple trustees; *Venkatanarasimha Bhattachariar* v. *Parthasarathy Iyengar,*[102] which was finally disposed of by the court in September 1922, was filed by one section of the priestly lineage at the temple against the trustees and the other section of the same lineage; *Ranganadham Chetty* v. *Parthasarathy Iyengar,*[103] which was resolved in March 1923, was a suit by one of the trustees against his co-trustees; *Venkatanarasimha Bhattachariar* v. *Parthasarathy Iyengar,*[104] which was settled by compromise in April 1925, was another suit by one section of the priesthood against the trustees; *Anna Rangachariar* v. *Parthasarathy Iyengar,*[105] which was finally adjudicated in November 1925, was a suit brought against the trustees to establish the rights of those Teṉkalai Brahmins who recited the Prabandam poems in the daily service at the temple (the *attiyāpakās*); and finally, *Viraraghavachariar* v. *Parthasarathy Iyengar*[106] was filed by some Brahmin "worshippers and voters" against the trustees and was settled by the final formation of a new scheme for the governance of the temple in December 1925.

But it is not only in a chronological sense that these cases overlapped each other. The issues represented in them were also intimately interconnected and reflected the precipitous fragmentation of the community interested in the temple. The most salient points of the final scheme[107] fixed by the High Court of Madras, in *Viraraghavachariar* v. *Parthasarathy Iyengar,* for the temple were: the establishment of a Board of Supervision, also elected, with extensive powers of supervi-

[100] C.S. 111 of 1918, High Court of Judicature at Madras.
[101] C.S. 843 of 1919, High Court of Judicature at Madras.
[102] C.S. 860 of 1920, High Court of Judicature at Madras.
[103] C.S. 559 of 1922, High Court of Judicature at Madras.
[104] C.S. 442 of 1923, High Court of Judicature at Madras.
[105] C.S. 349 of 1923, High Court of Judicature at Madras.
[106] C.S. 527 of 1924, High Court of Judicature at Madras; see Appendix C for the full text of this final scheme.
[107] Scheme in C.S. 527 of 1924.

sion over the trustees; the restriction of the tenure of trustees to five years; the (implicit) shrinkage of the electorate by insisting on literacy as well as a cash fee for participation in elections.

In principle, the nature, extent, and means of control by the Teṉkalai community over the Śrī Pārtasārati Svāmi Temple had become legally fixed. But to understand the serious fragmentation that was concealed by this collective and constitutional charter for local sect control over the temple, it is necessary to consider, from a structural point of view, the tensions *within* the community that evolved between 1916 and 1925 and the means by which the court helped to legally reify these tensions. This can best be done by considering the structural tensions surrounding five groups of individuals during this period who had, or aspired to, systematic shares in temple control: (1) the trustees, (2) the priests, (3) the *attiyāpakās* (Brahmin hymnists), (4) non-Brahmin voters and worshippers, and (5) the Vaṭakalai residents of Triplicane. These five focuses of tension are considered serially below.

The judges of the High Court of Madras continued to expect from temple trustees standards of behavior consonant with managers of English charitable trusts. These expectations were perhaps best expressed by Justices Madhavan Nair, Kumarasami Sastriar and Srinivasa Iyengar, when they passed judgment in *Viraraghavachariar* v. *Parthasarathy Iyengar*:

> In this connection we may take leave to observe that it is highly regrettable that trusteeships of temples and similar institutions should be looked upon as places of prestige and profit and that people should be found who are desperately anxious to be elected to such places or to continue to stick to them in spite of the onerous and serious responsibilities thereof. The true spirit in which such offices should be accepted or retained is the spirit of service and sacrifice in the interests of the public and of the institutions. So long as such offices are regarded not as posts of duty and responsibility but as opportunities of personal aggrandisement the affairs of such institutions are bound to be unsatisfactory.[108]

This judicial expectation that trustees were to act in a selfless and public-spirited way was both naïve and culturally unsound. Trustees, as the evidence of this chapter has shown, were personally "interested" in many aspects of the redistributive process of the temple. This did not offend any indigenous cultural principles, for their "protective" role also encompassed an active, personal set of

[108] Judgment, May 1, 1925, in C.S. 527 of 1924, High Court of Judicature at Madras.

transactions with the deity. In this respect, their combination of protective and personal interests in the temple was a natural extension, and survival, of the dual role of Hindu kings with respect to temples in pre-British South India.[109] But in the heightened atmosphere of conflict in the temple after the 1870s, this dual role became itself the focus of contention and criticism.

This was nowhere clearer than in the problem of the relationship of the Vanamamalai family to the building known as the Gānkaikkoṉṭāṉ Maṇṭapam, which surfaced repeatedly between 1895 and 1925. In discussions surrounding this issue, the problem was a simple one: Where did the role of the representative of this family as trustee end and his prerogatives as a donor in the spatial and ritual context of Gānkaikkoṇṭān Maṇṭapam begin? Although many opponents of this family, in the litigation over a thirty-year period, were willing to cast aspersions on the inappropriate ways in which this family manipulated the relationship between the temple and this particular building, no petitioner *ever* cast a doubt on the appropriateness of a trustee being simultaneously a donor with an active share in the redistributive process of the temple.

It is this cultural expectation, namely, that protection and endowment can honorably be combined in the activities of a trustee, that accounts for the immense number of ways in which trustees were willing to express factional interests, use their power to reward their clientele, and manipulate the "shares" of their opponents in the redistributive process of the temple. This is not to say that no standard of morals attached to the role of the trustee. Certainly, acts of outright peculation of endowed funds or explicit denial of shares to legitimate participants in the temple was considered offensive and improper. The point remains, however, that trustees, like other participants in the world of the deity, were not expected to sacrifice their own transactional relationship with the deity in the interests of a homogenous "public."

The response of the courts to this inexorable duality in the interests of trustees was to make numerous attempts to increase their accountability, both to their larger constituency, the Teṉkalai "voters and worshippers," and after 1925 to a supervisory body, the Board of Supervision, which lasted until 1946. In both these respects the actions of the courts had unintended consequences. The evidence displayed in cases throughout this period suggests that voters

[109] See Chapters 1 and 2.

never were, in their corporate capacity, able to make trustees accountable to them. Voters generally had to return to court in order to have any hope of rendering the trustees accountable to them. More often than not, however, these voters represented an anti-trustee alliance, rather than some disinterested and homogeneous electorate. Thus the courts' attempts to write trustee accountability into its schemes had the unintended consequence of providing both fuel as well as mechanisms for the legal pursuit of political conflicts, rather than providing for any genuine accountability of the trustees to the mass electorate.

Much the same was true with judicial attempts to subject the trustees to supervision from above. A short-lived Committee of Revision, created by the court during the case of *Parthasarathy Iyengar* v. *Appasawmy Pillay,* made pathetic appeals to the court for help in keeping the trustees in check.[110] Much the same was true of the Board of Supervision created by the court during the course of *Viraraghavachariar* v. *Parthasarathy Iyengar*. In April 1927 the board was already complaining to the court about the utter indifference of the trustees to their powers and prerogatives and their complete failure to place the trustees under any systematic scrutiny.[111] The Board of Supervision remained utterly helpless throughout the 1930s and 1940s, with the trustees simply, and successfully, resisting all attempts at systematic audit from above.[112]

Further, the internal relations among the trustees, intrinsically factious because of their lack of "public spirit," was exacerbated by the court in *Partharsarathy Iyengar* v. *Appasawmy Pillay,* where, as we noted already, it was established that the majority would prevail over the minority in cases of indecision among the trustees. This piece of legal codification had the unforeseen effect of freezing the "two versus one" factional propensity within the trusteeship. For the rest of the period under consideration, as well as throughout the 1930s, 1940s, and 1950s, the terms *majority* and *minority* came to describe the two factions within the trusteeship and lost all connection to the original tool of convenience that they should have been.

The most important problem of the trusteeship, which was made very clear in the period from 1916 to 1925, was its authority over

[110] Affidavit of G. Venkataranga Rao, August 10, 1923, in C.S. 111 of 1918.

[111] Affidavit of Rao Bahadur C. Dinadayalu Mudaliar, April 7, 1927, in C.S. 527 of 1924, para. 13.

[112] This is attested in a considerable volume of correspondence between the Board of Supervisors and the trustees, now in the Record Room, SPS Temple.

other groups who had fixed roles in worship and redistribution.[113] This was particularly true in respect to the priests and the *attiyāpakā*s. When faced with a direct threat to their authority from one section of the priesthood, the trustees pleaded that "unless the authority of the trustees is maintained and their hands strengthened to preserve order, the temple administration is absolutely impossible."[114] In a similar way, the trustees found themselves struggling for their own power when the *attiyāpāka* group made a systematic bid for the codification of their own rights in *Anna Rangachariar* v. *Parthasarathy Iyengar*. In the course of this suit, V. Parthasarathy Iyengar, the Brahmin trustee, said:

> I say that it is absolutely untrue that the Adhyapakas were exercising any control or supervision over the ceremonial worship or distribution of prasadams. They are the functions of the trustees and no such right was put forward or recognized in any of the Scheme decrees relating to this temple.[115]

But in respect to both the priests and the *attiyāpakā*s, the documented legal past as well as the proclivities of the court redounded to their benefit, and their privileges in opposition to the trustees were legally strengthened and codified.

The basic cultural elements and sociological profile of the priesthood at this temple were presented in Chapter 1.[116] A single lineage had, in the course of the nineteenth century, become divided, and thus in the early decades of this century there were three "shares" divided among, theoretically, three subdivisions of this lineage of priests.[117] In practice there had come to be two subsections, which shared the right to perform priestly services, and in a major civil suit in 1917, the specific and detailed privileges of these two subsections of the priesthood were codified by the City Civil Court of Madras.[118] These two subsections came to be known as the *Cinna Murai* (Small Turn) and the *Periya Murai* (Big Turn), because of the proportion of the ritual calendar they respectively monopolized in terms of the right to perform priestly service.

In *Venkatanarasimha Bhattachariar* v. *Parthasarathy Iyengar* and *Venkatanarasimha Bhattachariar* v. *Parthasarathy Iyengar*[119] the conflict

113 See Chapter 1 for a synchronic discussion of this problem.
114 Counteraffidavit of first defendant, August 6, 1923, in C.S. 349 of 1923.
115 Ibid.
116 See pp. 25–6, 38, and 48.
117 O.S. 485 of 1917, City Civil Court of Madras, provides detailed documentation of this process.
118 Judgment, October 8, 1919, in O.S. 485 of 1917.
119 C.S. 860 of 1920 and C.S. 442 of 1923, respectively.

between the subsections, stimulated by legal codification, provided the backdrop for serious conflicts between the priests of the *Periya Murai* and the trustees, who were themselves thoroughly factionalized. In the second case, Venkatanarisimha Bhattachariar, one of the priests, defined the autonomy of the priesthood in the following terms:

> The trustees had no power at any time to superintend or to control either the mode or form of worship in the said temple or the Gumustahs (agents) employed by any Archaka office-holder, the Archaka office-holder being always responsible to the Trustees for the due performance of the worship and for the safety of the jewels and other articles of worship entrusted to him.[120]

His request to the court that he should be allowed to do his share of the worship without interference from the trustees and that the trustees had no right to appoint agents for the performance of worship during his "turn" were granted and legally codified.[121] The systematic use of the legal past by the priests can be seen in the conclusion of their plaint, where the conflict was rooted in a crucial overlap of the "turns" of the two sections of the priesthood, which the trustees used as an opportunity to suspend the chief priest of the *Periya Murai*:

> That the defendants 1 to 3 herein [i.e., the trustees], their agents and servants may be restrained by an injunction of this court from interfering with the plaintiff and his agents in the discharge of the duties appertaining to the Periamurai as usual in the said temple in accordance with the decrees in C.S. 860 of 1920 on the file of this Hon'ble Court and City Civil Court Suit No. 485 of 1917.[122]

However, the compromise with which this suit was ended,[123] as well as the previous decisions, had unintended results. The codification of the rights of the two sets of priests, as well as of their prerogatives with respect to the trustees, achieved in these cases provided a charter and stimulus for such conflict throughout the 1930s, 1940s, and 1950s.[124]

But the trustees were not the only group from which the priesthood had something to fear. Another group with whom the priests had an uneasy relationship, which in subsequent decades grew into

[120] Plaint, November 19, 1920, in C.S. 860 of 1920, para. 10.
[121] Plaint, July 13, 1923, in C.S. 442 of 1923, paras. 10–13.
[122] Ibid., para. 32(c).
[123] Affidavit of K. Narasimha Bhattachari, April 21, 1925, in C.S. 442 of 1923.
[124] See, for example, the discussion of C.S. 241 of 1933 in Chapter 1.

open antagonism, was the group of Teṉkalai Brahmin males who monopolized the right of reciting the Prabandam corpus of Vaisnava devotional hymns, the *attiyāpakās*.[125] In Chapter 1, reference was made to the role of this group in ritual today and to the immense list of paraphernalia, in terms of duties and honors, that they claimed for themselves in *Anna Rangachariar* v. *Parthasarathy Iyengar* of 1923.[126]

The context for this extraordinary assertion of their rights and privileges by the *attiyāpakās* in the 1920s was an intense conflict between them and some of the trustees, wherein the entire balance of power in the temple was at stake. The specific claims of this group in *Anna Rangachariar* v. *Parthasarathy Iyengar* were set in the following sweeping context:

> From time immemorial the Thengalai Vaishnava residents of Triplicane have been interested in and have had rights of control over the temples of Sri Parthasarathy Svami in Triplicane and the plaintiffs and other Thengalai Vaishnava adult male Brahmins have under the title of sthalathars by immemorial right and long enjoyment been entitled to the mirasi offices of (1) Adyapakam (2) Arulapadu (3) Puranam (4) Vedaparayanam (5) Kattiyam in the temple . . . and to receipt of perquisites, emoluments and honors as set out in Schedule A and to perform the duties as set out in Schedule B hereto.[127]

Given this sweeping claim, it is not surprising that the *attiyāpakās* felt able to assert that "the trustees have no authority over the adhyapakas in respect of the recitation of prabandhams and vedas."[128] In some cases the attempts of this group for autonomy in ritual were supported by outright Brahmin superiority arguments: "I say that the Dharmakarthas, most of whom are non-Brahmins, have no manner of control over the Adhyapakas who are spiritually superior to them."[129]

The conflict between the *attiyāpakā* group and some of the trustees, which resulted in the filing of *Anna Rangachariar* v. *Parthasarathy Iyengar*, was no calm legal affair. Accounts from both sides testify to the fact that it involved public violence and disruption of ritual.[130] Its nature was furthermore considerably influenced by the current

[125] Counteraffidavit of Archaka Srinivasa Bhattachariar, August 6, 1923, in C.S. 349 of 1923.

[126] Chapter 1.

[127] Plaint, April 27, 1923, in C.S. 349 of 1923, para. 5.

[128] Affidavit of V. M. Lakshminarasimhachariar, April 27, 1923, in C.S. 349 of 1923, para. 22.

[129] Affidavit of T. Ramanujachariar, March 15, 1924, in C.S. 349 of 1923, para. 6.

[130] Plaint, March 27, 1923, paras. 11, 13, 15, and 16; affidavit of V. M. Lakshminarasimhachariar, paras. 12 and 13; affidavit of P. S. Parthasarathy Iyengar,

factional conflict among the trustees, as well as by the preceding conflicts between the trustees and the priests, because the *attiyāpakā* group had supported one section of the priests against the other section and some of the trustees.[131] It is sufficient to note the following incidents, which characterized the conflict between the *attiyāpakā*s and the trustees between 1922 and 1925: (1) attempts by the trustees to set up their own partisans as bona fide *attiyāpakā*s, who could then publicly, and disruptively, claim honors owed to the acknowledged leader of the *attiyāpakā*s; (2) claims by the two trustees opposed to this group that certain portions of the recital of the Prabandam were being performed contrary to custom and that this warranted the dismissal of some of the prominent *attiyāpakā*s; (3) specific attempts by some of the partisans of these trustees to withhold or divert some of the honors owed to the *attiyāpakā*s, thus causing them public humiliation and involving the interference of the police on several occasions.

Both sides invoked an immense mass of documentary evidence, including the Rules and Regulations formulated by the Board of Revenue in 1800, which were referred to in Chapter 3.[132] But the court found the largely negative evidence on behalf of the *attiyāpakā*s considerably more persuasive than the evidence cited by the trustees, and, accordingly, the judgment and the decree in this case were highly favorable to their interests.[133] The detailed codification of their duties, perquisites, and honors by the court in this case has ever since been a major charter for the proud autonomy of this group and still is today. This decree was reaffirmed in the final scheme for the overall management of the temple, ratified by the court in *Viraraghavachariar* v. *Parthasarathy Iyengar.*[134]

It was partly this major bid for legally ratified privileges by the *attiyāpakā*s, who are fervent Teṉkalai Brahmins, that partially provoked a final, abortive attempt by the Brahmin Vaṭakalai residents of Triplicane to carve out a place for themselves in the redistributive process of the temple. This attempt was also no doubt

March 27, 1923, paras. 8–10; affidavit of first plaintiff, July 30, 1923, passim; counteraffidavit of defendants one and two, July 30, 1923, passim; affidavit of C. K. Rangachari, July 24, 1923, passim. (All these documents are filed in C.S. 349 of 1923.)

131 Plaint, April 27, 1923, in C.S. 349 of 1923, para. 10.

132 Chapter 3; also see Appendix A of this study for the full text of these Rules and Regulations.

133 Judgment, May 1, 1925, and Decree, November 12, 1925, in C.S. 349 of 1923.

134 See this final scheme in Appendix C.

encouraged by the general and fluid atmosphere of conflict over rights in court by all the other groups involved with the temple. The last serious attempt by the Vaṭakalai community to gain a legitimate share in temple control had been in the 1830s when a Vaṭakalai resident of Triplicane made a futile application to the collector of Madras for the then vacant trusteeship.[135] After that, there is no evidence of any such attempt by the Vaṭakalai community of Triplicane, and the assumption and concept of Teṉkalai control over the temple gained increasing bureaucratic and judicial legitimation and concrete meaning. But in the intense ferment of 1924–5, the Vaṭakalai residents of Triplicane saw the opportunity for themselves to make one more attempt to gain a share in control over the Śrī Pārtasārati Svāmi Temple.

During the proceedings in *Anna Rangachariar* v. *Parthasarathy Iyengar* (the *attiyāpakā* case) and in *Viraraghavachariar* v. *Parthasarathy Iyengar* (the final "scheme" suit), there were three attempts by Vaṭakalai residents of Triplicane to enlist legal help in advancing their cause.[136] Given the complete failure of these attempts, only three points of interest are revealed by the evidence. First, that some of the trustees might have encouraged Vaṭakalai attempts to interfere with the ritual process as a way of defusing the growing power of the *attiyāpakā*s, who represented the height of Teṉkalai exclusivity.[137] Second, the use of the past by the Vaṭakalai litigants to make their case was fascinating: they attempted to legally legitimize the use of the verse beginning with the words "Rāmānuja Dayāpātra" at the commencement of Prabandam recitation[138] (it will be recalled that the genesis of the pan-regional Vaṭakalai movement at the beginning of the eighteenth century was associated with a royal order endorsing the use of this verse in Vaiṣṇava temple ritual).[139] The third point of interest is the decisiveness of the judges of the High Court of Madras, who flatly rejected all Vaṭakalai claims to any systematic role in the control of this temple.[140] This is the most eloquent testimony to the complete victory of the concept of "Teṉkalai

[135] Chapter 4.

[136] Affidavit of M. Venkatachariar, December 18, 1924, in C.S. 349 of 1923; reply affidavit of M. Venkatachariar, July 28, 1925, in C.S. 349 of 1923; affidavit of E. Raghunathachariar, November 30, 1925, in C.S. 527 of 1924.

[137] Written statement of the first defendant, October 3, 1923, in C.S. 349 of 1923, para. 10.

[138] Affidavit of M. Venkatachariar, December 18, 1924, para. 4.

[139] Chapter 2.

[140] Judge's Order, December 19, 1924, in C.S. 349 of 1923; Decree, November 12, 1925, in C.S. 349 of 1923; final scheme in C.S. 527 of 1924.

control" over this temple by 1925. Since then, to my knowledge, there have been no similar attempts by Triplicane Vaṭakalais to gain a share in the control of this temple.

One last example of fission in the temple, encouraged by judicial activity, remains to be considered: the growing rift between Brahmin and non-Brahmin worshippers. There is no doubt that this development was part of the larger cultural, social, and political mobilization of the non-Brahmin community in Madras city and in the Madras presidency in the second decade of this century but particularly after 1915.[141]

During the proceedings in *Parthasarathy Iyengar* v. *Appasawmy Pillay*, where the previous scheme fixed in 1895 was being reconsidered, several non-Brahmin members of the Teṉkalai community of Triplicane reacted adversely to proposals that a literacy requirement and a cash fee should be imposed on the electorate, claiming that these proposals were part of a Brahmin conspiracy to throttle the rights of non-Brahmins in the temple. One non-Brahmin argued that some of these "Brahmin proposals" were "looked upon by several of my caste men with apprehensions and suspicions [as calculated to] . . . cut off the rights of non-Brahmins of their legitimate shares in the due administration of the temple."[142] Similarly, four non-Brahmin deponents argued that "these are measures cunningly and mischievously introduced by plaintiffs who are all Brahmins to minimize the non-Brahmin franchise."[143] In the opinion of these and some other non-Brahmin participants in the suit, these alterations "would practically vest the management in the hands of a few Brahmins hanging around the temple."[144] All these non-Brahmin allegations were couched in terms of the legal history of the temple, and their argument was held to be an assertion of rights held from "time immemorial."

After the election of V. Ranganatham Chetty to the trusteeship in June 1919, two of the non-Brahmin deponents in *Parthasarathy Iyengar* v. *Appasawmy Pillay* (C.S. 111 of 1918) filed the case of *Vijayaraghava Mudaliar* v. *Ranganadham Chetty*,[145] arguing that the election was invalid. The major factual basis of their complaint was

[141] Eugene F. Irschick, *Politics and Social Conflict in South India: The Non-Brahmin Movement and Tamil Separatism, 1916–1929* (Berkeley, 1969), Chaps. 1–5, esp. p. 17.

[142] Affidavit of C. Krishnaswami Chetty, February 20, 1920, in C.S. 111 of 1918.

[143] Affidavit of N. M. Vijayaraghava Mudaliar and others, February 17, 1920, in C.S. 111 of 1918.

[144] Objections and suggestions of defendants nine through eleven, November 22, 1921, in C.S. 111 of 1918.

[145] Plaint (no date), in C.S. 843 of 1919.

an extension of the earlier "conspiracy" theory: They claimed that in the list of voters for this election, the names of seven hundred non-Brahmins who had voted in the previous election had been arbitrarily excluded and the names of one hundred Brahmin voters added.[146] But this charge was not carefully documented or discussed before the case was dismissed on a technicality.[147]

After the passage of the final scheme in *Viraraghavachariar* v. *Parthasarathy Iyengar,* in which monetary and literacy requirements for the voters were legally incorporated, a number of non-Brahmins attempted to move the case to the Privy Council in England.[148] Their lengthy argument painted the court, after 1918, as having been utterly insensitive to the rights of the non-Brahmin community interested in the temple and viewed all the changes made since then in the management of the temple as part of a Brahmin conspiracy against non-Brahmin rights.[149] This appeal was rejected, and the scheme suit of 1924 did become binding on the entire community.

This particular piece of legal codification meant that a large proportion of the poor and illiterate non-Brahmin section of the Teṉkalai community was henceforth excluded from the electoral process at the temple. It is hardly surprising that in the subsequent decades and up to the present non-Brahmin sentiment has focused directly on their share of honors in the redistributive process. This movement has been discussed in Chapter 1.[150]

What was the outcome of the interaction in the period from 1878 to 1925 between the Śrī Pārtasārati Svāmi Temple and the High Court of Madras? First, the idea that the Teṉkalai community of Triplicane was to control the temple was given concrete legal expression in a formal and elaborate electoral system. Second, however, a series of tensions within this community were legally stimulated and reified, involving the rights and relationships of trustees, priests, *attiyāpakās*, non-Brahmins, and Vaṭakalais.

These diametrically opposed consequences were largely unexpected. How are they to be explained? First, from beginning to end, the judges of the High Court viewed the temple, by analogy, as being

146 Ibid., para. 11.
147 Judgment, September 8, 1920, in C.S. 843 of 1919.
148 Memorandum of Grounds of Appeal to Privy Council, July 17, 1926, in C.S. 527 of 1924.
149 Ibid., paras. 1–7 and passim.
150 See pp. 45–6.

like a charitable "trust" in contemporary English terms. This implied a fundamental misunderstanding of the sovereign personality of the deity, which, by virtue of its *capacity* to confer legitimate authority and its *incapacity* to adjudicate conflicts involving such authority, is the major structural source of temple disputes. Thus, every legal attempt to resolve temple disputes in this period was a cure addressed to symptoms and not to causes. Second, these legal cures exacerbated the symptoms. The willingness of the court to codify both general schemes as well as particular sets of rights in the temple created a "ripple" effect, so that every act of codification, which temporarily satisfied one set of litigants, was a threat and therefore a stimulant to another set of individuals to bid for a similar codification of *their* rights. Thus, paranoia and emulation created a helical process of codification.

Finally, neither of these preceding factors would have had very serious consequences but for the general orientation of the Anglo-Indian legal system to "legislation" and to "precedent" as twin sources of legal decisions. This subordination of temple disputes to a set of general rules, which were constantly refined through accumulated precedents, encouraged native litigants to formulate their own concerns in increasingly sophisticated legal terms. Together, these three factors generated a dynamic framework that bound the temple to the court in increasingly subtle and complicated ways.

The legal "dramas" that provided the empirical and narrative basis for this chapter permitted a series of dense glimpses of this evolving framework. Like Turner's "social dramas," they are simultaneously indices and vehicles of change, and as in his examples, they permit us to grasp some structural sources of tension, some changes in social equilibrium, through the concrete ambitions and interests and successes and failures of a host of particular individuals.

6

RETHINKING THE PRESENT: SOME CONTEXTUAL IMPLICATIONS

This conclusion is divided into three sections. The first section reconsiders and refines the argument concerning continuity and change, which was briefly previewed in the Introduction. The second section places the findings of this study in relation to some important new work in the political history of colonial South India. The last section concerns the implications of this case study for certain issues in South Asian anthropology as well as in the wider context of the anthropology of colonialism.

Authority, continuity, and change

It was suggested in the Introduction to this study that the temple is best defined as a combination of three attributes: spatial, processual, and symbolic. The five substantive chapters that followed suggested the following review and refinement of this definition. Both the architecture of the temple and the ritual dramas that occur within it suggest that the last two centuries have not altered the indigenous conception of the temple as a royal abode (*kōyil*), enshrining a paradigmatic sovereign. The temple, therefore, continues to be conceived as a "sacred" space for many of the same reasons as it was in the Vijayanagara period. Second, the redistributive process of the temple has undergone no *formal* change:[1] Its core is still the ongoing relationship of exchange, in which goods and services are gifted to the deity, transformed in the process of worship, and reallocated to the worshippers in the form of shares, which are culturally demarcated by publicly received honors. These honors appear today to have the same powerful constitutive and denotative power that they had in the pre-British period. Third, as a system of symbols, the temple does not appear to have lost its powerful "metasocial" and

[1] There has been, of course, considerable change in a *substantive* sense in this process: The profile of donors has obviously undergone changes in this period; similarly, the ratio of cash gifts to land grants has probably changed, although this study has not dealt with that issue; old festivals have possibly become defunct for lack of funding, and new ones have probably been added. None of these changes, however, has affected the cultural form or significance of exchange.

reflexive quality with respect to its social context as a result of changes in the last two centuries. Temple disputes and especially conflicts over temple honors are the continuing index of this "metasocial" charter. For in these conflicts, groups and individuals self-consciously debate their respective privileges, refine their "pasts," alter their prospects, and renew their self-understandings. Conversely, however, these conflicts are always set in a context of cooperation. Today, as in the pre-British past, such conflicts would be disastrous if they did not coexist with cooperative behavior ("sharing"), whereby diverse groups and individuals subsidize different portions of a *single* ritual process oriented to a *single* overarching deity. In thus providing a continuing arena for *both* conflict and cooperation between diverse (sometimes opposed) groups and interests, the temple continues to be a "metasocial" arena, an arena of condensed, public, and dramatic processes, in which individuals are encouraged to exaggerate their *separate* identities while simultaneously subordinating them to a *common* ritual process.

What is the shared essence of three attributes of the temple, the spatial, the processual, and the symbolic? It is the idea of the sovereign personality of the presiding deity, who commands the generosity of worshippers but is generous in return; who involves the worshipper in a task of radical cooperation with his fellowmen but also actively helps to constitute his separate identity; who is made of stone but lives in a palace and eats, sleeps, processes, governs, and blesses. To make sure a figure the supreme embodiment of authority suggests a "theology" that only the comparative religionist can fully explore.[2] But one consequence of adherence to this system of beliefs does fall within the province of this study, namely, how can such a system be maintained, managed, and controlled?

Authority, temple control, and change

It is one thing for human beings to enshrine a stone figure as a paradigmatic sovereign and make it the focus of a complex and dramatic ritual and redistributive process. It is quite another matter to come to organized terms with the day-to-day management and

[2] For example, one of the paradoxes that might be resolved by a comparative religionist involves the relationship between the *multiplicity*, even within small areas, of such "paradigmatic sovereigns" and the attribution of universal sovereignty to each of them. Actors in the cultural system do not appear to see this paradox as a problem, but to the outside analyst, it does constitute a difficulty.

authoritative human control required to maintain such a process. For this cultural model of authority does not clearly specify a set of rules for temple control. In Chapter 1 temple control was defined as "the acknowledged competence of an individual or an agency to authoritatively allocate the roles, rights, and resources involved in the ongoing maintenance of worship." The absence of such an explicit set of understandings has made the temple particularly dependent on its social context, specifically on the state and more generally on the prevailing ideology of dispute arbitration with respect to the temple. This dependence has been the major stimulus to change in the last two centuries in the rules and mechanisms of temple control.

In the pre-British period the Śrī Pārtasārati Svāmi Temple, like many others, provided one node in a triangular set of relationships between warrior-kings, sectarian leaders, and temples, which was dynamic and even divisive in its effects on the Śrī Vaiṣṇava community in South India but which nevertheless rested on a coherent and shared ideology. The key elements of this shared ideology were: (1) Temples were fundamental to the maintenance of human kingship through the exchange of royal gifts for temple honors; (2) the links between kings and temples were provided by mobile sectarian leaders; (3) the day-to-day management of temples was left in the hands of local (generally sectarian) groups, although kings were responsible for the "protection" of the deity, that is, for the ultimate resolution of temple disputes; and (4) kingly action in regard to temples, whether expressed in gifting or dispute arbitration, was, in a particular ethnosociological sense, not legislative but administrative.

Thus, the elaborate, enduring, and widespread relationships of Hindu kings to South Indian temples implied a continuous dependence of the sovereignty of human rulers on their transactions with the paradigmatic sovereigns enshrined in temples. However, royal orders and judgments in respect to temples were not legislative, insofar as they were always addressed to specific groups and individuals, were not of general applicability, were subject to alteration or repeal according to the current needs of kingship, and could not fix the law or even strictly serve as an illustration. Furthermore, the "administrative" actions of the Hindu king in respect to the South Indian temple were context sensitive and context bound in an organizational sense as well. Thus, there does not appear to have been at any time a single, centralized, permanent bureaucratic organization (on the Weberian model). Instead, there was a temporary affiliation of a number of local groups, constituted by, or in the name of, the king and empowered to make public decisions on specific matters.

This intimate, yet delicate, relationship between state, sect, and temple was altered in four key respects with the introduction of British rule. First, at the normative level, temples were not essential to the authoritative basis of British rule in South India. Consequently, the public exchange of gifts and honors between king and deity largely ceased to exist.[3] Accordingly, and by extension, the early English mercantile regime did not transact in any systematic way with local sectarian leaders or groups but preferred the intermediary aid of "natives" who were brokers in the new colonial economy. Second, unlike their Hindu predecessors, who preferred to leave the day-to-day control of temples in local hands but did not hesitate to arbitrate temple disputes of whatever sort, the British gradually expanded (given their growing revenue bureaucracy) their day-to-day involvement with temples but grew increasingly reluctant to resolve temple disputes. Third, the institutional separation, under British rule, of "executive" from "judiciary" created ambiguities in the arbitration of temple disputes. Such ambiguities did not exist in the previous royal context, given the unification of "judicial" and "administrative" functions in the powers of the Hindu king. And fourth, given the contrast between the context-bound nature of Hindu royal orders made to resolve temple disputes and the generalizing tendencies of the case law of the British courts (which grew immensely important after 1870), it is no surprise that the temple and the Anglo-Indian judiciary grew entangled in a growing cycle of interactions, which resolved little but provoked much new conflict.

These four contrasts between the British regime and its Hindu predecessors had serious consequences on an arena that was intrinsically ill-defined, namely, temple control. In the case of the Śrī Pārtasārati Svāmi Temple, there is no better way to chart the consequence of these changes than to review the changes in the meaning of the term *Teṉkalai* in its application to temple control.

In the pre-British period, the term *Teṉkalai* appears to have indicated a pan-regional schism in the Śrī Vaisnava community in

[3] Of course, as the evidence in Chapter 3 suggests, the break was gradual and not a self-conscious result of British policy. Many structural features of the earlier relationship between king and temple did, de facto, persist, but the normative changes gradually had structural effects, the most important of which was the "withdrawal" of the British bureaucracy from temple affairs in the 1840s.

South India, which had temple control as one of its competitive expressions. In the early British period, at least in the Śrī Pārtasārati Svāmi Temple, it appears to have become a primary and *contrastive* category, whereby certain Śrī Vaisnavas in Triplicane resisted the attempts of other Vaisnavas called Vaṭakalais to share in the control of the temple. In the first half of the nineteenth century, through the actions of British revenue officials, this de facto eighteenth-century Teṉkalai victory was made the basis of a potentially far-reaching piece of bureaucratic codification, whereby the election of trustees for the temple was henceforth to be "left to the suffrage of the community of the Tengala sect as has heretofore been customary." By this time, the term *Teṉkalai* had lost its pan-regional, theological, and ritual connotations and become a potential sociopolitical category, denoting the local constituency that was to control the temple.

In the period between 1878 and 1925, this local, political, and electoral connotation of the term *Teṉkalai* became the dominant theme of the interaction between the temple and the Anglo-Indian judiciary, so that, by 1925, the right of the Teṉkalai Srī Vaisnava community of Triplicane to manage the Śrī Pārtasārati Svāmi Temple was clearly and "constitutionally" established. This final scheme contained absolutely no role for the state in the management of this temple. This was all well as long as the "secularist" British Empire prevailed. But even with the formation of a Hindu Religious Endowments Board in 1925 (composed of Indians), this situation was already potentially problematic.

With the formation of a full-scale Hindu Religious and Charitable Endowments (Administration) Department in 1951, the imbalanced consequences of British rule became apparent. In Chapter 1 the problem of temple control from 1951 to the present was posed in terms of the conflict between the local Teṉkalai community in Triplicane and the HRCE Department. The course of this conflict, the arguments of the two sides, and the clear-cut victory of state over sect can now be better understood.

Put briefly (and the substance of Chapters 2 through 5 is the basis for this interpretation), both the state and the local sect today have a legitimate case for monopolistic and mutually exclusive control of the Śrī Pārtasārati Svāmi Temple. On the side of the state, there is the "protective" mandate of pre-British Hindu rulers, the British bureaucratic version of that royal mandate, the logic of centralization introduced by British rule, and the contemporary force of pan-regional legislation, which can override many local factors. All these historical factors are responsible for both the present structure of the HRCE Department and its multilayered rhetoric in its claims to the control of public temples in Tamiḻnāṭu. But both its structure and its arguments reveal a complex accretion of features from the "past": a mixture of Vijayanagara royal models of behavior, British bureaucratic structure, British and post-British legislative mandates, and the restorationist ideology of the Drāvita Munnēṟṟa Kalakam, which prevailed until 1976.[4]

The case of the Teṉkalai community of Triplicane, in its battle for control of the Śrī Pārtasārati Svāmi Temple, is equally complex and legitimate. Its appeal to "ancient and immemorial usage" can be documented from at least the second half of the eighteenth century. In subsequent decades, the idea of Teṉkalai control over this temple was increasingly axiomatized and clarified. But the artificial nature of the final court-sponsored mandate for Teṉkalai control of the temple in 1925 is revealed in the June 1968 petition by a Teṉkalai litigant against the state. This petitioner pleads that "every time there was a threat to the rights of the Thengalai denomination or community of Triplicane, steps were taken to prevent the same and so far there has been a *measure of protection*" (emphasis added). The irony, of course, is that the only real protection afforded to the Teṉkalai community by organs of the state in the eighteenth, nineteenth, and early twentieth centuries was against Vaṭakalai incursions into the management of the temple. In this case, what was required was "protection" against the archprotector, the state itself.

But the reasons for the failure of the Teṉkalai community to successfully resist the inroads of the HRCE Department are not simply a matter of the strength and rhetorical skills of the state. They also have to do with the somewhat artificial connotations of the category "the Teṉkalai community of Triplicane." In fact, although the Anglo-Indian judiciary defined an entity called the Tenkalai community, which was supposed to exercise control over the Śrī Pārtasārati Svāmi Temple, it also sufficiently aided the fragmentation of this community, so that it reduced the scope of the *common interests* of this community in the management of the temple. Continuing conflicts up to the present (some of which were described in Chapter 1) between trustees, priests, Brahmin *attiyāpakās*, and non-Brahmin

[4] See Franklin Presler, "Religion Under Bureaucracy: The State and Hindu Religious Endowments in Tamilnadu, India" (Ph.D. diss., University of Chicago, 1978).

worshippers are at least partly traceable to the rather divisive codifying tendencies of the Anglo-Indian judicial system in the 1916–25 period. Given this fragmented twentieth-century heritage, it is not surprising that only some members of the Teṉkalai community of Triplicane were actively involved in the battle against the state. Other elements in the community were either indifferent or actively supportive of the state. This divided state of the Teṉkalai community in the last decade, as much as the justice of its claims, has substantially resulted from the outcomes of court cases in the period from 1878 to 1925.

In short, the situation today in respect to temple control at the Śrī Pārtasārati Svāmi Temple is an uneasy compromise between the local agents of the state, the trustees (who are Teṉkalais appointed by the state and not elected by the community), and the other internally conflicted groups involved in temple service. In part, this situation owes itself to the inherent structural problem of temple control, namely, how do common servants (including representatives of the state) of the sovereign deity resolve conflicts among themselves? But this inherent problem has been no doubt greatly exacerbated by the innovations of the last two centuries, which have become superimposed in a complicated way upon earlier models and understandings. As a consequence, the major groups involved in some aspect of temple control today possess divergent "pasts," composed of varying combinations of their common history. This makes temple control today a delicate and often tense affair.

It is, of course, not surprising that in situations of tension in a single complex institution, different groups and individuals should construct different, and sometimes, opposed, "pasts." What is striking in this case is the peculiar tendency of British bureaucratic and judicial institutions to codify, reify, and thus complicate the recorded past. Furthermore, the institutional changes in the mode of dispute arbitration and temple control that occurred under British rule have created genuine ambiguities and contradictions. These, when juxtaposed with *contemporary understandings* of the pre-British past, tend to encourage complex and conflicted versions of the past.

In the temple today, when conflicts do arise between groups (see the examples in Chapter 1), such complex versions of the past are particularly prone to surface. It has already been noticed that representatives of the HRCE Department support their interests in temple control through a complex portrait of the past, combining Vijayanagara royal models, nineteenth-century bureaucratic precedents, and twentieth-century legislative and judicial charters. Some members of the Teṉkalai community of Triplicane, similarly, base their rights to control the temple on a version of "immemorial usage," composed of vague allusions to the pre-British past, references to the 1843 bureaucratic charter for Teṉkalai control over the temple, and a series of judicial decisions in the 1878–1925 period. The *attiyāpakā* group of Brahmin males, who recite the Prabandam poems in daily service, construct a complicated picture of *their* rights, which starts with the Rules and Regulations framed in 1800 by the Board of Revenue (Appendix A) and culminates in the judgment in *Anna Rangachariar* v. *Parthasarathy Iyengar*[5] (discussed in Chapters 1 and 5). The two segments of the Vaikānasa priesthood in the temple, similarly, base their fierce concern for their rights, depending on the context, on one or another of the judgments delivered by the Madras High Court in the 1917–33 period. Lastly, the non-Brahmin worshippers at the temple (whose recent protests were analyzed in Chapter 1) see their rights as rooted equally in the Bhakti egalitarianism of Teṉkalai Śrī Vaisnavism in the pre-British period and in the judicial egalitarianism of the High Court schemes for the governance of the temple after 1878.

Looked at as ethnohistorical material for an understanding of contemporary tension in the arena of temple control, it is these multiple pictures of the past that constitute, in the Geertzian sense, "winks upon winks upon winks." To these pictures of the past, with their multiple meanings and references, of course, must be added contemporary and specific grievances, alliances, and ambitions in every given case of conflict to provide a full account. In this study, the interpretive guides for such an analysis have been provided, although a complete ethnography of contemporary conflicts has not been attempted.

Culture and social structure

The contemporary problem of authority in the temple can now be rephrased in terms of the general distinction between "culture" and "social structure" (following Geertz's definition) made in the Introduction.

It seems reasonable to argue that in the context of at least one South Indian temple the set of ideas and symbols that focus on the

[5] C.S. 349 of 1923.

sovereign personality of the deity constitute the "cultural system" of the temple. Similarly, the set of regularities associated with what has here been glossed as "temple control" constitute the core of the "social system" of the temple. The history of this South Indian temple exhibits the kind of incongruity and tension between these two domains that Geertz discovered in his analysis of a funeral ritual in Java. The cultural aspect of the temple has remained fundamentally the same, but its sociostructural aspect has undergone important changes.

This incongruity produces tension because both these aspects of the temple happen to focus on a single problem, namely, the problem of authority. Insofar as the deity, conceived as a paradigmatic sovereign, continues to be a powerful repository of authority, the temple continues to attract donors, inspire awe, and command the interests and the sentiments of a large body of worshippers. A certain cultural perception of authority in South India is thus the key to continuity in the temple, as a space, a process, and a symbol. But authority in another sense, in the sense of that set of behavioral regularities that assure the ongoing maintenance of worship as a cooperative enterprise, has become fragmented. Consensus concerning authority in this latter sense is fragile and easily disturbed. This fragmentation of authority, in the social-structural sense, is largely a product of the impact of colonial ideas and institutions on the temple. The dual capacity of the temple, to express enduring cultural understandings as well as to embody serious and recent tensions, is probably the key to its unqualified importance in contemporary South Indian life.

The political history of the region

Like keyholes, intensive local studies in a large civilization are a mixed blessing, for they necessarily sacrifice breadth of perspective to intensity of focus. But recent work on the political history of South India during the colonial period presents an opportunity for at least a programmatic correction of this tendency. In an important set of closely interwoven publications,[6] David Washbrook and Christopher Baker have presented a fascinating and detailed analysis of political

[6] D. A. Washbrook, *The Emergence of Provincial Politics: The Madras Presidency 1870–1920* (New York, 1976); C. J. Baker, *The Politics of South India 1920–1937* (New York, 1976); C. J. Baker and D. A. Washbrook, *South India: Political Institutions and Political Change 1880–1940* (New Delhi, 1975).

change in the Madras presidency from 1870 to 1937. Because South Indian temples do play a role in their larger arguments concerning political change, addressing their arguments is a useful way to place the findings of this case study against the larger backdrop of regional politics under British rule.

At one level the results of this local study serve to illuminate and to expand upon, from the point of view of a single institution, the larger processes of change that Washbrook and Baker have amply identified. Specifically, the Triplicane temple, in the period from 1878 to 1925, certainly fits into the pattern of urban philanthropy proposed by Washbrook.[7] Furthermore, the steady intensification of temple politics at Triplicane in the late nineteenth and twentieth centuries supports the regional argument of these scholars about the place of temples in political change, especially as regards the scenario of tumult, manipulation, and shifting alliances across caste boundaries.[8]

Yet, when we consider *why* Hindu temples should continue to play a vital role in local (and increasingly provincial) politics, Washbrook and Baker offer less satisfaction. They concede, of course, that temples differed from local boards, government offices, and local committees for self-government insofar as they represented the institutional opportunity for increments in resource control *as well as* in prestige and honor. Yet their explanation of the continued importance of temples in politics leans heavily toward their usefulness for resource and patronage distribution, in keeping with the general perspective that these authors take on political change in the presidency.

This leaning has two serious flaws. In the first place, it overlooks precisely the *specific* link between status, resources, and authority that temples *uniquely* represent to their patrons and their mass constituencies, a matter to which I shall return in the following section. Taken by itself, this is a weak criticism, because their account is accurate as far as it goes and is entirely adequate to their avowed purposes, which are those of the political historian rather than those of the anthropologist or social historian. But this flaw has a second ramification that is certainly germane even within their own terms of discourse and investigation. This second problem can be

7 Washbrook, *Emergence of Provincial Politics*, pp. 106-8.

8 Ibid., pp. 183–90; Baker, *Politics of South India*, pp. 58–62 and passim; Baker, "Temples and Political Development," in Baker and Washbrook, *South India*, pp. 69–97.

put as follows. Why should temples generate intense conflict between local men of power, their publicists, and their lawyers at just the period when *new* arenas for the accumulation and disposal of resources (created by the administrative and political changes they so ably describe) are multiplying? Clearly, to simply assert that temples continue to be local repositories of power and resources, as they have always been, ought not to satisfy Washbrook and Baker's purposes, even if it were to satisfy those of this writer. In that case, there are only two possible lines of explanation. One would be to argue that the proportional share of temples in the overall economy was growing and, therefore, that temples represented *growing* targets for entrepreneurship and control. This approach would fit with neither their documentation of changes in the economy nor my own impressions.

It is necessary, therefore, to take a second line of argument, which this study suggests but by no means proves within its case-oriented limits. From even the narrow perspectives of donors, brokers, and publicists, whose ambitions far transcended the temple walls, temples came increasingly to represent the *sole* arena in South Indian society to combine the three following features: (1) *cultural continuity*, as the enduring virtue of public affiliation with the royal authority of the deity and the persistent understanding that such affiliation was a culturally valid base for the redistribution of privileges and resources (in a growing bureaucratic and material economy, this constituted a steadily shrinking resource); (2) *structural virtuosity*, by which I mean the facility to absorb and utilize the requirements and potentialities of the new electoral mode of local politics *in combination with* the older cultural model of royal generosity and ritual appropriateness, and (3) inherent *political utility*, in the sense that the organization of worship in most major temples always represented to any donor or manager a culturally appropriate mode for alliance on a political basis and for the attraction of cross-caste and suprafamilial followings *beyond* those already in the possession of such magnates in their home grounds (both rural and urban).[9] Taken together, these features account more persuasively for the intensified and competitive concern over temple control in the late nineteenth and twentieth

[9] The role of donative activity in group formation in Hindu temples has been argued by Carol A. Breckenridge in "The Śrī Mīnākṣi Sundarēsvarar Temple: A Study of Worship and Endowments in South India, 1800–1925" (Ph.D. diss., University of Wisconsin, 1976). I am indebted to Dr. Breckenridge for bringing this aspect of the political function of South Indian temples to my attention.

centuries than the homogeneous and static patronage model of temple politics proposed by Washbrook and Baker.

Without a doubt, those interested in the control of the Triplicane temple after 1870 had larger interests and occupations that affected both the nature and the tactics of their activities in the temple. Washbrook's study of Madras politics provides an excellent guide to what this larger arena of interests might have been. But the point is that temples provided the political focus for a variety of notables not simply as another till to plunder but because they represented a special type of resource. Individuals sought the honors provided by Hindu temples because these were culturally valued markers of the recipient's status as the leader of his group, as a partial replica of the sovereignty of the deity, and as a co-sharer in a larger system of gift and honor in which other notables were involved.

The late nineteenth and twentieth centuries offered many new opportunities for political men but provided few corresponding new understandings about entitlement to such opportunities, especially given the end of warfare and the eclipse of the political legitimacy of indigenous kings. In this context, temples represented a last resort for working out political entitlement in an old and well-understood cultural framework. Temple honors, of course, took on added significance because access to them was neither automatic nor uncontested, and those who gained them gained both the benefits of temple resources (in men, money, and property) and a source of new followings and allies, generated in and through donation to, and management of, the temple.

Increasingly, in the course of colonial rule, obedience to the commands of a few by the many was not simply a matter of economic dependence. Throughout South Indian history, rural magnates and their urban counterparts participated in temple worship not only because of private motives of piety or instrumental reasons of profit but also because authority is not simply a matter of sanctions but also of incentives for the follower. Such incentives invariably have a cultural form. In South India a major form that such incentives have taken is the association of leaders with the ritual subsidy of deities whose sovereignty is viewed as primary, enduring, and, with appropriate efforts, accessible.

Some implications for anthropology

In the Introduction to this book it was suggested that the virtually exclusive concentration on caste by anthropologists of India has made it difficult to evaluate the relationship between the religious domain, on the one hand, and the economic and political domain, on the other. In analyzing this relationship in India, anthropologists have focused largely on issues of power, status, and hierarchy, as they are reflected in the caste system. In some of the discussions power has been treated as a straightforward cross-cultural category[10] or as one aspect of a complex indigenous conceptual system[11] or as a behavioral residuum of coercion quite apart from legitimate deference.[12] By extension, the problem of status has been rendered coterminous with the problem of rank in a scale of purity and pollution, and the problem of authority has largely been identified with the problem of hierarchy.[13]

None of these anthropological approaches comes to terms directly with the question of *authority* in India, especially insofar as it is related to the construction of ritual.[14] Even when the arena of religion has been considered distinct from that of caste, the theoretical concerns generated in the context of caste have largely overshadowed any serious treatment of worship in its own terms, the domain par excellence where ritual and authority come together. This case can best be made by reference to a recent essay by Christopher Fuller.[15]

Fuller's analysis of ritual in a South Indian temple takes issue with such previous anthropological analysts of Hindu religion as Edward Harper and Lawrence Babb. Harper was the first to explicitly argue that the hierarchy of purity and pollution, which underlay caste, had its source in a model of society in which various groups shared the labor of worshipping the gods.[16] Babb's important study of religion

[10] See, for example, A. Beteille, *Caste, Class and Power* (Berkeley, 1965).

[11] See, for example, S. S. Wadley, *Shakti: Power in the Conceptual Structure of Karimpur Religion* (Chicago, 1975).

[12] See, for example, Louis Dumont, *Homo Hierarchicus* (Chicago, 1970).

[13] This view runs through virtually the entire field and has now received a major formulation by Dumont.

[14] Recent work by historians and Indologists, as well as anthropologists, has begun to analyze these issues for premodern India. The situation is also rather different in the scholarship on Sri Lanka, as for example in the recent study of H. L. Senaviratne of the rituals of the Kandyan state. B. S. Cohn's ongoing research on British imperial ritual in India also promises important new insights into the problem of legitimacy in colonial India. These works and others that bear on the relationship between ritual and authority in South Asia are dealt with in a forthcoming essay in *Reviews in Anthropology* by this writer.

[15] C. J. Fuller, "Gods, Priests and Purity: On the Relation Between Hinduism and the Caste System," *Man*, n.s., 14 (1979):459–76.

[16] E. B. Harper, "Ritual Pollution as an Integrator of Caste and Religion," *Journal of Asian Studies* 23 (1964):151–97.

in central India extends and refines this model but generally supports the link between the hierarchy of caste and the protocol of Hindu worship.[17] Fuller claims to have transcended the caste bias of his predecessors in his analysis of South Indian worship, and it is therefore to his argument that I now turn.

In spite of Fuller's claim to have analyzed Hindu religion "in its own terms," his analysis of worship in a South Indian temple remains entirely bound by the vocabulary of power, purity, and rank, all terms derived from the study of caste. Thus, although he argues that there can be no reduction of the "conceptual apparatus of a highly developed religion" to its "significance in the social order," he concludes, at a cultural level, precisely by trying to stretch the meaning of such concepts as purity, pollution, rank, and divine power to encompass the peculiarities of worship in the temple. Little surprise, then, that in criticizing Harper and Babb for an excessively caste-centered view of religion, Fuller succeeds mainly in telling us what Hindu worship is *not*. In order to progress in analyzing Hindu worship in its own terms, it is not adequate to examine only the *ideology* of selected aspects of temple ritual that seem related to aspects of caste. It is necessary to examine precisely those meanings that underlie the ritual system *and* make the social organization of worship quite different from the social organization of caste. After all, it is not as if caste is "on the ground" and Hinduism is "in the head."[18]

My own study has sought to shift the focus from a priest-centered view of Hindu worship, in which purity and pollution play a disproportionate and distorting role, to a more general sociology of worship in which the power of the deity (rightly emphasized by Babb and Wadley, among others) takes its place in a larger system of rules and meanings that is quite different from that of the caste system. In this system, the sovereignty of the deity is the focus of a set of ideas concerning deference, authority, and redistribution, with relatively little emphasis on pollution, hierarchy, and rank as they appear in caste organization. It is of course true that certain common ideas characterize both domains. But the test of any effort to characterize Hindu worship "in its own terms" must be whether it captures those

[17] L. A. Babb, *The Divine Hierarchy: Popular Hinduism in Central India* (New York, 1975).

[18] Carol A. Breckenridge and I have presented the schematic outlines of such an approach in our essay "The South Indian Temple: Authority, Honor and Redistribution," *Contributions to Indian Sociology*, n.s., 10, No. 2 (Delhi, 1976):187–211.

beliefs that have the greatest saliency to the system under consideration when seen as a functioning cultural and organizational whole.

Needless to say, the nature of authority in the South Indian temple cannot entirely be divorced from considerations of the power of the deity, the purity of its ministrants, and the rank of human worshippers, and this study has pointed to the importance of these issues in the moral economy of the temple. Nor, however, can the problem of authority be reduced to these other issues or tacitly equated with them. What then constitutes authority in the South Indian temple? A simple formula would be: Authority is the capacity to mobilize collective ritual deference to a sovereign deity in such a way that the mobilizing actor partakes of divine authority in relation to those human beings who are either the instruments or beneficiaries of such worship. More simply still, authority is the capacity to command collectivities in the homage of the deity. Of course, given the sociological complexities of the ritual process and the incomplete jural capacities of the deity (whatever its "power" in indigenous eyes), such authority can never be monopolized by any one individual or group and must always be shared. Further, such authority, depending on the historical context, stands in a complex and shifting relationship to the capacities of the donor (*yajamāna*) in such other arenas as the field, the factory, the marketplace, and the municipality. But, as I argued in the previous section, such arenas lacked precisely this capacity to confer authority on a patron, certainly in the colonial period, if indeed they ever possessed it in prior periods of South Indian history. This is what accounts for the enduring importance of the South Indian temple as an arena for the construction of human authority in relationship to divine sovereignty.

These considerations lead to the second general anthropological concern on which the findings of this study have some bearing, the anthropology of colonialism. In spite of a recent revival of interest in Marxist approaches in social anthropology,[19] there is still a dearth of studies in what might be called the cultural dynamics of colonialism,[20] although there have been numerous historical monographs on

[19] See, for example, M. Bloch, ed., *Marxist Analyses and Social Anthropology* (London, 1975); T. Asad, ed., *Anthropology and the Colonial Encounter* (New York, 1973); M. Godelier, *Rationality and Irrationality in Economics* (New York, 1972) and *Perspectives in Marxist Anthropology* (London, 1977).

[20] For examples of those lonely exceptions that prove the rule, see Victor Turner, ed., *Profiles of Change: African Society and Colonial Rule* (Cambridge, 1971); J. Clammer, "Colonialism and the Perception of Tradition in Fiji," in Asad, *Anthropol-*

colonial societies and numerous institutional (as opposed to cultural) analyses of the impact of colonial rule on non-Western societies. From the cultural point of view, the central question for any study of colonial impact must be: In what way did the new arrangements of economic and political power affect the indigenous fabric of authority? There are, of course, two sides to this question. One involves the ways in which the colonial power comes to see itself and be seen as the legitimate superior power. This question, only implicitly touched on in the present study, has long been the central preoccupation of Bernard S. Cohn, whose current research on British imperial ritual in South Asia and its larger sociocultural framework promises important new insights.

But the other side of the question is: How did the ideology and institutional structure of colonial rule affect the perception and construction of authority in the smaller domains that were of no vital symbolic concern to the colonial power? The present study is a partial contribution to the investigation of this latter question. Its findings, summarized in detail in the first part of this chapter, can be restated as follows with an eye to their comparative implications. The cultural and political conditions of this particular colonial regime have fostered a lag between the cultural understanding of human and divine authority *and* the organizational rules for the management of the ritual construction of such authority. This lag, which is the outcome of both deliberate and inadvertent colonial policies, of planned as well as unplanned encounters between the languages of the rulers and the ruled, has had the peculiar result of perpetuating the vitality and cultural centrality of institutions (such as the South Indian temple), just as their relative economic importance is clearly diminishing. Such phenomena in the cultural constitution of authority cannot easily be classified either as blind atavisms or as deliberate acts of revitalization. Nor are they solely products of the encounter between British colonial ideas and South Asian institutions, for they appear to be important elements in the political culture of many "new nations." What then are we to make of them? In my view it would be premature to judge such findings as evidence for the argument, recently advanced by Dumont, of the continued "encompassment" of the political and economic domains by the

ogy and the Colonial Encounter, pp. 199–220; P. D. Curtin, *The Image of Africa* (Madison, Wisc., 1964); C. Geertz's many essays on the culture of politics in the "new states."

"religious" domain, at least in South Asia. To judge their meaning, it is essential that the findings of this study be juxtaposed with those of other studies of the cultural constitution of colonial societies, where the rulers were not English and the ruled were not South Asian. Such studies will be genuinely comparable to the extent that they combine the methods of anthropology and history in the manner proposed in the Introduction to this study, a proposal that I have only imperfectly been able to put into practice in this case.

APPENDIX A

RULES AND REGULATIONS OF 1800

Rules and regulations[1] to be observed in future respecting the distribution of Theertha Prasadam, or holy water, rice etc. at Triplicane Pagoda:

1. That in the distribution of theertham and prasadam to the goshti or congregation, no priority is to be observed: it is to be distributed among those who stand foremost unless any yathi or monk happens to be there, in which case he is entitled to the priority.

2. After the different kinds of prasadams are dedicated to the God Perumal, the swadantram or fixed portion therefrom to the church officers to be retained, and the remainder distributed among the congregation.

3. If any of the acharyapurushals or priests coming from the country, who are entitled to Sree Sadagopam, the cup of consecration being brought before them from the church, happens to be in the congregation, on that day only he is entitled to one thosa or cake from the viniyogam then distributing. Theertham and prasadam in preference to the congregation that is after the yathees, if no yathi happens to be in the congregation, an acharyapurushal of the said description if present, are entitled to theertham and prasadam in preference to the congregation.

4. If any of the acharyapurushals newly coming from the country, or those residing on the spot and those who are deserving the Sree Sadagopam from the church, happens to be at the congregation on the following festival days viz. the days of Garudeseva and Thirutheru in Brahmotsavam, the days Sauthoomara in Adinavutsam, Emberumanar and Manavala Mahamuni, the theertham and prasadam should be first given to them (if no yathees be present) and then distributed

[1] This document (discussed in Chapter 3) is recorded in the Board of Revenue Consultations (India Office Library), February 3, 1800, pp. 903 ff. A copy of this original is also contained in the printed documents filed in C.S. 241 of 1933, High Court of Judicature at Madras (Original Side, Record Room). The technical terms that occur are either self-explanatory or are explained elsewhere in the study.

to the congregation, but on all other days no priority is to be observed as it is to be distributed among those who stand foremost.

5. At the time of distributing the prasadam among the congregation, if the holders of the offices of mundrapushpam and vedaparayanam should be in the congregation, they are to have double viniyogam, and after it is distributed among the congregation double viniyogam is to be given to the panrupateyam (the manager of the church), then to the two officiating worshippers of Periya Koil etc. and in the next place double viniyogams to be distributed to soyempagi, paricharakam, dasanambi, kattiam, kanaku poligar etc. the servants of the church.

6. If sandal, flower and betal be dedicated to the God Perumal the archakals or worshipping Brahmins are first to be served and then a distribution is to take place among the congregation etc. as above described.

7. If any person of the respectability come into the church at any time, the churchwarden or his manager is at liberty to take out of the prasadam then distributing a small portion, and present the same to such person, but they are prohibited from taking out any prasadams at other times, an account of such small portion which the said churchwarden's manager is permitted to take out for the said purpose is to be kept by stala conecoply.

8. At the time of the feasts, if the church warden be under the necessity of sending prasadam to the natives of respectability at Madras he is to cause the same to be made from the stock of the church.

9. From the thaligai etc. which are made by the church warden at the expense of the church no share whatever is to be given to the said officers of the church.

10. The prasadam which has been dedicated to the God Perumal is not to be carried back to Madapalli where prasadam is made.

11. That the holy rice dedicated to the God Perumal at noon under the denomination of thesandry cutla exclusive of the fixed shares to the church, should be distributed among thesandry Brahmins or travellers, but the same is not subject to be distributed to the congregation.

12. The fixed rates of swadantram, or what the worshipping Brahmins and servants of the church are entitled to out of the different sorts of thaligai, viz. . . . [this portion of the manuscript allots shares to the priests, cook, priest's helper, clerk and accountant, totaling 3/16].

From the residue of 13/16 the ubayakar, the person who bears the expense of the feast, is entitled to have 8/16 and the remaining 5/16 to be distributed to the congregation.

The different sorts of cakes 60 pieces per each paddy to be distributed as follows: viz.:

To archakals	2 and 1/2
To Paricharakam	1/2
To Soyempagi	2
To Dasanambi and Kanaiupillai	1
To Poligar	1
Total:	7

From the remaining 53 ubayakar is to have 20 and 33 is to be distributed to the congregation. If the God Perumal should be carried out in procession, 2 pieces to Brahmins attending to divine service called Iyalpadu, 3 to sreepatham thangees of three villages and the remaining to be distributed to the congregation.

13. That the soyembagi is to dry the holy rice and cakes with care, and pay attention that no bits of stone or putty be mixed therewith, and with great purity in due time and without delay or neglect.

The holy rice and cakes should weigh as follows:

Holy rice of each thaligai:	
Pulyogara	7 and 1/2 visses
Thathiyothanam	8 visses
Sakkarapongal	7 and 1/2 visses
And all other thaligais	6 visses
Cakes:	
Each thosai	12 Palams
Appam	12 Palams
Vadai	4 Palams
Athirisam	5 Palams

That if the thaligai weigh 1/4 viss less or more and the cake called thosai and appam one palam more or less, vadai and athirisam half palam less or more, it is not to be considered as material difference in the weight when examined.

8th January 1800.

APPENDIX B

JUSTICE HUTCHINS'S SCHEME OF 1885

1. That all future appointments of Dharmakarthas of the temple of Śree Partasarathy Swamy at Triplicane in the plaint[1] mentioned shall be made by election in manner hereinafter appearing.

2. That all persons shall be entitled to vote who shall be:
   - (a) of the Tengalai persuasion
   - (b) of the male sex
   - (c) of the age of 18 years or upwards
   - (d) Resident in Triplicane and within the following boundaries viz. on the North the Wallajah Road; in the East the South Beach Road; on the south the Ice House Road and on the West Woods Road and Patters Road for at least six months within the twelve months immediately preceding the occurrence of the vacancy then about to be filled up.

3. That any person of the age of 25 years or upwards resident anywhere within the Municipal limits of Madras who would except for the requisition as to residence contained in Article 2 (d) of this scheme be entitled under the said Article 2 to vote at such elections shall be eligible for election to the office of Dharmakartha of the said temple provided that he shall not belong to or be of the same caste or, in the case of Sudras, of the same subcaste as either of the then surviving or continuing Dharmakarthas.

4. That no Dharmakartha shall hold any office of emolument in the Temple.

5. That within 14 days of the service upon them of the decree herein and within 14 days after the occurrence of any future vacancy in the office of Dharmakartha of the said Temple, the first or second Defendants or the other surviving or continuing Dharmakarthas for the time being shall notify the vacancy by affixing a notice to each of the two gates of the Temple and shall call upon the Headmen of all or any caste or castes resident in Triplicane within the limits afore-

[1] This judicial scheme was created in the course of the proceedings in C.S. 36 of 1884, High Court of Judicature at Madras. The context for its formulation has been discussed in Chapter 5.

said to furnish them with a list of persons belonging to his caste possessing the qualifications of voters above mentioned and shall by and with the aid of such lists if any as may be furnished within 14 days from date of such requisition prepare a preliminary list in Tamil of all persons qualified to vote under Article 2 hereof and shall make 3 copies of such list and each of such copies shall be signed by the said surviving or continuing Dharmakarthas and be dated as of the day on which it is so signed and they shall retain and keep one of such copies and shall post one of the remaining copies on each of the two gates of the said temple conspicuously and to each of such copies shall be appended a notice signed by the said surviving or continuing Dharmakarthas fixing a day and hour and place for the preliminary meeting hereinafter provided and the day and hour so to be fixed shall be some hour between 6 A.M. and 6 P.M. on the first Sunday after the 30th day after the date which such copies shall bear, and the place shall be the usual place where the business of the said temple is carried on or if there be no such place some convenient public place inside the temple to which all the said persons hereby entitled to vote may have free access provided that the place fixed shall be the place thereafter to be used as the polling station. The substance of such notices shall be proclaimed by beat of tom-tom outside the Temple and through the principal streets of Triplicane.

6. That any person or persons whose name or names shall be in the said Preliminary List or who shall claim to vote as hereinafter mentioned who shall object to any person or persons whose name or names shall appear in the said preliminary list on the ground that he or they is or are not entitled to vote at such elections shall state his or their objection or objections on paper to each of the said surviving or continuing Dharmakarthas and another copy thereof on paper to each of the persons objected three clear days before the day fixed as aforesaid for the said preliminary meeting.

7. Any person who shall claim a right to vote at such elections and whose name shall not appear in the said preliminary list shall in like manner state such his claim . . .

8. That a preliminary meeting shall take place and on the day and at the hour so fixed in order to settle the list of persons entitled to vote for the appointment of Dharmakarthas aforesaid and all persons whose names shall appear in the said preliminary list and all persons who shall have delivered claims as aforesaid shall be entitled to attend same, and at such meeting the Senior Dharmakartha of the said Temple shall preside and the other surviving or continuing

Dharmakartha and all Headmen of castes aforesaid shall be entitled to be present thereat to assist the said President and all objections and claims delivered as aforesaid shall be decided by the said President thereat and after the said President shall have decided on such objections and claims he shall draw up a final list of persons entitled to vote for the appointment of Dharmakarthas to the said temple according to such his decisions with the aid and assistance of the said Headmen if he shall require the same and two copies of such final list shall be made by the said surviving or continuing Dharmakarthas and each of such copies shall be signed by the said President and one such copy shall be posted conspicuously on each of the two said gates and the said President shall be at liberty to adjourn the said Preliminary Meeting for purposes of convenience to such day and hour or day and hours as he may appoint but so that the said final list shall be completed and posted as aforesaid at least 14 days before the day appointed for the actual voting.

9. On the first Sunday after the 14th day after the said final lists of voters shall have been posted or affixed as aforesaid an election shall be held by the said Senior Dharmakartha at the said temple between the hours of 7 and 11 A.M. Notice thereof shall be given by beat of tom-tom outside the said temple and by notice in writing signed by him notifying the hours at which the voting will begin and close, to be affixed to the two gates of the Temple seven clear days before the day fixed for the election and at such election only parties whose names shall appear in the said final list shall be entitled to vote.

10. Every voter shall hand in to the said Senior Dharmakartha a voting paper with the name of the person for whom he votes legibly inscribed thereon. Such paper shall be signed or marked by the voter and shall show his name or number in the said final list of voters.

11. There shall be no voting by proxy or otherwise than in person.

12. The said Senior Dharmakartha shall receive all votes and count them at the close of the elections in the presence of the other surviving or continuing Dharmakartha and of such of the Headmen as may choose to remain and if any two persons who shall have received an equal number of votes shall head the poll the said President shall have a casting vote and the President shall immediately declare the name of the person who shall have received the largest number of votes or the person in whose favour he shall have given his casting vote as aforesaid to have been elected by affixing a notice signed by himself to each of the two gates of the Temple and thereupon the person so declared to have been elected shall be

deemed to be duly appointed and to be a Dharmakartha of the said Temple.

13. The other surviving or continuing Dharmakartha and the headmen aforesaid shall be at liberty to be present at the voting and the delivery to and receipt by the said Senior Dharmakartha of the said voting papers and to bring to the notice of the said Senior Dharmakartha any instances of personation. Any person whose name is in the final list shall also be entitled to bring any instance of personation to the notice of the said Senior Dharmakartha provided that no such objection shall be taken after the voting has been once accepted and passed by the Senior Dharmakartha.

14. On any such objection being taken the Senior Dharmakartha shall mark such voting paper and shall enquire into the matter and shall either allow or disallow such vote at his discretion and shall state and sign each such objection with his decision thereon.

15. The appointment of Dharmakartha of the temple shall be vacated only by (a) resignation, (b) insolvency i.e. on filing his petition and schedule and being adjudicated a bankrupt under the provisions of the present Act for the Relief of Insolvent Debtors at Madras or any Insolvency or Bankruptcy law which may hereafter come into force in Madras, (c) nonresidence within the Municipal limits of Madras for any purpose other than a pilgrimage, in which case a Dharmakartha may remain absent for a year without vacating office or (d) death.

16. The affairs of the Temple shall be under the control of the Dharmakarthas of the Temple for the time being and they shall have the appointment and dismissal of all servants and the management of the affairs of the Temple and the receipt and expenditure of the income thereof as heretofore.

17. The Dharmakarthas shall make in a form to be approved of by this Court and file on record in this suit within two months from the date of the decree:

- (a) A list of the officers or servants of the said temple with their salaries if any.
- (b) A balance sheet showing the actual receipts and disbursements for the twelve months ending the 13th day of July 1885.
- (c) An inventory of all the property of the said temple including all endowments thereof and all the landed property, jewels, vahanums, furniture, utensils and all property whatsoever of or belonging to the said temple.

18. The list of voters shall be revised as hereinafter provided on

the occurrence of every vacancy in the Dharmakarthaship or, if no such vacancy shall occur within five years, from date of the said final list or from date of the last revised list registered under the provisions of this article on the 1st day of March next after the expiry of such term of 5 years and the Dharmakarthas shall keep a register of voters in a book or books especially set apart for that purpose by copying into such book or books the said final list, and every subsequent revised list as and when revised and each of the Dharmakarthas for the time being shall sign such copy lists in such book or books and the rules and provisions herein contained and provided for the preparation and posting of the said final list shall (*mutatis mutandis*) be observed at each such revision. But if a vacancy shall occur within twelve months from the date of the last registered revised list no revision thereof shall be required or made but the election to fill up such vacancy shall proceed upon such last registered revised list and the next revision shall be made five years after the date of such last registered revised list as if no such vacancy had occurred.

19. The Dharmakarthas for the time being shall also make or cause to be made in a book or books to be kept for that purpose a full and complete copy of the said inventory of all the property of the said temple including all endowments thereof and all the landed property and vahanums, furniture, utensils and all property whatsoever and such inventory shall be checked, altered and corrected and rewritten once in 3 years in the said book or books and this shall be signed by the Dharmakarthas and kept among the records of the temple.

20. The Dharmakarthas for the time being shall also keep full and complete books of account of the income and expenditure of the said temple and within three months after the close of each official Revenue year, a balance sheet showing the income and expenditure of the temple during such year, beginning with the said balance sheet for the 12 months ending the 13th July 1885, shall be made out in the said book or books kept for that purpose and signed by the Dharmakarthas for the time being and by the auditor to be appointed as hereinafter mentioned and certified by him as correct and copy thereof signed by the said Dharmakarthas and countersigned by the auditor to be appointed as aforesaid, shall be posted to each of the said Gates and allowed to remain there for at least four weeks.

21. The said register of voters and the books containing the inventory of temple property ordered by this decree and annual

balance sheets aforesaid shall be kept in the temple premises and shall be open to the inspection of any person or persons whose name or names may appear in the register of voters for the time being between the hours of 12 and 2 on the first Sunday of each month and any such person or persons shall be at liberty to take copies thereof or extracts therefrom.

22. Once at least in every year the temple accounts shall be examined by an auditor to be appointed by the Dharmakarthas for the time being and the correctness of the said annual balance shall be ascertained and testified by him and his remuneration shall be fixed and paid by the said Dharmakarthas out of the said Temple's funds.

APPENDIX C

FINAL JUDICIAL SCHEME OF MANAGEMENT, 1925

1. This revised scheme[1] and the modifications made herein and hereby in the scheme now in force relating to the said Śrī Pārthasārathy Svāmi Temple shall come into force from the commencement of 1926.

2. The management and affairs of the temple shall be carried on by a body of Dharmakarthas under the supervision and control of a Board of Supervision as hereinafter constituted, with powers as defined hereinafter.

3. The Dharmakarthas shall be three in number and the Board of Supervision shall consist of seven members. Of the Dharmakarthas, one shall be a Brahmin, one an Arya Vysia (Komiti) and one a non-Brahmin non-Arya Vysia.

4. Provided always that nothing done or purported to be done by the said Dharmakarthas or the Board of Supervision shall be illegal or invalid merely by reason of the fact that the number of Dharmakarthas at any time is less than three or of the Board of Supervision less than seven.

And provided also that on the occurrence of any vacancy or vacancies the surviving or continuing Dharmakartha or Dharmakarthas or the surviving or continuing members of the Board of Supervision shall have all the rights and be liable to discharge all the duties of the Dharmakarthas and the Board of Supervision respectively until such vacancy or vacancies are filled up.

In case of difference of opinion amongst the Dharmakarthas the opinion of the Majority shall prevail.

A Dharmakartha or a Member of the Board of supervision shall hold office a period of 5 years from the date of his appointment.

5. A retiring Dharmakartha or a retiring member of the Board of Supervision may, however, be re-eligible for office provided he is, at

[1] This scheme for the management of the Śrī Partasārati Svāmi Temple was part of the final decree in C.S. 527 of 1924, High Court of Judicature at Madras (see Chapter 5).

the time of his re-appointment, eligible for such office under the other provisions of this scheme.

6. The Dharmakarthas and the Members of the Board of Supervision of the said temple shall be elected in a manner hereinafter appearing.

7. Every person shall be entitled to vote at any such election whose name stands on the date of such election, registered in the "List of Voters" maintained at the temple and hereinafter so referred to, and no one shall be entitled to vote at any such election whose name does not stand so registered.

8. All persons shall be entitled to have their names registered in the "Lists of Voters" who are:

(a) Vaishnavas of the Thengalai sect;
(b) of the male sex;
(c) of the age of 21 years or upwards;
(d) resident of Triplicane and within the following boundaries namely, on the north by Wallajah Road, on the east by South Beach Road, on the south by Ice House Road and on the west by the Woods Road and Patters Road and who have been so resident for at least six months immediately preceding the publication of the year's preliminary electoral roll hereinafter referred to; and
(e) able to sign their names.

Provided always no person shall be entitled to have his name registered or continued to remain registered in the "List of Voters" unless he has at any time made a payment of Rs.3/- as registration fee in lieu of the annual fee of annas four hereinafter referred to or else paid a sum of annas four for the fasli year on or before the 31st December of such fasli year, or within a month of the publication of the preliminary list for the year hereinafter referred to.

9. No person shall be eligible to be appointed as Dharmakartha or Member of the Board of Supervision of the said temple who is not

(a) of the Thengalai sect;
(b) of the male sex;
(c) of the age of 25 years or upwards and
(d) a resident either within the Municipal limits of Madras or within a radius of 15 miles beyond such limits; and
(e) the owner in his own rights of lands paying annual revenue or rent of not less than Rupees one hundred or does not pay municipal or local taxes of not less than rupees fifty per

annum, or in occupation of premises as tenant paying an annual house rent not less than Rs.240/- or who does not pay some income-tax.

Provided also further that a person shall be disqualified to be appointed as such Dharmakartha or Member of the Board of Supervision if such person,

(a) had been convicted of any non-compoundable offense involving moral turpitude; or

(b) is at the date of his appointment – (1) an undischarged insolvent, or (2) already a Dharmakartha or Member of the Board of Supervision of said temple, or (3) has been removed for misconduct by an order of Court from the trusteeship of any temple.

10. No Dharmakartha or Member of the Board of Supervision shall hold any office carrying emoluments in the temple.

11. The Board of Supervision shall, in every fasli year before the end of February of such year, prepare what shall be called the preliminary list of registered voters and such preliminary lists shall include the names of all persons who according to the rules herein contained and to the knowledge of the members of the Board of Supervision are entitled to vote at any election for such fasli year and shall be prepared not only from the previous list of registered voters but also from the applications, if any, for registration as voters since received.

12. Four copies shall be made of such preliminary lists and each being signed by the President or the secretary of the Board and dated two copies shall be posted conspicuously one on each of the two main gates of the said temple and the other two copies shall be retained in the temple office. To each of the said copies shall be appended a notice signed by the President or Secretary of the Board fixing the date, hour and the place for the final revision of the said list. The hours to be so fixed shall [be] between 8 A.M. and 7 P.M. on some Sunday in the month of April. The substance of such notices shall also be published by circulation of hand-bills proclaimed by beat of tom tom outside the temple and through the Principal streets of Triplicane. One of the said preliminary lists to be kept in the office of the Board of Supervision shall for a period of one month after its preparation and publication be open for inspection of the worshippers at the said temple. It shall be open to any worshipper at the temple to object to the inclusion in the list of the voters of any name appearing in the preliminary list. But such objection shall be in

writing setting out the grounds of the objection and at least three clear days before the date fixed for the final settlement of the list of voters one copy of such writing signed by the objector, shall be filed in the office of Board of Supervision and another copy served on the person the inclusion of whose name is objected to.

13. Any person whose name has been improperly left out in the said preliminary list shall also be entitled to claim the inclusion of his name in the final list, but he should at least within three clear days before the date fixed for the final settlement of the list file in the office of the Board of Supervision an application for such inclusion setting out the grounds on which he claims such inclusion.

14. The final list of voters shall be settled at and by a meeting of the Board of Supervision. Such meeting shall be convened at the place, on the day and between the hours fixed in the notice already referred to, or may be adjourned and held or continued at such time and on such dates as may be duly notified.

15. The said meeting shall, after hearing the various objections if any, draw up a final list of voters entitled to vote at the elections of Dharmakarthas and members of the Board of Supervision. After the list of voters is finally settled as aforesaid and four copies thereof shall be made and all the same being signed by the President of the Board and the Secretary, two copies thereof shall be posted conspicuously one on each of the two gates of the said temple and a third copy shall be retained by the Board of Supervision. The list of voters when finally settled or revised as aforesaid shall be in force until a fresh list is again finally settled in the manner aforesaid. The list of voters shall not be amended, altered or added to except at the annual revision as herein before provided.

16. On the occurrence of a vacancy in the office of the Dharmakarthaship of the temple or the membership of the Board of Supervision, the Board of Supervision shall, within fourteen days of the receipt of information of the occurrence causing the vacancy, post copies of notices in Tamil, Telugu and English on the two temple gates and also publish notices in the said languages in Tamil, Telugu and English daily newspaper[s] in Madras respectively, to the following effect:

(a) that a vacancy has occurred in the office of Dharmakarthaship or the Membership of the Board of supervision, as the case may be;
(b) that an election to fill up such vacancy will be held on a Sunday to be specified therein;

(c) that nominations setting out the qualifications to such vacancy signed by two of the registered voters setting out the qualifications and showing how the nominee or nominees is or are possessed of the qualifications for being elected to such vacancy together with a consent in writing of such nominee or nominees should be filed in the office of Board of Supervision on a date to be fixed in such notice which shall not be earlier than fourteen days from the date of such notice.

17. All nominations received later than the day specified as aforesaid shall be invalid and the Board of Supervision shall, within seven days of such date, publish the names of the persons nominated as candidates by affixing copies on the two temple gates and also be distributing hand-bills in Tamil, Telugu and English within the local area and also be publishing notices in three local daily newspapers of Madras, one in Tamil, one in Telugu and one in English.

18. The scrutiny by the Board of Supervision of the list of nominees and their decision and declaration with regard to the candidates for the election shall be final, and so far as the qualifications of the nominees are concerned, conclusive of the possession of such qualifications by the nominees.

19. The elections to fill up the vacancy as aforesaid shall be fixed for and held on some Sunday not later than four weeks after the publication of the names of the candidates as aforesaid between the hours of 7 A.M. and 7 P.M. except for an interval of one hour between 12 noon and 1 P.M.

20. Notice of the date of the election with the names of the candidates shall also be given by distributing hand-bills in Tamil, Telugu and English and also in three daily newspapers of Madras, in Tamil, Telugu and English respectively and also by beat of tom tom in the principal streets of the local area mentioned in clause 8 above.

21. Such notices of election shall also be affixed to the temple gates.

22. Notwithstanding anything contained above no election shall be held invalid merely for the reason that the date of the election was not fixed within the time of limit as aforesaid or that the names of the candidates or the list of voters were not published on the dates hereinbefore fixed for the same.

23. The Board of Supervision shall nominate one or more of their members to be Returning Officers to preside over and conduct the elections at the polling stations.

24. Every voter on his signing his name in the book kept at the polling station by the Returning Officer shall receive at the polling station a voting paper containing in printing the names of the candidates in English, Tamil and Telugu and shall record his vote. The voting shall be by ballot and the voting papers shall be placed in a ballot box.

25. No voting by proxy or otherwise than in person shall be permitted.

26. On any objection being taken as to false personation either by a voter or by a candidate, such objection shall be noted and shall be enquired into and shall either be allowed or disallowed by the Returning Officer whose decision shall be final and no such objection shall be taken after the voting paper has been accepted, and passed by the said person.

27. The Returning Officer or Officers shall, after the close of the election, count the votes in the presence of such of the candidates or their authorized agents for the election not exceeding two for each candidate as may choose to be present at such counting and the said officer or officers shall declare after the counting is over the name of the person who shall have received the largest number of votes to have been duly elected. In case two or more candidates shall have received an equal number of votes, the election shall be made by casting of lots and the name of the successful candidates shall be declared. The Returning Officer or Officers shall communicate the result to the Board. The Board shall publish the result of the election by affixing notices to each of the two gates or in such other manner as they may deem fit.

28. The office of a Dharmakartha or a Member of the Board shall be vacated (a) by his death, (b) by his resignation, (c) by his insolvency, (d) by his non-residence within the radius of 15 miles outside the Municipal limits of Madras for a continuous period of six months (e) by his being convicted of a non-compoundable offense involving moral turpitude and (f) by efflux of time.

29. The Members of the Board of Supervision shall elect amongst themselves a President and a Secretary. The President shall ordinarily preside at all meetings of the Board and in his absence the Members may elect any Member present as Chairman for the time being.

30. The Secretary of the Board shall transact business of the Board, convene meetings, record minutes and generally look after its affairs.

31. The Board of Supervision shall have the rights and be subject to the duties hereinafter set out:

(a) To sanction or to modify the annual budget to be set by the Dharmakarthas.
(b) To sanction leases of over three years or sales of immovable property or securities belonging to the temple when such sale would otherwise be legal.
(c) To sanction generally or specifically the modes of the investment of the temple funds in authorized securities.
(d) To conduct elections.
(e) To appoint the auditor and fix his remuneration.
(f) To prescribe the forms in which the accounts of the temple and other books and registers shall be maintained.
(g) To decide references made to them by the majority of Dharmakarthas, or by individual Dharmakarthas relating to any breach of trust, or any violation of the provisions of this scheme.
(h) To determine on appeal any dispute and differences relating to rituals and other observances.
(i) To determine any appeal by temple servants suspended or dismissed or fined in any sum exceeding Rs.5/- by the Dharmakarthas.
   (i) The Board of Supervision shall also have such powers as may be necessary for the due carrying out of the matters set out in clause 31 (i) above.
   (ii) The Trustees shall, on the requisition of the Board of Supervision, furnish them with such funds as the Board may consider necessary for the due carrying out of their duties.
(j) To frame such by-laws and rules for the despatch of business by the Board and for elections as are not inconsistent with the provisions of this scheme.
(k) To call for any information from the Dharmakarthas regarding any matters relating to the temple or its management.

32. The Board of Supervision shall meet at least once in a month to transact business. In cases of differences of opinion amongst the Members of the Board of Supervision, the opinion of the majority shall prevail. In cases of equality of votes the President for the time being of the Board shall have a casting vote. An accurate record shall be maintained of the proceedings of the Board of Supervision.

33. The Dharmakarthas shall keep full and complete account books of the income and expenditure of the said temple in the form prescribed by the Board. The Dharmakarthas shall maintain or cause to be maintained vouchers in respect of all such matters and in such manner as may be prescribed by the Board of Supervision.

34. The temple accounts for each official year shall be examined by a certified Auditor who shall be appointed at least four weeks before the termination of the fasli year by the Board of Supervision for the time being of the said temple. The Dharmakarthas shall give the Auditor all books, vouchers and other documents required for the audit and the said auditor shall prepare a balance sheet before the 30th of September, showing the assets and liabilities of the temple as also the income and expenditure for the year and the said balance sheet shall be signed by the Dharmakarthas for the time being and by the said Auditor and shall be certified by him as correct and shall be forwarded to the Board before the 30th September. The Auditor for the time being shall, while submitting the balance sheet, make his report thereon. The auditor shall also check the inventories of the properties of the temple and also make his report thereon. The remuneration of the Auditor shall be fixed by the Board and shall be paid out by them from and out of the temple funds. The Board shall affix a copy of the same at the temple gates within 30th of June and shall before that date publish an advertisement in an issue of an English daily paper that such balance sheet is published and posted at the gates of the temple.

35. In a book that shall be kept for the said purpose by the Board the annual balance sheet shall be entered and the Dharmakarthas for the time being shall affix their signatures to the entries of the balance sheets in the said books. The register of voters of the temple, the account books of the temple and inventories and such other books and papers as may be determined by the Board of Supervision shall be allowed to be inspected by any worshipper at the temple on the last Sunday of each month between the hours of 2 and 6 P.M. on payment of a fee of one Rupee.

36. Any Dharmakartha or Member of the Board of Supervision of the temple, or with the previous sanction in writing of the Advocate-General, any five or more worshippers at the temple may, by notice of motion entitled in this suit, apply to this court for any alteration or amendment of this scheme or any provision contained herein and the court shall thereon be entitled to pass such orders as it deems fit.

37. The first Board of Supervision shall be appointed by the

Court. Two out of the seven to be so appointed, to be determined by lot cast by the Board, shall retire with the 30th June 1928, and two out of the remaining five, to be determined by lot cast by the Board, shall retire with the 30th June 1929 and the remaining three or such of them as may survive shall retire with the 30th June of 1930.

38. The first Board of Supervision to be so appointed by the Court shall, within two weeks of their appointment, prepare a preliminary list and proceed thereupon to settle the final list of voters as hereinbefore provided.

BIBLIOGRAPHY

Primary sources

Inscriptions

Archaeological Survey of Mysore: Annual Report 1938. Bangalore: Government Press, 1940.

Cennai Mānakara Kalveṭṭikal Madras City Stone Inscriptions. Edited by R. Nagaswamy. Madras: Madras Government Archaeological Survey, 1970.

Selected South Indian Inscriptions: Tamil, Telugu, Malayalam and Kannada. Edited by V. R. R. Dikshitar. Madras: University of Madras, 1952.

South Indian Inscriptions. Edited by E. Hultzsch and others. Madras: Government Press, 1890– .

South Indian Temple Inscriptions. 3 vols. Edited by T. N. Subramanian. Madras: Government Oriental Manuscripts Library, 1953–7.

Tirumalai-Tirupati Devasthanam Epigraphical Series. 6 vols. Madras: Tirupati Sri Mahant's Press and Tirumalai-Tirupati Devasthanams Press, 1931–8.

Administrative records

Board of Revenue Consultations. London: India Office Library; Madras: Tamiḻ Nāṭu Archives, 1799–1860.

Correspondence between T. K. Ramanujadoss and Temple Trustees, 1960–1. Triplicane, Madras: In the possession of T. K. Ramanujadoss.

Diary and Consultation Book, Fort St. George. Madras: Government Press, Vol. 83 (1754).

Temple Correspondence 1940–1973. Madras: Śrī Pārtasārati Svāmi Temple, Record Room, Miscellaneous Files.

Court cases

Unless otherwise specified, the following cases occurred in the High Court of Judicature at Madras, and the documents pertaining to these cases were consulted in the Record Room, Original Side, High Court of Judicature at Madras.

Anna Rangachariar v. Parthasarathy Iyengar (C.S. 349 of 1923).

Condiah Chetty v. Raghavachariar (C.S. of 1891).

Kistnamah Charry v. Vencatanarayana Pillay (C.S. 36 of 1884).

Krishnasawmy Moodeliar v. Rajaruthnum Naidu (C.S. 169 of 1905).

Parthasarathy Iyengar v. Appasawmy Pillay (C.S. 176 of 1916).

Parthasarathy Iyengar v. Appasamy Pillay (C.S. 111 of 1918).

Rajaruthnum Naidu v. Venkatarangam Naidu (C.S. 137 of 1895).

Ramanjulu Naidu v. Parthasarathy Iyengar (C.S. 233 of 1911).

Ranganadham Chetty v. Parthasarathy Iyengar (C.S. 559 of 1922).

Srinivasachariar v. Raghavachariar (C.S. 122 of 1897).
Srinivasa Ayyangar v. Raghavachariar (C.S. 293 of 1895).
Srinivasachariar v. The Commissioner of HRCE (O.S. 2910 of 1968); City Civil Court of Madras; (printed documents from this case consulted at the Śrī Pārtasārati Svāmi Record Room).
Vencatanarayana Pillay v. Secretary of State for India in Council (C.S. 486 of 1878).
Venkatanarasimha Bhattachariar v. Srinivasa Bhattachariar (O.S. 485 of 1917); City Civil Court of Madras; (printed documents from this case consulted at the Śrī Pārtasārati Svāmi Temple Record Room).
Venkatanarasimha Bhattachariar v. Parthasarathy Iyengar (C.S. 860 of 1920).
Venkatanarasimha Bhattachariar v. Parthasarathy Iyengar (C.S. 442 of 1923).
Venkatanarasimha Bhattachariar v. Narasimha Bhattachariar (C.S. 241 of 1933).
Vijayaraghava Mudaliar v. Ranganadham Chetty (C.S. 843 of 1919).
Viraraghavachariar v. Parthasarathy Iyengar (C.S. 527 of 1924).

Secondary sources

Books

Annangarachariar, P. B. *Rāmānujā Dayāpātrā*. Kancipuram, 1954.
Annual Reports on South Indian Epigraphy. Archaeological Survey of India. Madras: Government Press, 1886–1945.
Asad, T., ed. *Anthropology and the Colonial Encounter*. New York: Humanities Press, 1973.
Babb, L. A. *The Divine Hierarchy: Popular Hinduism in Central India*. New York: Columbia University Press, 1975.
Baker, C. J. *The Politics of South India 1920–1937*. Cambridge: Cambridge University Press, 1976.
Baker, C. J., and Washbrook, D. A. *South India: Political Institutions and Political Change 1880–1940*. New Delhi: Vikas, 1975.
Beck, B. E. F. *Peasant Society in Konku: A Study of Right and Left Subcastes in South India*. Vancouver: University of British Columbia Press, 1972.
Beteille, A. *Caste, Class and Power*. Berkeley: University of California Press, 1965.
Bloch, M., ed. *Marxist Analyses and Social Anthropology*. London: Malaby Press, 1975.
Broughton, L. P. D. *The Code of Civil Procedure Being Act X of 1877 With Notes and An Appendix*. Calcutta: Thacker, Spink, 1878.
Carman, John B. *The Theology of Rāmānujā: An Essay in Interreligious Understanding*. New Haven, Conn.: Yale University Press, 1974.
Census of India 1961. Vol. 9, "Madras," Parts I–XI. Madras: Superintendent of Census Operations, 1964–9.
Chetty, V. R. *History of Triplicane and the Temple of Sri Parthasarathi Swamy*. Triplicane, Madras: Giri Press, 1948.
Conlon, Frank F. *A Caste in a Changing World: The Chitrapur Saraswat Brahmans 1700–1935*. Berkeley: University of California Press, 1977.
Crole, C. S. *Manual of the Chingleput District*. Madras: Lawrence Asylum Press, 1879.

Cross, R. *Precedent in English Law*. Oxford: Clarendon Press, 1961.

Curtin, P. D. *The Image of Africa*. Madison: University of Wisconsin Press, 1964.

Derrett, J. D. M. *Hindu Law Past and Present*. Calcutta: Mukherjee, 1957.

Religion, Law and the State in India. London: Faber and Faber, 1968.

Desikacharya, N. *The Origin and Growth of Śrī Brahmatantra Parakāla Mutt*. Bangalore: Bangalore Press, 1949.

Diehl, Carl Gustav. *Instrument and Purpose: Studies on Rites and Rituals in South India*. Lund, Sweden: Gleerup, 1956.

Dikshitar, V. R. Ramachandra. *Hindu Administrative Institutions*. Madras: University of Madras, 1929.

ed. *Selected South Indian Inscriptions: Tamil, Telugu, Malayalam and Kannada*. Madras: University of Madras, 1952.

Douglas, Mary. *Implicit Meanings: Essays in Anthropology*. London and Boston: Routledge, Kegan and Paul, 1975.

Dumont, Louis. *Une sous-caste de l'Inde du Soud: organisation sociale et religion des Pramalai Kallar*. Paris: Mouton, 1957.

Homo Hierarchicus: The Caste System and Its Implications. Chicago: University of Chicago Press, 1970.

Fallers, Lloyd A. *Law Without Precedent: Legal Ideas in Action in the Courts of Colonial Basoga*. Chicago and London: University of Chicago Press, 1969.

Frykenberg, R. E., ed. *Land Control and Social Structure in Indian History*. Madison: University of Wisconsin Press, 1969.

Geertz, Clifford. *The Interpretation of Cultures*. New York: Basic Books, 1973.

Ghosh, A. *The Law of Endowments (Hindu and Mohameddan)*. 2nd ed. Calcutta: Eastern Law House, 1938.

Godelier, M. *Rationality and Irrationality in Economics*. New York: Monthly Review Press, 1972.

Perspectives in Marxist Anthropology. London: Cambridge University Press, 1977.

Gonda, Jan. *Aspects of Early Viṣṇuism*. 2nd ed. Utrecht: Oosthoek, 1954.

Viṣṇuism and Sivaism: A Comparison. London: Athlone Press, University of London, 1970.

Hari Rao, V. N. ed. *Kōil-Oḻugu: The Chronicle of the Srirangam Temple with Historical Notes*. Madras: Rochouse and Sons, 1961.

Hart, H. L. A. *The Concept of Law*. Oxford: Clarendon Press, 1961.

Hayavadana Rao, C. *History of Mysore*. 4 vols. Bangalore: Government Press, 1943–6.

Heras, Henry. *The Aravidu Dynasty of Vijayanagara*. Madras: Paul, 1927.

Hubert, Henri, and Mauss, Marcel. *Sacrifice: Its Nature and Function*. Translated by W. D. Halls. Chicago: University of Chicago Press, 1964.

Inden, Ronald. *Marriage and Rank in Bengali Culture: A History of Caste and Clan in Middle-Period Bengal*. Berkeley: University of California Press, 1976.

Irschick, Eugene F. *Politics and Social Conflict in South India: The Non-Brahmin Movement and Tamil Separatism, 1916–1929*. Berkeley: University of California Press, 1969.

Iyer, P. R. Ganapathy. *The Law Relating to Hindu and Mohameddan Endowments*. 2nd ed. Madras: Modern Printing Works, 1918.

Jain, M. P. *Outlines of Indian Legal History*. 3rd ed. Bombay: Tripathi, 1972.

Kane, P. V. *History of Dharmasāstra (Ancient and Mediaeval Religious and Civil Law)*. 2nd ed., 5 vols. Poona: Bhandarkar Oriental Research Institute, 1930–62.

Kessinger, Tom G. *Vilyatpur, 1848–1968: Social and Economic Change in a North Indian Village*. Berkeley: University of California Press, 1973.

Krishnaswami, A. *The Tamil Country Under Vijayanagara*. Annamalainagar: Annamalai University, 1964.

Lal, Nand. *The Code of Civil Procedure (Act V of 1908), With the Case-Law Thereon*. 3 vols. Lahore: Lahore Law Journal, 1926.

Leach, E. R. *Political Systems of Highland Burma: A Study of Kachin Social Structure*. Boston: Beacon Press, 1965.

Leonard, K. I. *Social History of an Indian Caste: The Kayasths of Hyderabad*. Berkeley: University of California Press, 1978.

Levi-Strauss, Claude. *Structural Anthropology*. New York: Basic Books, 1963.

Lingat, Robert. *The Classical Law of India*. Translated by J. D. M. Derrett. New Delhi: Thomson Press; Berkeley, Los Angeles, and London: University of California Press, 1973.

Love, H. D. *Vestiges of Old Madras*. 3 vols. Madras: Murray, 1913.

Madras Tercentenary Commemoration Volume. Madras: Oxford University Press, 1939.

Madras University Tamil Lexicon. 8 vols. Madras: Law Journal Press, 1925–63.

Mahalingam, T. V. *South Indian Polity*. Madras: University of Madras, 1967.

Mahar, J. Michael, ed. *The Untouchables in Contemporary India*. Tucson: University of Arizona Press, 1972.

Markose, A. T. *Judicial Control of Administrative Action in India*. Madras: Madras Law Journal Office, 1956.

Mauss, Marcel. *The Gift: Forms and Functions of Exchange in Archaic Societies*. Translated by Ian Cunnison. New York: Norton, 1967.

Mudaliar, Chandra Y. *The Secular State and Religious Institutions in India: A Study of the Administration of Hindu Public Religious Trusts in Madras*. Wiesbaden: Steiner, 1974.

Nārāyaṇasāmi Nāyaṭu, T. K., ed. *Srī Pillai Lōkācāriyār Srī Vacana Pūcaṇam Maṇavāḷa Māmunikaḷ Viyākkiyāṉam: Tamiḻ Ākkam*. Madras: Kabeer Printing Works, 1970.

Nelson, J. H. *A View of the Hindu Law as Administered by the High Court of Judicature at Madras*. Madras: Higginbotham, 1877.

Commentaries on the Code of Civil Procedure, Act No. X of 1877. Madras: Higginbotham, 1878.

A Prospectus of the Scientific Study of the Hindu Law. London: Kegan Paul, 1881.

Indian Usage and Judge-Made Law in Madras. London: Kegan Paul, Tranch, 1887.

O'Kinealy, J. *The Code of Civil Procedure Being Act XIV of 1882, As Amended by Acts VI, VII and X of 1888, with Notes and an Appendix.* Calcutta: Thacker, Spink, 1889.

O'Malley, L. S. S., ed. *Modern India and the West.* London: Oxford University Press, 1941.

Owen, David. *English Philanthropy 1660–1960.* Cambridge: Harvard University Press, 1964.

Pathar, S. Viraswami. *Temple and Its Significance.* Tiruchi: Vani Vilas Press, 1974.

Pirammātīca Varucattiya Utsava Vivaram 1973–1974. Triplicane: Sri Partasarati Svami Devastanam, 1973.

Ramanuja Dasan, K., et al. *Tiruvallikkēni Tivyatēsa Ūlalkal (Akramañkal), [Decadences and Irregularities in the Triplicane Temple].* Madras: Selvarangam Press, 1944.

Ramanujan, A. K. *Speaking of Siva.* Baltimore: Penguin Books, 1973.

Ramaswamy Tatachar, D. *The Vanamamalai Temple and Mutt.* Tinnevelly: Hilal Press, 1937.

Rangacharya, V. *A Topographical List of the Inscriptions of the Madras Presidency.* 3 vols. Madras: Government Press, 1919.
1931, Vol. 11, Pt. 2.

Rangacharya, V. *A Topographical List of the Inscriptions of the Madras Presidency.* 3 vols. Madras: Government Press, 1919.

Rangaswami Aiyangar, Kovalgudi S. *A Second Collection of the Papers Relating to Sri Ranganadhasvami Temple, Its Management, etc.* Trichinopoly: Southern Press, 1894.

Row, T. V. Sanjiva. *The Code of Civil Procedure, 1908 (Act V of 1908) With the Case-Law Thereon.* 2 vols. Madras: Law Printing House, 1909.

Rudolph, Lloyd I., and Rudolph, Suzanne H. *The Modernity of Tradition: Political Development in India.* Chicago: University of Chicago Press, 1967.

Sahlins, M. D. *Stone Age Economics.* Chicago: Aldine, 1972.

Saletore, B. A. *Social and Political Life in the Vijayanagara Empire 1346–1646.* 2 vols. Madras: Paul, 1934.

Setalvad, M. C. *The Common Law in India.* Bombay: Tripathi, 1970.

Sills, David L., ed. *International Encyclopaedia of the Social Sciences.* Glencoe, Ill.: Free Press, 1968.

Stein, Burton, ed. *South Indian Temples: An Analytical Reconsideration.* New Delhi: Vikas, 1978.

Strange, T. *Hindu Law.* 2 vols. London: Parbury, Allen, 1830.

Subrahmanya Sastry, S. *Report on the Inscriptions of the Devastanam Collection with Illustrations.* Madras: Tirupati Sri Mahant's Press, 1930.

Sundaram, K. *Studies in Economic and Social Conditions of Medieval Andhra (A.D. 1000–1600).* Machilipatnam and Madras: Triveni, 1968.

Turner, Victor. *Schism and Continuity in an African Society: A Study of Ndembu Village Life.* Manchester: Manchester University Press, 1957.
Dramas, Fields and Metaphors: Symbolic Action in Human Society. Ithaca and London: Cornell University Press, 1974.

Turner, Victor W., ed. *Profiles of Change: African Society and Colonial Rule.* Cambridge: Cambridge University Press, 1971.

Varadachari, K. C. *Āḻvārs of South India*. Bombay: Bharatiya Vidya Bhavan, 1966.
Viraraghavacharya, T. K. T. *History of Tirupati (The Tiruvengadam Temple)*. 2 vols. Tirupati: Tirumalai-Tirupathi Devasthanams Press, 1953–4.
Wadley, Susan S. *Shakti: Power in the Conceptual Structure of Karimpur Religion*. Chicago: University of Chicago, 1975.
Washbrook, D. A. *The Emergence of Provincial Politics: The Madras Presidency 1870–1920*. New York: Cambridge University Press, 1976.
Weber, Max. *The Religion of India*. Glencoe, Ill.: Free Press, 1958.
The Theory of Social and Economic Organization. Translated by A. M. Henderson and Talcott Parsons. Edited by Talcott Parsons. New York: Free Press, 1964.
Max Weber on Law in Economy and Society. Edited by Max Rheinstein. New York: Simon and Schuster, 1967.

Articles

Allott, A. N. "Legal Personality in African Law." In Max Gluckman, ed., *Ideas and Procedures in African Customary Law*, pp. 179–95. London: Oxford University Press, 1969.
Appadurai, Arjun. "Right and Left Hand Castes in South India." *Indian Economic and Social History Review* 11, Nos. 2–3 (June–September 1974):216–59.
"Protest and Participation: Non-Brahmins in a South Indian Temple." Paper presented at the Twenty-seventh Annual Meeting of the Association for Asian Studies, San Francisco, March 24–26, 1975.
"Kings, Sects and Temples in South India, 1350–1700 A.D." *Indian Economic and Social History Review* 14, No. 1 (January–March 1977): 47–73. Reprinted in Burton Stein, ed., *South Indian Temples: An Analytical Reconsideration*. New Delhi: Vikas, 1978.
Appadurai, Arjun, and Breckenridge, Carol Appadurai. "The South Indian Temple: Authority, Honor and Redistribution." *Contributions to Indian Sociology*, n.s., 10, No. 2 (Delhi, 1976):187–211.
Barnett, S. A. "The Process of Withdrawal in a South Indian Caste." In M. Singer, ed., *Entrepreneurship and the Modernization of Occupations in South Asia*, pp. 179–204. Durham, N.C.: Duke University Press, 1974.
Beteille, A. "Social Organization of Temples in a Tanjore Village." *History of Religions* 5, No. 1 (1965):74–92.
Breckenridge, Carol Appadurai. "Betel-Nut and Honor: Exchange-Relationships and Temple-Entry in a South Indian Temple." Paper presented at the Twenty-seventh Annual Meeting of the Association for Asian Studies, San Francisco, March 24–26, 1975.
"The Śrī Mīnākṣi Sundarēsvarar Temple: A Study of Worship and Endowments in South India, 1800–1925." Ph.D. diss., University of Wisconsin, 1976.
Clammer, John. "Colonialism and the Perception of Tradition in Fiji." In T. Asad, ed., *Anthropology and the Colonial Encounter*, pp. 119–220. New York: Humanities, 1973.

Cohn, Bernard S. "From Indian Status to British Contract." *Journal of Economic History* 21 (December 1961):613–28.
"Anthropological Notes on Law and Disputes in India." *American Anthropologist* 67, No. 6 (December 1965):82–122, Pt. 2.
"Ethnohistory." In David L. Sills, ed., *International Encyclopaedia of the Social Sciences*. 6:440–8, New York: Free Press, 1968.
Dikshitar, V. R. R. "Around the City Pagodas." In *Madras Tercentenary Commemoration Volume*. Madras: Oxford University Press, 1939.
Dirks, Nicholas B. "Political Authority and Structural Change in Early South Indian History." *Indian Economic and Social History Review* 13, No. 2 (1976):125–58.
Dumont, Louis. "The 'Village Community' from Munro to Maine." *Contributions to Indian Sociology* 9 (Paris, 1966):66–89.
Fuller, C. J. "Gods, Priests and Purity: On the Relation Between Hinduism and the Caste System." *Man*, n.s., 14 (1979):459–76.
Galanter, Marc. "Law and Caste in Modern India." *Asian Survey* 3, No. 11 (1963):544–9.
"The Abolition of Disabilities – Untouchability and the Law." In J. Michael Mahar, ed., *The Untouchables in Contemporary India*, pp. 227–314. Tucson: University of Arizona Press, 1972.
Gopinatha Rao, T. A. "Soraikkavur Plates of Virupāksha: Saka Samvat 1308." *Epigraphia Indica* 3 (1905–6):298–306.
"Dalavāy-Agrahāram Plates of Venkatāpatidēva Mahārāya I: Saka-Saṁvat 1508." *Epigraphia Indica* 12 (1913–14):159–87.
Govindacarya, A. "The Astadasa-Bhedas, or the Eighteen Points of Doctrinal Differences between the Tengalais (Southerners) and the Vadagalais (Northerners) of the Visistadvaita Vaishnava School, South India." *Journal of the Royal Asiatic Society of Great Britain and Ireland* (1910): 1103–12.
"Tengalai and Vadagalai." *Journal of the Royal Asiatic Society of Great Britain and Ireland* (1912):714–17.
Govindacarya, A., and Grierson, G. A. "The Artha-Panchaka of Pillai Lokacarya." *Journal of the Royal Asiatic Society of Great Britain and Ireland* (1910):565–97.
Hanchett, S. "Hindu Potlatches: Ceremonial Reciprocity and Prestige in Karnataka." In Helen E. Ullrich, ed., *Competition and Modernization In South Asia*, pp. 27–59. New Delhi: Abhinav, 1975.
Hari Rao, V. N. "A History of Trichinopoly and Srirangam." Ph.D. diss., University of Madras, 1948.
"Vaishnavism in South India in the Modern Period." In O. P. Bhatnagar, ed., *Studies in Social History (Modern India)*, pp. 116–35. Allahabad: St. Paul's Press Training School, 1964.
Harper, E. B. "Ritual Pollution as an Integrator of Caste and Religion." *Journal of Asian Studies* 23 (1964):151–97.
Hultzsch, E. "Ranganatha Inscription of Goppanna: Saka-Samvat 1293." *Epigraphia Indica* 6 (1900–1):322–30.
Jagadeesan, N. "History of Śrī Vaiṣṇavism in the Tamil Country (Post-Rāmānujā)." Ph.D. diss., University of Madras, 1967.

Levi-Strauss, C. "History and Anthropology." In *Structural Anthropology*, pp. 1–28. New York: Doubleday, 1967.

Lewandowski, Susan. "Urban Growth and Municipal Development in the Colonial City of Madras, 1860–1900." *Journal of Asian Studies* 34, No. 2 (February 1975):341–60.

"Changing Form and Function in the Ceremonial and the Colonial Port City in India: An Historical Analysis of Madurai and Madras." *Modern Asian Studies* 2, No. 2 (1977):183–212.

Lindsay, Sir Benjamin. "Law." In L. S. S. O'Malley, ed., *Modern India and the West*, pp. 107–337. London: Oxford University Press, 1941.

Marriott, M., and Inden, Ronald. "Caste Systems." *Encyclopaedia Britannica*, 15th ed. Chicago: Encyclopaedia Britannica (1974), 3:982–91.

Martin, James L. "The Cycle of Festivals at Pārthasārathi Swami Temple." In Bardwell L. Smith, ed., *Journal of the American Academy of Religion: Asian Religions* (1971):223–40.

Presler, F. "Religion Under Bureaucracy: The State and Hindu Religious Endowments in Tamilnadu, India." Ph.D. diss., University of Chicago, 1978.

Rangachari, V. "The History of the Naik Kingdom of Madura." *Indian Antiquary* 43 (1914):7.

"The Life and Times of Srī-Vēdānta-Dēsika." *Journal of the Bombay Branch of the Royal Asiatic Society* 24 (1914–15):277–312.

"The Successors of Rāmānujā and the Growth of Sectarianism among the Śri-Vaishnavas." *Journal of the Bombay Branch of the Royal Asiatic Society* 24 (1914–15):102–36.

"The History of Śri Vaishnavism: From the Death of Srī Vēdanta Dēsika to the Present Day." *Quarterly Journal of the Mythic Society* 7, No. 2 (January 1917):106–18, and No. 3 (April 1917):197–209.

"Historical Evolution of Sri Vaishnavism in South India." In H. Bhattacharya, ed., *The Cultural Heritage of India*. 2nd ed., 4 vols. Calcutta: Ramakrishna Mission Institute of Culture, 1953–58; 4 (1956):163–85.

Saletore, B. A. "The Sthānikas and Their Historical Importance." *Journal of the University of Bombay* 7 (July 1938): 29–93, Pt. I.

Sontheimer, Gunter-Dietz. "Religious Endowments in India: The Juristic Personality of Hindu Deities." *Zeitschrift fur Vergleichende Rechtswissenschaft* 67 (1964): 45–100, Pt. 1.

Spencer, George W. "Religious Networks and Royal Influence in Eleventh Century South India." *Journal of the Economic and Social History of the Orient* 12 (January 1969): 42–56, Pt. I.

"Royal Initiative Under Rajaraja I." *Indian Economic and Social History Review* 7, No. 4 (December 1970): 431–42.

Stein, Burton. "The Economic Function of a Medieval South Indian Temple." *Journal of Asian Studies* 19, No. 2 (1960): 163–76.

"Social Mobility and Medieval South Indian Hindu Sects." In J. Silverberg, ed., *Social Mobility in the Caste System in India; An Interdisciplinary Symposium*, pp. 78–94. Paris: Mouton 1968.

"Integration of the Agrarian System of South India." In R. E.

Frykenberg, ed., *Land Control and Social Structure in Indian History*, pp. 175–216. Madison: University of Wisconsin, 1969.

"Temples in Tamil Country, 1300–1750 A.D." *Indian Economic and Social History Review* 14, No. 1 (1976): 11–45. Reprinted in Burton Stein, ed., *South Indian Temples: An Analytical Reconsideration*. New Delhi: Vikas, 1978.

"The Segmentary State in South Indian History." In Richard G. Fox, ed., *Realm and Region in Traditional India*, pp. 3–51. Durham, N.C.: Duke University Press, 1977.

van Buitenen, J. A. B. "On the Archaism of the *Bhāgavata Purāna*." In Milton Singer, ed., *Krishna: Myths, Rites and Attitudes*, pp. 23–40. Chicago: University of Chicago Press (Phoenix Edition), 1968.

Venkataraman, K. R. "The Vaikhānasas." In H. Bhattacharya, ed., *The Cultural Heritage of India*, 2nd ed., 4 vols. Calcutta: Ramakrishna Mission Institute of Culture, 1953–58; 4 (1956): 160–2.

Vijayaraghavachari, S. "A Few Inscriptions of Lakshmikumara Tatacharya." *Journal of Indian History* 25 (April 1947): 121–31, Pt. 1.

INDEX

and "protection" of SPS Temple, 125, 136–8, 152; and advocate general's perception of collector–Pillay dispute, 128–9; and *mirasi* rights, 142–4; and Teṉkalai control claims, 145–6; and 1840 honors dispute, 146–7, 153; and trustee succession, 157–62, 184; *see also* Collector of Madras
Board of Supervision, 60, 200, 202, 203, 238–46
Boddam, Justice, 193–5, 197; *see also* Civil Suit 108 of 1905
Boscowen, Admiral, 107
brahmadēyas, 64
Brahmatantra Parakāla Tantra Svāmi Maṭam, 97
Breckenridge, C. A., viii, 9–10n, 20n, 25n, 222n, 225n
Broughton, L. P. D., 173n, 175n
Bukka Oḍeyar, 50n, 65
bureaucracy, British, 69–71, 105, 214–15, 218; growth of, 109, 215; and temple management, 110, 139, 162–4; arbitration of temple disputes by, 114; *see also* Board of Revenue; Collector of Madras; East India Company; state, colonial

Carman, J. B., viii, 74n, 75n, 76n, 77–8n, 82n
case-history, extended, 3–4
caste, 75, 112, 131, 177, 222; studies of, 6–8, 9, 223–6; authoritative basis of, 7–8; and SPS Temple churchwardenship, 155, 156; and SPS Temple trusteeship, 158, 181, 186, 187–92; and Anglo-Indian law, 169; *see also* elections of trustees; festivals at SPS Temple; non-Brahmin worshippers; state, colonial
Ceṭṭi, Tampu, 103
charity: *see* trusts and charities, legal concepts of
Charities Procedure Act of 1812, 174
Charity Commission, 174
Chetti merchants of Triplicane, 131–2
Chetty, Murugappa, 194
Chetty, V. R. 13n, 23n, 27n, 104n, 209
Churchwarden of SPS Temple: and Board of Revenue, 111, 113–14, 118, 124–7, 142–4, 146, 149–53; formal relationship to Collector of Madras of, 115, 119–21, 124–7, 129–30, 142–4, 148, 150–3; as "trustee," 126, 127; as "public servant" 149–50; caste affiliation of, 155–7; and sect affiliation, 155–7; *see also* Pillay, Annaswamy; temple servants; trustees of SPS Temple
City Civil Court of Madras, 38n, 55n, 60n
Civil Procedure Code of 1877, 170–2, 174–5
Civil Procedure Code of 1882, 170–2, 174–5, 185, 196
Civil Procedure Code of 1908, 170–3, 174–5
Civil Suits: 29 of 1914, 199; 36 of 1884, 185–8, 190, 232n, *see also* Justice Hutchins's Scheme of 1885; 108 of 1905, 197–8, 199; 111 of 1918, 200, 203, 209; 137 of 1895, 193–5; 161 of 1891, 162, 177n, 189–93, 199; 169 of 1905, 197; 176 of 1915, 198–9; 211 of 1933, 38–9; 233 of 1911, 199; 241 of 1933, 38–9, 205n; 293 of 1895, 195–6, 197; 349 of 1923, 39n, 40–4, 200, 204, 206–8, 219; 442 of 1923, 200, 204–5; 485 of 1917, 205; 486 of 1878, 160–2, 182–5, 199; 527 of 1924, 55–9, 60, 200–1, 203, 207, 210, *see also* schemes for temple management; 559 of 1922, 200; 843 of 1919, 200, 209–10; 860 of 1920, 200, 204–5
Clammer, J., 226n
codification, legal, 165, 167, 170, 175, 193, 210, 218; of priests's rights, 38, 204–5; of *attiyāpakās*' rights, 40–5, 200, 204, 206–8; as stimulative of conflict, 148, 211; of Teṉkalai control at SPS Temple, 164, 177
Cohn, B. S., viii, 4n, 7n, 8n, 168n, 169n, 224n, 227
Cōḻa dynasty, 64
Collector of Madras, 110, 159; and disputes at SPS Temple from 1800 to 1820, 114–16; as administrator of Madras temples, 117–18,

LaVergne, TN USA
11 January 2011
211906LV00003B/18/A